Through Ebony Eyes

Through Ebony Eyes

What Teachers Need to Know But Are Afraid to Ask About African American Students

Gail L. Thompson

JOSSEY-BASS
A Wiley Imprint
www.josseybass.com

Published by Jossey-Bass
A Wiley Imprint
989 Market Street, San Francisco, CA 94103-1741   www.josseybass.com

Jossey-Bass books and products are available through most bookstores. To contact Jossey-Bass directly call our Customer Care Department within the U.S. at 800-956-7739, outside the U.S. at 317-572-3986, or fax 317-572-4002.

Jossey-Bass also publishes its books in a variety of electronic formats. Some content that appears in print may not be available in electronic books.

Library of Congress Cataloging-in-Publication Data

Thompson, Gail L., date.
  Through ebony eyes : what teachers need to know but are afraid to ask about African American students / Gail L. Thompson.— 1st ed.
      p. cm. — (The Jossey-Bass education series)
Includes bibliographical references and index.
  ISBN-13 978-0-7879-7061-1 (alk. paper)
  ISBN-10 0-7879-7061-1 (alk. paper)
  ISBN-13 978-0-7879-8769-5 (paperback)
  ISBN-10 0-7879-8769-7 (paperback)
  1. African American students. 2. Teaching—United States. I. Title.
II. Series.
  LC2771.T56 2004
  371.829'96073—dc22

                                                        2003027616

Printed in the United States of America
FIRST EDITION
HB *Printing* 10 9 8 7 6 5
PB *Printing* 10 9 8 7 6 5 4 3 2 1

The Jossey-Bass Education Series

Contents

Appendices

List of Tables

Acknowledgments

Writing a book is a time-consuming, difficult process that requires much sacrifice and diligence. This book became a reality as a result of the support, encouragement, and prayers of many individuals. My husband, Rufus, and my children, Nafissa (who read the entire manuscript), NaChé, and Stephen were overwhelmingly encouraging and supportive throughout the process. My mentor and colleague, David E. Drew, read several chapters and advised me on how to improve the quality of the book. Margaret Goss, an exemplary veteran teacher and teacher specialist, read the book, gave me invaluable feedback, and reminded me that the truth still needs to be told, even if some people are resistant to hearing it.

My friends Cynthia Hebron (who left encouraging messages on my answering machine and sent me uplifting notes), Sharon Holmes-Johnson, and Deborah Tavasti read the entire manuscript and gave me many great suggestions. Marga Madhuri, one of my graduate students, and Virginia Leon read the entire manuscript and offered much encouragement and useful feedback.

My great aunt, Ebbie Crear; my sister, Tracy Smith; and my friends Wanda Foster and Camille Mayers read sections of the book and told me that it could make a positive difference in the schooling experiences of African American children. My little niece, Elyse Harris (an outstanding sixth grader in Atlanta), is one of my biggest supporters. My aunts Dorothy Taylor, Wilma Hester, and Lillian

Mitchell said that they were proud of my professional accomplishments. My friends Malinda West and Melody Lark and my beautician, Eva Duncan, have continued to cheer me on. I am also extremely grateful to Sylvia Durbin of the Mountainview School District for giving me many positive messages about my work, and for telling me that as a Latina she can relate to the stories in my books.

My Claremont Graduate University students in my fall 2002 ED 564 and spring 2003 ED 437 classes—particularly Carrie Allen, Carol Dickerson, Martha Ikner (who gave me a wonderful suggestion for the book's title), Saundra Kirk, T-Fox, Will Kratt, Kathleen Vaughn, Monica Turner, Jonathan Daehnke, Jennifer Zarougian, Tracy Mendoza, Bettina Casad, and Tami Foy—listened to me talk about the book each week, expressed enthusiasm for its contents, and gave me great suggestions and words of encouragement.

Lesley Iura, my editor at Jossey-Bass, was enthusiastic about the project, supportive, and encouraging; I have enjoyed working with you, Lesley. Thanks for your invaluable contributions about the book's organization and its tone.

Several of my colleagues, among them Dean Mary Poplin in the School of Educational Studies and President Steadman Upham, as well as Jewell Plummer-Cobb, a trustee, at the Claremont Graduate University also expressed enthusiasm about this project.

The Author

Gail L. Thompson, Ph.D., taught in public junior high and high schools for fourteen years. During this time, she won a civic award for outstanding teaching, as well as teaching awards from student organizations. Thompson served as a district-selected mentor teacher and later developed an after-school literacy program for struggling elementary school students. She is an associate professor in the School of Educational Studies at the Claremont Graduate University, and the author of *African American Teens Discuss Their Schooling Experiences*, *What African American Parents Want Educators to Know*, and numerous journal articles. In 2002, one of her essays, "Teachers' Cultural Ignorance Imperils Student Success," was published in *USA Today*.

In addition to serving as a guest editor for *Educational Horizons*, *The Urban Review*, and *The High School Journal*, Thompson has appeared on National Public Radio and KXAM radio in Scottsdale, Arizona, and has been quoted in several newspapers. She serves as a reviewer for *The Reading Teacher*, *The California Reader*, *The High School Journal*, and *The Journal of Adolescent and Adult Literacy*. In addition to serving as a keynote speaker for many organizations, she has presented papers at numerous national, regional, and state conferences and done consultant work in many K–12 schools. She is married to Rufus, an educator, and they have three children: Nafissa, a college student, and NaChé and Stephen, high school students.

Through Ebony Eyes

Introduction

Persistent Problems

Today, nearly a half-century after the U.S. Supreme Court mandated that public schools be desegregated and decades after the end of the civil rights movement, race, culture, and related topics continue to generate controversy and discomfort for many Americans. In 1954, the *Brown* v. *Board of Education of Topeka, Kansas*, decision set off a chain of events whose repercussions can still be felt today.[1] Since then, the public school system, like the larger society, has continued to grapple with issues pertaining to race and ethnicity, diversity, and multiculturalism. These issues are important because students of color constitute a substantial percentage of the U.S. school-age population. Although the *Brown* decision sought to make public schools more equitable, inequality of educational opportunity has continued to be a problem in public schools, and race-related problems persist.

In its Tools for Schools study, the U.S. Department of Education examined twenty-seven school reform models that were funded by the National Institute on the Education of At-Risk Students. However, of the twenty-seven reform models that were described in the study, fewer than 40 percent focused on issues relating to cultural diversity, and only a third made social skills a primary educational objective. Moreover, the reforms including cultural diversity as a main objective tended to approach it from the standpoint of improving teachers' knowledge, attitudes, and instructional practices for students of color. Few, if any, targeted race relations between teachers and students or among students and their peers specifically.[2]

Goertz, Floden, and O'Day conducted a study involving twelve "reforming schools" in California, Michigan, and Vermont. Each state approached school reform in a different manner, yet certain characteristics surfaced among the three states. All three had a primary objective of raising academic standards for students and addressing the needs of lower socioeconomic status students, English language learners, and students with disabilities. Although the researchers did not specifically recommend that reform efforts also seek to improve race relations among members of the school community, they did suggest that policy makers focus on diversity, recruiting teachers of color, and preparing teachers to better address the needs of students from nonmainstream backgrounds.[3]

One reason that education reform may fail to focus on racial issues is that race is still a volatile topic in America.[4] However, according to Hacker, race has always occupied a dominant role in the history of the United States.[5] Recently, some students and organizations have become more vocal about racist school polices and practices. In California, for example, the American Civil Liberties Union (ACLU) filed a lawsuit on behalf of a group of African American and Latino students who were systematically denied access to advanced placement courses.[6] In other cases, attempts to address racist practices have resulted in opposition. For example, in North Carolina a federal mandate resulted in "detracking" English courses. Although the court order was designed to improve the schooling experiences of African American students who had historically been subjected to inequality of educational opportunity, the mandate met opposition from a coalition of parents and teachers who wanted to maintain the status quo.[7]

Walker examined interracial relations in three high schools and one middle school and found that interracial conflicts and tensions were common. When a racially diverse group of teachers formed a committee and developed a program that was designed to improve interracial relations, they were criticized by some teachers and staff members. Walker concluded, however, that interracial conflicts can be beneficial if school leaders use them as a catalyst to change the school environment and create a structure that will ensure lasting change.[8]

Glasser developed the Glasser Quality School reform model, which has been implemented successfully at eight schools. At the core of this reform model is the theory that schools can become successful only when they improve the relationships among the individuals within the school community. Glasser attributed low performance and discipline problems to poor relations between teachers and students.[9] A related example surfaced in the work of Orange and Horowitz, who contrasted the beliefs of a group of teachers with those of a group of African American and Latino male students. They found that as a result of misunderstandings an "academic standoff" existed between teachers and their African American and Latino male students.[10]

In recent decades, one way that educators have attempted to reduce racial tension in schools throughout the United States is to promote cultural diversity, tolerance, and multiculturalism. Many school leaders are undeterred in their quest to help teachers improve their efficacy with students of color. Often, they use their professional development options as a way to achieve this goal, and also to narrow the great cultural divide that exists between some teachers and students. The gulf seems to be widest between many teachers and African American students. This ongoing problem became the catalyst for this book.

Why This Book Is Needed

This book is needed for two primary reasons. The first, and more obvious, is that the achievement gap between blacks and whites continues to exist. Many poor children, African Americans, Latinos, and other students of color in schools throughout the nation are subjected to inequality of educational opportunity, which limits their future options and socioeconomic advancement. Second, a high percentage of teachers are underprepared to work effectively with students of color. Hence there is often a cultural mismatch between teachers and African American students that has many negative consequences. However, as a result of the No Child Left Behind Act (NCLB),[11] the federal government has created a comprehensive plan that promises to hold teachers accountable for educating "all" children. Although the plan has numerous components, it fails to address both the cultural mismatch between teachers and students of color and the impact that this mismatch has on the black-white achievement gap. Nevertheless, many school leaders have noticed not only that this mismatch exists but that it does indeed affect student-teacher relations, instructional practices, and achievement.

For these reasons, school administrators at four schools (a middle school and three high schools; see Appendix I) who became familiar with some of my previous research, who heard me speak at conferences, or who knew of my work from colleagues invited me to conduct professional development inservice trainings at their schools. The goal was for me to share research and strategies that could help teachers increase their efficacy with African American students. The training was conducted in two California cities; two school districts were represented. The middle school training was in central California; the high school session, which was held for three high schools at the same time, took place in a southern California city.

This book is the result of data that I collected from 175 educators at the participating schools at the end of each training. Each group of educators attended a one-day, six-hour inservice during the summer of 2002. At the end of the inservice, participants completed a questionnaire consisting of thirty-four items. The questionnaire, which used a four-point Likert scale, was designed to measure these factors:

- The participants' attitudes, before and after training, about being required to attend an inservice that focused solely on issues pertaining to African American K–12 students
- Pretraining beliefs about their relations and efficacy with African American students
- Pretraining beliefs about African American parents
- Posttraining beliefs about the short-term impact of the inservice, and their professional development plans
- Demographic information about the participants

The participants also had an opportunity to write additional comments on the questionnaire, and many submitted written questions throughout the day.

As with most of my previous research, the purpose of this book (which contains much of the information that I presented to the 175 middle school and high school teachers) is to help several groups—individuals who are contemplating becoming teachers, prospective teachers who are currently enrolled in teacher training institutions, and teachers who already have their own classrooms—increase their efficacy with African American students, particularly those who are enrolled in urban public schools nationwide. Furthermore, because the book contains the main components of the model that I created and that I present at schools, school administrators and district officials can also use the book for professional development at K–12 schools and at the district office to train teacher specialists. Because I am always adding new information to my inservice model, the book contains additional stories and research that I have added to the model since I presented it for the four groups in 2002. Because the model is a work in progress, I am not so naïve as to believe that it is perfect. I do think, however, that it can be extremely useful to educators. Finally, the book might be useful to other researchers who write about culturally sensitive issues and who conduct related workshops in schools.

The Book's Organization

Although this book is grounded in research, the tone is intended to be conversational, like the tone that I use when conducting trainings. Teachers are less likely to tune out or ignore a message if it speaks to them plainly rather than in academic jargon. Moreover, in addition to citing related research throughout the book, as I do during trainings, I also provide numerous examples and personal stories related to the topics that are covered in this book. I often find that the stories that I share have a greater impact on some teachers than the research and scholarly studies that I cite. The personal stories give the participants a two-pronged "human touch." They illustrate that, although I am African American, as an educator I have experienced some of the same problems and situations that concern them. Furthermore, the stories illustrate that during my childhood, adolescence, and young adulthood I also experienced some of the same problems that many of their African American students face.

This book is divided into two parts. In Part One ("The Basics"), Chapter One presents theories that have been used to explain the underachievement of African American students. It includes related stories and examples, and it underscores the fact that teachers' beliefs and attitudes have an impact on African American students' schooling experiences.

Chapter Two describes effective instructional practices for African American students. The chapter begins with an example of an African American eighth grader who was failing her algebra class and in danger of retention because of her math teacher's ineffective practices. The chapter presents research about effective teaching strategies in general, as well as specific reading, math, and writing strategies and related stories and examples.

In addition to presenting a brief summary of research about the huge number of teachers who have weak classroom management skills, Chapter Three explains why some African American students misbehave in class, how teachers often unwittingly contribute to their misbehavior, and effective classroom management strategies that teachers can use. Moreover, the chapter gives specific examples of common discipline problems and related practical solutions.

In Part Two, numerous culturally sensitive issues and questions that surface during inservice trainings are explored. For example, Chapter Four uses research but is primarily the story of the elementary school teacher who changed the direction of my life during my difficult childhood; this is offered as an example of how teachers can reach African American students from challenging backgrounds. The chapter underscores two important facts: (1) one committed and dedicated teacher has the power to change the direction of a child's life, and (2) choosing to become a powerful and influential life-changing teacher is an option available to every educator.

Chapter Five revisits the controversy over Ebonics versus Standard English and addresses the issue of whether or not teachers should force African American students to speak Standard English in class. The chapter includes pertinent stories, summarizes key points from related research, and describes how teachers' actions can actually become counterproductive. The chapter also includes recommendations regarding how teachers can motivate African American students to acquire Standard English skills without silencing them or devaluing their "home" language or dialect. The chapter begins with a related example from my first year of junior high school.

Chapter Six focuses on the controversy surrounding the use of the "N word" by African American students, and whether or not teachers should permit them to use it in class. Numerous teachers are quite confused about this topic. This chapter includes research about the origins and uses of the N word, related examples, and practical advice to teachers about whether or not they should permit African American students to call each other this word.

"What should I do when African American students accuse me of being racist?" a question regularly asked during teacher training of this kind, is addressed in Chapter Seven. The chapter presents a brief history of the word *racism*, definitions of the word, examples of racism in schools, some reasons why African American students might accuse teachers of being racist, and how teachers can handle these accusations. The chapter includes several related examples from my own personal experiences—as a student who once accused an instructor of being racist and as an educator who has been accused of discrimination. It concludes with a lesson plan for teachers and an explanation of how they can use an accusation of being racist to foster their own personal and professional growth and their students' personal growth.

Chapter Eight presents the reasons why African American students need a culturally relevant education. The chapter includes background information about the origins and purposes of multicultural education, related controversial issues, the reasons some teachers are opposed to multicultural education, counterproductive actions by teachers, related examples of how multicultural education can be used to harm African American students or help them, and a definition of "culturally relevant teaching."

Chapter Nine describes other controversial issues that teachers raised during the 2002 trainings, as well as related suggestions and stories. The following questions are addressed in this chapter:

- Are African American teachers more effective with African American students than nonblack teachers?
- Black or African American: Which term should we use?
- Why do so many African Americans have a bad attitude?
- Why can't we call them "monkeys"? (to offend or not to offend)
- Why are African American students so loud?

The chapter is designed to describe some of the gray areas that cause teachers to (perhaps unwittingly) offend African American students. It presents the case of a teacher who unknowingly made a culturally insensitive statement, the outcome, the lesson she learned, how she handled the situation, and the responses and reactions to this story by two other teachers.

In the Conclusion, key points, recurring themes, a summary of the 175 middle school and high school teachers' pre- and postinservice beliefs, implications for educators, ways in which school leaders can improve professional development practices, and lessons for researchers whose work focuses on racial and culturally sensitive issues are discussed. The chapter concludes with a three-part, long-term professional development plan for educators who want to continue their professional growth related to African American students.

Finally, because teachers are often inundated with theories and scholarly research when what they really want are actual strategies and hands-on activities, the Appendices include selected activities that teachers can use with all students, not just African American students. I used these assignments with my own secondary students, and most can be modified for elementary students.

In short, this book is a description of how educators can face challenging issues that could empower them. The book is an opportunity for prospective teachers, current teachers, and other educators to face the same issues that were addressed during the training that I conducted for the 175 teachers and to examine their own beliefs, attitudes, and relations with African American students. Furthermore, it gives school leaders and state and national education officials an opportunity to examine current approaches to professional development for teachers and suggestions about how to narrow the great cultural divide that persists in schools and in the larger society. Finally, although the incidents, personal experiences, and results may be interpreted differently by others, the book offers a candid view through "ebony eyes" (my own and those of other African Americans who are mentioned in this book) of the bittersweet lessons that teacher trainings and my own teaching experiences have taught me about race relations in America. Thus it can serve as a guidepost for others—particularly researchers of color—who are considering doing similar work or who are already doing so.

PART ONE

The Basics

1

If African American Kids Aren't Dumb or Lazy, Why Are They Still Underachieving? Related Theories

For decades, researchers have sought to explain the causes of the black-white achievement gap. At least ten theories have been posited:

1. The deficit-deprivation theory
2. The theory of structural inequality
3. Tracking
4. The theory of cultural discontinuity
5. "Fourth grade failure syndrome"
6. The "acting white" theory
7. The peer-pressure-and-the-lure-of-street-life theory
8. The parents-are-at-fault theory
9. Underprepared teachers
10. Low teacher expectations

During the workshops that I conduct in schools I describe each of these theories, but my goal is to emphasize that regardless of students' backgrounds, teachers' beliefs, attitudes, and expectations have been shown to become a self-fulfilling prophecy for students.

The Deficit-Deprivation Theory

The deficit-deprivation theory was one of the first. The basic premise is that there is a hierarchy of intelligence that starts with whites and Asians at the top and ends with blacks at the bottom. This theory has been supported by eugenics advocates and proponents of biological determinism and hereditarianism. Hence, deficit-deprivation theorists argue that African Americans are incapable of excelling at the same academic level as whites or Asians because they are genetically inferior to these groups. In *The Mismeasure of Man*, Gould traces the origins of the deficit-deprivation theory and illustrates how standardized tests have been used to validate it. In so doing, however, Gould shows how the inherent biases of standardized tests and their misuse have contributed to inequality of educational opportunity, particularly for African American students.[1] Although this theory has existed for at least a century, it is still believed by numerous researchers and educators. The celebrated child psychiatrist Dr. James Comer confirmed this: "In our culture we believe that the life outcome of an individual is due almost entirely to genetically determined intelligence and will. . . . We deny or downplay all other determinants."[2] According to Loewen, "The very essence of what we have inherited from slavery is the idea that it is appropriate, even 'natural,' for Whites to be on top, blacks on the bottom. In its core, our culture . . . tells all of us . . . that Europe's domination of the world came about because Europeans were smarter. In their core, many Whites and some people of color believe this."[3]

The Theory of Structural Inequality

The theory of structural inequality has also been used to explain the black-white achievement gap. This theory maintains that schools were designed to perpetuate class differences that exist in the larger society.[4] Therefore, since African Americans are disproportionately represented among those at the lowest socioeconomic level, by and large schools prepare them to remain at this level.[5] Because schools use middle-class norms as benchmarks and standardized tests as a primary way of measuring aptitude, poor children and African American and Latino children are at a disadvantage from the first day they enter school. In addition to common testing practices, ability grouping and tracking are two other ways in which the theory of structural inequality becomes evident.[6]

Tracking

Much has been written about the effects of tracking on the schooling experiences of African American children.[7] The general consensus is that African American and Latino students are disproportionately represented among the students who are placed in lower academic tracks. Conversely, they are less likely than white students to be placed in the highest tracks and thereby receive a college preparatory education.[8] The tracking system has been widely used to prepare students for their socioeconomic future. Students who are identified as "gifted" are usually "tracked" for college and higher paying jobs. Those who are identified as special education students are usually tracked for less prestigious and lower-paying jobs. African American students are disproportionately represented among the students in special education classes.[9]

The Theory of Cultural Discontinuity

The theory of cultural discontinuity maintains that there is a clash or mismatch between the home culture of African American students and other students of color and the school culture.[10] According to Ladson-Billings, "The clash between school culture and home culture becomes evident in judgments and labels that teachers place on students with non-mainstream speech and styles of discourse, and through teachers' use of instructional practices and classroom management strategies that are at odds with community norms."[11] Cattani wrote: "Schools can only reflect their larger societies, and schools' problems of racial difference mirror those elsewhere. . . .

Specifically, urban students may face many of the same difficulties that they face in the workplace, including discrimination and cultural misunderstanding."[12]

In *Culturally Responsive Teaching: Theory, Research, and Practice*, Gay described how the traditional educational system promotes achievement for white middle-class students by building on the positive aspects of European culture. However, the same system has promoted underachievement for many students of color by ignoring the strengths of their cultures. Therefore, "conventional reforms" are destined to fail because they continue to view students of color as deficient. According to Gay, "The best-quality educational programs and practices can never be accomplished if some ethnic groups and their contributions to the development of U.S. history, life, and culture are ignored and demeaned."[13] What is needed is a curriculum based on a culturally responsive, holistic approach to educating students. "Culturally responsive teaching," Gay stated, "can be defined as using the cultural knowledge, prior experiences, frames of reference, and performance styles of ethnically diverse students to make learning encounters more relevant to and effective for them."[14] Chapter Eight presents more details about this theory.

"Fourth Grade Failure Syndrome"

A number of researchers have argued that school has a deleterious effect on the achievement of African American children. These researchers have found that achievement for African American children actually decreases over time. For example, Kunjufu described the phenomenon of "fourth grade failure syndrome," which many African American boys experience. Although these boys may exhibit high achievement and show strong potential for academic success in kindergarten, by fourth grade many have been relegated to special education or labeled as "underachievers."[15] In *Bad Boys: Public Schools in the Making of Black Masculinity*, Ferguson described the trajectory of common school practices, cultural differences, and underlying messages that actually set up African American boys for school failure. In Ferguson's ethnography, this failure became most evident for African American boys during fourth grade. She wrote, "It is my contention that this diminished motivation to identify [oneself] as a 'scholar' is a consequence of the inhospitable culture of school that African American children encounter, rather than a consequence of peer pressure."[16]

The "Acting White" Theory

Researchers have also stated that some African American students underachieve because they equate school success with being required to "act white." In other words, these students infer that they have to reject their home culture to succeed academically. Fordham's work was instrumental in explaining this theory.[17] In *Bad Boys*, Ferguson described how African American fourth and fifth grade boys made a conscious choice to "disidentify" with the school, as a result of negative schooling practices. Like many of the students in Fordham's study, the boys in Ferguson's study concluded that the price they would have to pay for school success was much too high. According to Ferguson, "African American youth know that what they bring to school from family and community is seen as deficient, is denigrated, devalued. They know that their family background, their experience, their modes of expression—both verbal and nonverbal—are detrimental to their achievement. . . ."[18]

Acting white is diametrically opposed to the "cool pose" coping mechanism that some African American males adopt. According to Majors and Mancini-Billson, the cool pose or "cool mask" enables the African American male to "deal with the closed doors and negative images of himself that he must confront on a daily basis."[19] This pose or mask is characterized by aloofness, lack of emotion, fearlessness, detachment, power, and style. Among the positive consequences are that it serves as a protective mechanism, gives African American males a sense of pride, and serves as a form of social competence. However, the negative consequences often surface through underachievement and behavioral problems in school.[20]

In the fall of 2002, one of my African American graduate students expressed the exasperation that illustrates what some other African Americans who have used education to "improve" their lives may have felt. "We do not fit in anywhere," she stated. "The whites never fully accept us, no matter how much education we have, and many African Americans reject us because of our education." I told her that she was absolutely correct and urged her to consider conducting a related study. What was most interesting to me was that the student learned this valuable lesson at a much younger age than I did.

When I went away to college during the late 1970s, I naïvely assumed that all of my family, friends, and acquaintances would be happy for me, if not proud. Upon returning home periodically for breaks and vacations, I learned otherwise. I was shocked when one of my younger brothers was not only unimpressed that I was a college student but accused me of "just trying to be like white people" for going to college in the first place.

Since then, I have noticed that my educational accomplishments have generated a predictable pattern: many whites tend to treat me more respectfully when they learn that I am "educated" as opposed to being an "ordinary" African American. Conversely, many less-educated and even some highly educated African Americans are suspicious; I have to prove to them that I do not act white and have not forgotten my urban roots.

I am convinced that like the aforementioned graduate student, many African American students from urban backgrounds are a lot wiser and more prescient than I was at their age. Unlike myself, they can see ahead of time the great price that must be paid if they are to become highly educated in the traditional sense. Perhaps they can foresee the fact that a formal education might separate them from their natural style of speaking, their culture, community, family, and friends, and they conclude that the price might be too high to pay. This topic is revisited in Chapter Five.

The Peer-Pressure-and-the-Lure-of-Street-Life Theory

Another theory that has been used to explain African American student underachievement posits that peer pressure and the lure of street life cause many African American students to reject school and a formal education. In *What African American Parents Want Educators to Know,*[21] several parents described how peer pressure had a negative effect on their own schooling experiences and those of their children. One mother said that, in less than a year, her daughter went from being a good student who was close to graduating from high school to a student who would not graduate on time. The daughter had earned failing grades and was lacking numerous course credits. The cause, according to her mother, was a boyfriend of whom the parents did not approve.

Another parent said that he dropped out of school during eleventh grade because of a boring curriculum and unqualified teachers, harassment by school security, and the lure of street life. Regarding school, he stated: "The only thing I could say about the educational system is we need more qualified teachers. . . . I could say that in junior high and high school, some of the teachers . . . knew about as much as I knew. That's probably one reason why I left, because I felt like I was not learning anything."[22] Nevertheless, peer pressure and the lure of street life also contributed to his decision to drop out: "When I was in high school . . . I was harder. I wanted to run the streets more then. I wanted to be bad, like everybody else. I wanted the fast money like everybody else and fast cars. I wanted all the girls to look at me."[23] Consequently, he dropped out of school and became a drug dealer, which resulted in a five-year prison sentence that eventually caused him to change his lifestyle.

Another parent said that the desire to have the material possessions many of her friends had and the desire to fit in with her friends led to her decision to drop out of school. She stated: "I wore bifocals until I was in the tenth grade. In eleventh grade, I lost my bifocals. I wanted to do what my friends were doing. I wanted to hang out. I wanted my own job, and I wanted to get what I could get."[24] Although her mother tried to dissuade her from dropping out of school, she did so anyway. She explained: "The pressure, the pressure was getting to me. My friends were doing this, so I said, 'I'm stopping everything. I'm going to do what my friends are doing.' I went and got a job, and kept on working. Then I got pregnant."[25] In each of these cases, the parents were extremely concerned about the effects of peer pressure on their own children's schooling experiences.

Despite the fact that the lure of the street has always competed with schools for the minds of African American youths, as evidenced by the previous examples, today that lure appears to be stronger than ever. In *The Hip Hop Generation: Young Blacks and the Crisis in African American Culture,* Bakari Kitwana, a former magazine editor and the editorial director of a book publishing company, gave a detailed description of how the situation has changed. Kitwana stated that during previous eras "Black youth were more likely to derive values and identity from such traditional community institutions as family, church, and school. . . . Today, the influence of these traditional purveyors of Black culture [has] largely diminished. . . . Now media and entertainment are among the major forces transmitting culture to this generation of Black Americans."[26]

One result has been the emergence of the black hip hop generation. This generation, according to Kitwana, consists of African Americans who were born between the years 1965 and 1984. Their examples, values, attitudes, and worldview have influenced many of today's youth from all socioeconomic levels. The black hip hop generation's "complex worldview" includes "a severe alienation between the sexes," an openness "to family arrangements other than the traditional family," "Black pride," and a preoccupation with materialism. Kitwana wrote that "like our White peers [we] are more likely than our parents' generation to be obsessed with our careers and getting rich. For us, achieving wealth by any means necessary is more important than most anything else. . . ."[27]

According to Kitwana, this preoccupation with getting rich quickly stems from at least two sources. The first is the high unemployment rate in urban black communities. In many cases, the education system has failed to prepare young blacks for the workforce or for college. Moreover, some black youths conclude that even with a high school diploma finding a job that pays enough to live comfortably is difficult. Furthermore, Kitwana asserted that because of racism many black youths find it difficult to even find a job in a store in their own community. "Until these employment issues are addressed," he wrote, "Black youth must continue to explore creative options."[28] One of these "creative options" is selling drugs, which is directly related to the high rate of prison incarceration among African Americans.

Another source of this preoccupation with getting rich quickly is the frequency with which rags-to-riches stories are reported by the media. According to Kitwana, "Professional athletes and entertainers routinely secure million-dollar contracts. It's nearly impossible to find a kid on the block who doesn't think he can be the next Puff Daddy or Master P., Chris Webber, or Tiger Woods."[29]

In spite of much negativity—including misogyny, disrespect, glorification of gangs, the prison culture, and gangsta rap—a strong political agenda remains one of the black hip hop generation's top priorities, according to Kitwana. In addition to the goal of increasing employment opportunities for black youths and adults, developing a strong economic infrastructure in urban communities, eliminating poverty and disease among black youths, and improving the public, and private, K–12 and higher education systems are also part of their agenda. Kitwana wrote, "As many hip hop generationers struggle to make a living in today's world, they support any changes at the elementary and secondary levels . . . that will prepare young blacks for employment options in a high-tech global economy."[30] These changes must include improvements that not only prepare students for college but make college more affordable.[31]

Although it is true that peer pressure and the lure of street life compete with schools for the minds of African American and other youths, several cautionary notes are needed. First, these problems are not new. Second, in spite of these strong and often negative influences, countless African American youths are able to withstand these pressures. Third, many of them continue to be strongly influenced by positive values from their parents, extended family members, and religious and community-based organizations that promote cultural pride and good citizenship.

The Parents-Are-at-Fault Theory

Numerous researchers have found that there is a positive correlation between parent involvement and academic achievement. Moreover, the U.S. Department of Education identified several other benefits of parent involvement: a higher rate of homework completion, an increased rate of high school graduation, and a higher college attendance rate, as well as a positive effect on students' attitudes and behavior.[32]

In spite of the well-documented benefits of parent involvement, many teachers are dissatisfied with the amount of involvement of some parents in their children's schooling. A common belief among educators is that certain children perform poorly in school because their parents do not care about their education. In most cases, these assumptions are made about poor parents, African American parents, and Latino parents.[33] I believe that many teachers assume the majority of their African American students have parents who do not care. In fact, as noted in Appendix I, 34 percent of the inservice participants at the four schools blamed parents for African American student underachievement. To address the question "Do African American parents really care about their children's education?" in that training I presented related points from other researchers as well as my own *African American Teens Discuss Their Schooling Experiences*[34] and *What African American Parents Want Educators to Know*.[35]

In *African American Teens Discuss Their Schooling Experiences*, high school seniors were asked to rate the level of their parents' or guardians' involvement in their elementary, middle, and high school education. Seventy-four percent of the students rated their parents' or guardians' involvement in their elementary school education as "excellent" or "good," 62 percent of the students rated their parents' or guardians' involvement in their middle school education as "excellent" or "good," and nearly 60 percent rated their parents' or guardians' involvement in their high school education as "excellent" or "good." During the interview phase of the study, participants described specific ways in which their parents and guardians assisted them academically, such as by modeling reading and reading to them, and by encouraging them to attend college.[36]

In *What African American Parents Want Educators to Know*, the 129 participants were given numerous opportunities to describe their involvement in their children's education. Eighty percent of the parents and guardians rated their involvement in their children's education as "excellent" or "good." There were eleven specific ways the majority of parents and guardians offered academic assistance to their children. Four common practices (listening to children read, buying books for children, reading to children, and encouraging children to read) pertained to literacy. In other words, helping their children become better readers was an important goal for most of the parents and guardians. Other strategies that the majority of the parents and guardians used regularly were talking to their children about school, contacting teachers, encouraging children to attend college, helping with homework, encouraging children to check their class work and homework, limiting television viewing, and helping their children study for tests.[37]

Two additional findings that surfaced in *What African American Parents Want Educators to Know* provide important information about the discrepancy, on the one hand, between what many teachers believe about African American parent involvement and on the other hand the high ratings that the African American students gave in the first study, and the ratings parents and guardians in the second study gave to their involvement. Several parents and guardians inferred from their treatment by school personnel that they were not really welcome on campus. For example, one African American father said that whenever he went to visit his son's middle school, school personnel were clearly intimidated by his presence.

Although he dressed conservatively, teachers and school security were always suspicious of him. He stated: "They were intimidated because I'm a big African American man. When I walk on campus, I'm always asked a lot of questions by security guards and different teachers. . . . They don't make eye contact with me, even though I dress very conservatively."[38]

A mother said that whenever she offered to serve as a classroom volunteer she was told that her help was not needed; yet teachers would often complain about her children. "I ask the teachers if they need any extra help," she said. "I tell them that if my kids need help, I'll be there and I will help. And do you know what the teachers tell me? 'We don't need help.' But at the end of the school year, they have a problem with my kids."[39] Thus, like the aforementioned father, this mother concluded that teachers feared her: "I think it's that I'm intimidating to the teachers because they aren't teaching fair. I do not know if they're fearful or what. I've offered my help several times. . . . They let other parents come and volunteer their services. But I have never once been asked to come and sit in the classroom. There are things that they don't want me to see, but I see a lot."[40]

The second finding was that teachers appear to be measuring parent involvement through a very limited paradigm. Hence, they equate nonattendance at "back to school night" and "open house" with a lack of parental concern about their children's education. In actuality, however, most of the parents and guardians in the study were engaging in practices at home to assist their children academically of which teachers were ignorant.[41]

In *Learning While Black*, Hale presented numerous examples of how schools can actually deter African American parents from being visibly involved in their children's formal education. She wrote, "If you were to listen to educators talk among themselves, you might believe that everything that is wrong with the education of lower-income African American children is the fault of their parents."[42] Conversely, Hale found that common school practices often serve as deterrents to parent involvement and cause many

African American parents from upper, middle, and lower socioeconomic backgrounds to become frustrated "as they try to cut through
the 'psychobabble' they hear from teachers about their children."[43]
Moreover, Hale found that even many highly educated African
American parents "do not have the training in education that
would enable them to cut through teachers' attempts to project
their own incompetence back onto the child. How much worse
must be the outcomes for children whose parents . . . are overwhelmed by what it takes to keep their heads above water emotionally, psychologically, and financially."[44]

In my own research, observations, and experiences, I have concluded that most African American parents do care about their
children's education, and that some African American parents express caring differently from how white middle-class and upper-class
parents do. A good example is the contrast between how my mother
expressed caring about my education and how I have seen white
parents do so.

During my childhood, my mother, a single parent of six children whose main priority was to keep us fed, clothed, and with a
roof over our heads, expected the older children to do their homework and then assist the younger children with theirs. She often
asked, "Did you do your lesson?" and expected that we had completed the homework. She did not check over our work, but she
gave us feedback about each report card and clearly took our education seriously. Conversely, when I became a parent I was shocked
to see how far some upper-class and middle-class parents of private
school students (of all races and ethnicities) would go to give their
children the "unfair educational advantages" that Hale described.
When my children were assigned to build a replica of a California
mission or to create a dinosaur from scratch, my husband and I purchased the materials they needed, gave them advice, and answered
related questions. In the case of the dinosaur project, I even helped
my son dip the strips of newspaper into the papier mâché paste,
apply the gooey strips to his model, and mount and paint it. However, believing that it would be dishonest to do more, and that

doing the projects themselves would help our children become more responsible students, my husband and I did little else to assist them. When my children took their projects to school, they became ashamed of their work, for many of their classmates turned in masterpieces that they openly bragged had been created by their parents. During one school year, a second grade teacher became so exasperated by this common practice that she actually sent a letter home asking parents to please let their children do the work themselves.

These experiences led me to conclude that there are cultural differences in how upper-class and middle-class parents and many African American parents define "parent involvement." Some parents of color believe that since teachers have received formal training to educate students, most of the burden should be placed on the teachers' shoulders. However, although they are receiving paychecks to educate all children, many teachers would prefer for the parents to do more than some are capable of doing.

One of the main conclusions I have drawn from my study of African American parents can be summarized by an old Native American proverb: "Never judge a man until you have walked a mile in his moccasins." I can understand the frustration of teachers who struggle to teach African American children, often without seeing the desired results. Nevertheless, just as it would be wrong for African American parents to make assumptions about what goes on behind the closed doors in a teacher's home, it is just as wrong for educators to assume without proof that African American parents do not care about their children's academic welfare—and missing back to school night or open house is not adequate proof.

Underprepared Teachers

As a result of the No Child Left Behind Act,[45] one of the U.S. Department of Education's most pressing goals is to ensure that every child has a "highly qualified teacher." The most obvious reason is that countless students throughout the nation are relegated to classrooms in which their teachers are underqualified or underprepared to teach. Although it is convenient and popular for many educators, researchers, and the public to attribute African American student underachievement to parents and students, it has been well documented that poor children and African American and Latino students in urban schools are disproportionately represented among the students whose teachers tend to be underqualified and underprepared.

According to "Meeting the Highly Qualified Teachers Challenge," a report by the U.S. Secretary of Education in 2002, "Nationwide six percent of teachers lack full certification, but the share of uncertified teachers is higher in high poverty schools and certain fields like special education, math, and science."[46] In this same report, Rod Paige, the secretary of education, cited numerous studies that linked teacher qualifications to student academic achievement. In another study, Ingersoll drew a similar conclusion, stating "The quality of teachers and teaching is undoubtedly one of the most important factors shaping the learning and growth of students."[47] Among the consequences of the out-of-field teaching (teachers teaching subjects in which they did not major or minor) that has been common in middle schools and urban schools that Ingersoll listed were a negative learning environment, low achievement, and a lack of critical thinking instruction.[48] In another report, "Eliminating Barriers to Improving Teaching," the U.S. Department of Education declared, "Research shows that the quality of teaching in our classrooms is the most important in-school factor in improving student achievement."[49] However, the department admitted that "despite increased awareness of our teacher-quality challenges and earnest efforts to address them, we as a nation are still far from having a caring and competent teacher in every classroom."[50]

Low Teacher Expectations

Although only 9 percent of the inservice participants (see Appendix I) admitted to having low expectations for their African American students, low teacher expectations are common in public schools. For poor children and children of color, there is a greater likelihood of being subjected to low teacher expectations. According to Hale, "Inferior educational outcomes are tolerated for African American children day in and day out, in inner-city, suburban, and private school settings."[51]

In summarizing the recurring themes in research about teacher expectations, Gay identified five:

1. Teacher expectations significantly influence the quality of learning opportunities provided to students.

2. Teacher expectations about students are affected by factors that have no basis in fact and may persist even in the face of contrary evidence.

3. Assumptions about students' aptitude are difficult to change.

4. Teachers tend to believe that white students and some Asian American students are smarter than other students.

5. Teachers who feel less confident about their teaching ability are more likely than others to have low expectations for students.[52]

A white elementary school principal once told me that many of the teachers at her predominantly Latino elementary school said they did not offer the children a challenging curriculum because "they felt sorry for them." Several years ago, I conducted a workshop at another school where the teachers felt the same way. When I asked why, the teachers told me they believed that most of their students would not live past ninth grade, as a result of the high degree of gang-related violence in the community.

The tone about expectations is often set by administrators. The result is that teachers who choose to have high standards become the bad guys. A good example of this involves the son of a friend of mine. This friend, an African American, is one of the best teachers and most well-respected educators I know. She passed this love of and dedication to teaching onto one of her sons. As a new teacher, he went into his middle school classroom with passion, conviction, high standards, and a strong desire to help his students (who were primarily African Americans and Latinos) soar academically. However, he was derailed and destined to fail. He encountered much resistance and pressure to lower his standards. Ironically, the pressure did not come from his students. It came from his principal, a Latina; and an African American veteran teacher who urged him to "just let students pass the class." The principal told him that his standards were too high and that he was expecting too much from "these" kids. This pressure and lack of administrative support eventually drove a promising young teacher completely out of the teaching force.

Like so many other aspects of teaching, teacher expectations can become a self-fulfilling prophecy. The work of Marva Collins is illustrative of this point. Collins, a nationally known Chicago educator, demonstrated that African American students in urban communities can excel academically if teachers raise their expectations and use effective instructional practices.[53] Conversely, when administrators and teachers set low standards for students, they fail to equip them with the skills and knowledge that they will need to compete for high-paying jobs and admission to four-year colleges and universities. When teachers choose or are forced to assign passing grades to students just for showing up to class or are forced to engage in grade inflation, they are doing a great disservice to their students—and, if they have a conscience, to themselves as well.

Teachers' Negative Beliefs About African American Students

As shown repeatedly throughout this chapter, many theories have been used to explain African American student underachievement. I strongly believe that teachers' attitudes and negative beliefs resulting in low expectations and a nonchallenging curriculum contribute to this underachievement. I have drawn this conclusion from my own research and that of other scholars. I have also drawn it from my teaching experience, schooling experience, and stories that others have shared with me. Although only 10 percent of the teachers who attended the inservices I conducted during summer 2002 said they believed that most of their African American students did not want to succeed academically, I suspect that a much higher percentage of educators actually believe this.

Laziness, apathy, and a lack of interest in learning are some of the ways that some teachers would explain African American underachievement. I agree that some African American students are lazy, and I agree that some are apathetic. However, I also know for certain that the same is true for some white, Asian, and Latino students. What I disagree with is the argument that African American students do not want to learn, for in all of my years of teaching I have never met a student—of any race or ethnicity—who did not want to learn. I have seen students at all levels (including teachers and administrators enrolled in graduate school) who wanted to receive a grade they did not earn, and I have seen students who did just enough work to get by. However, I have never ever seen a student who wanted to sit in a classroom for any length of time and not learn anything meaningful. One reason some teachers assume African American students do not want to learn is that students may covertly or overtly engage in acts of resistance to a boring, non-challenging, and culturally irrelevant curriculum, a topic that is revisited in Chapters Three and Eight. Another reason is that students may infer negative messages from teachers that result in a self-fulfilling prophecy. Two negative schooling experiences that made a lasting impact on my husband, Rufus, occurred during elementary school. They illustrate how teachers' beliefs can affect students' outlooks and attitudes.

Unlike my husband, since childhood I have been an avid reader. I love reading biographies, autobiographies, and books about history. I believe one of my greatest accomplishments as a parent is that I passed my love for reading on to my children, who enjoy reading and receiving books as gifts and visiting bookstores in shopping malls. In fact, my oldest daughter is an English literature major at a university. Whereas my children and I love reading and discussing books, my husband, Rufus, is the opposite of us in this respect. As the technology director for a school district, he enjoys reading materials and magazines pertaining to technology and fly-ing airplanes. Beyond this, he finds little enjoyment in reading. What is most ironic about this is that he started out as a bibliophile. Although he was reared by grandparents who were functionally il-literate because they had to drop out of elementary school to work in the fields, he developed an early love of reading. This love of reading started in church.

Before he even started school, the Sunday School teacher at his small church instilled in him a strong desire to read. Each week, every child received a little card that contained a Bible story and a related picture. Once the children were old enough to read the cards on their own, they took turns reading orally. Later, when he started school, because they lived in a rural area that did not have schools within walking distance Rufus and the other African Amer-ican children from his neighborhood rode buses to the predomi-nantly white schools in the southern part of the city.

Several years after Rufus learned to read, his second grade teacher announced that every two weeks prizes would be awarded to the student who had read the most pages for recreational reading. Be-cause he already loved to read, the promise of a prize galvanized him. He began to read more than ever. When the teacher asked the children the number of pages they had read during the previous two weeks, it turned out that Rufus had read the most pages. Another African American second grader, a girl, had read the second high-est number of pages.

To Rufus's dismay, instead of receiving praise or a prize for his accomplishment, the teacher accused him of lying. According to Rufus, the teacher said, "Rufus, you know that you did not read that many pages." Almost immediately, this little second grader, one of the few African American children in this predominantly white class, went from elation to dejection. He had read numerous books and enjoyed doing so, but the prize that he deserved would not be awarded to him, merely because his teacher believed that the little African American boy from an impoverished background, in which his guardians were elderly and uneducated, could not have possibly read more books than his white classmates—or even more than an African American girl. From that point on, the act of reading became associated with pain and humiliation for him. "I was done," he remarked. "It was the second time that this had happened to me. In first grade it had happened with a spelling word. I enjoyed most of my education, but after going through universities and graduate school, and teaching for seventeen years, these two incidents stand out in my mind."

According to Rufus, the first incident occurred the preceding year, when he and his classmates were participating in a routine in-class spelling bee. He explained:

There were two of us left, a white kid and myself. The teacher accused me of misspelling a word. But I didn't misspell it. She told me to sit down, but I knew that I had not misspelled the word. Because my grandparents had taught me to respect authority, I sat down, even though the teacher had disrespected me. So, I waited until recess and got the dictionary. I showed her the word in the dictionary. In order to look things up in the dictionary, you have to have some clue as to how to spell the word. I knew that I did not misspell it. When I showed it to her, the teacher said, "Oh, you're right." No apology; nothing. That was it. The way that she dealt with it was wrong. I was very upset and felt that I had been treated unfairly. It didn't matter that I had not won the spelling bee. What mattered was that she had falsely accused me in front of the whole class, so she should have apologized in front of the class. She was the teacher. I eventually told all of my classmates what had happened. This was the same teacher who forced me to become right-handed. I was writing with my left hand, and she walked up to me and took the pencil out of my left hand, and said, "You won't make it in this world writing left-handed." And she forced me to become right-handed.

Although most of his elementary school teachers treated him fairly, Rufus attributed the problems that he had with these two teachers to a case of mistaken identity, in which he was falsely accused of pushing an African American girl into a trashcan during first grade and to "that whole black boy threat thing to women. This is a gender thing, a perception thing," he explained. In both cases, he believed the teachers disbelieved him, primarily "because of stereotypes about African American boys, and boys in general." Still, after being falsely accused of pushing the girl into the trashcan, he found that the principal, unlike his teacher, gave him a chance. He explained: "The principal interviewed me and then closed the door. She said 'Rufus, I believe you. I'm going to hit my hand real hard with this paddle, like I'm swatting you. Every time I hit my hand, I want you to scream like I'm hitting you.' And that's what she did. She gave me three swats, but she didn't hit me; she hit her hand and then said, 'Go back to class.'"

Summary of the Review

The review of theories that have been used to explain the causes of African American students' underachievement illustrates several salient points. First, there is no simple answer; instead, multiple theories exist. Second, the research can be divided into two categories.

One category pertains to research that blames "the victims" (students and their parents) for African American students' underachievement. As noted in Appendix I, 10 percent of the inservice participants said they believed that most of their African American students did not want to succeed academically. Furthermore, 34 percent said that, prior to attending the inservice, they believed African American parents and guardians were mainly responsible for African American students' underachievement. Therefore, the teachers in both of these groups would probably agree with research supporting the first category of explanations. The second category comprises research attributing African American underachievement to schooling factors. These factors illustrate the many ways in which inequality of educational opportunity is perpetuated.

Both categories of research became evident in California during the 2002–03 school year. When the results of the California High School Exit Exam were published, the fact that the majority of Latino and African American students failed caused a huge public debate. The exam results were important because they revealed that the majority of Latino and African American students who took it were in jeopardy of not graduating on time. Consequently, some individuals suggested that the students should be required to complete an extra year of high school. Others recommended that enforcement of the exam be postponed. One of the most sobering and rational voices that weighed in on the dilemma was that of Jeannie Oakes, a UCLA professor who has written about the effects of inequality of educational opportunity—particularly through tracking—for decades. In an opinion essay published in the *Los Angeles Times*, Oakes and Rogers maintained that instead of blaming students for their failure to pass the exam, critics should consider other factors: the high percentage of underqualified teachers, overcrowded classrooms, and the lack of textbooks and other instructional materials in the schools the Latino and African American students attended.[54]

Necessary Attitudes and Beliefs

Teachers' beliefs about African Americans and other students have far-reaching consequences. However, as a result of deficit theories, many Americans believe that children from nonmainstream backgrounds are innately inferior to middle-class and upper-class white children. Unfortunately, some teachers have the same belief. Delpit said, "We say we believe that all children can learn, but few of us really believe it."[55] Conversely, Nieto said, "A small number of these teachers may believe that their unsuccessful students are genetically or culturally inferior. But I am convinced that the vast majority of teachers do not harbor such racist and classist beliefs."[56] Regardless of the number of teachers who hold negative beliefs about African American students' aptitude, the main point is that their beliefs and attitudes affect student achievement through the curriculum and through instructional practices. For example, teachers who believe that African American students do not have the aptitude to excel academically are likely to have low expectations and offer a watered-down curriculum, which directly contributes to the underpreparedness of African American students.[57] According to Gay, "Over time, negative teacher attitudes and low expectations cultivate 'learned helplessness' among African American students."[58] But as Comer concluded, "We can't begin to make the degree of change that is needed . . . without dismantling our paralyzing myths."[59]

When it comes to African American and Latino students, in my opinion, too many teachers waste time focusing on their perceived deficits, which often are merely cultural differences that teachers measure against middle-class norms. One of the recommendations I always make to teachers who want to increase their efficacy with students of color is to stay away from the negative teachers on campus. At each school, there is usually a group of teachers who can find nothing good in students of color. They sit in the teachers' lounge or in someone's classroom—often the classroom of the ringleader of the negative group of teachers—and spend their lunch time criticizing the home life, behavior, styles of discourse, community, and aptitude of students of color as if they and their own homes, culture, and families were perfect. As a result, I tell teachers to stay away from this group; otherwise their negativity will spread like poison and soon corrupt the most optimistic of teachers. Before long, optimism is replaced with hopelessness and despair about the students.

In conclusion, numerous researchers have found that there are several attitudes and beliefs that teachers must have if they are to work effectively with African American students. Among them are the beliefs:

- That all children can learn
- That African American children are not *tabula rasa* (blank slates); they arrive at school with cultural capital and talents that should be built upon
- That most African American parents do care about their children and often assist them academically in ways that are invisible to teachers
- That it is the teachers' job to do their best with all students; it is not their job to judge students' culture, family, and so forth, as Hale so aptly stated[60]
- That it is not wrong to recognize racial and cultural differences among individuals; when it comes to viewing people, colorblindness does not exist (teachers who claim they are colorblind are merely in denial)[61]
- That most African American children do want to learn, and when teachers seek the best in them that is usually what they find, as Marva Collins and other educators have proven[62]

Like Collins and other researchers, A. Wade Boykin, a researcher at Howard University, stressed the need for an additive pedagogy for African American students.[63] Unlike the traditional model of schooling, which uses a "talent-sorting, weeding-out approach," Boykin's talent development model encourages teachers to build on students' strengths and use their cultural capital to improve their academic achievement. The eight components of Boykin's model, as well as my suggestions earlier in this chapter, can be combined with the strategies in Chapter Two to help teachers increase their efficacy with African American students:

1. High standards for all students
2. Multiple determinants of students' success
3. Building on the assets that students bring to school

4. A developmentally appropriate education
5. An active, constructivist approach to learning
6. A thematic and interdisciplinary curriculum
7. Preparation for the demands of the twenty-first century
8. Promotion of school as a caring community that focuses on students' academic and personal well-being[64]

2

Effective Instructional Practices

In April 2002, one of my beauticians, an African American mother of two school-age children, told me an interesting story. Her daughter, Lynn (not her real name), an eighth grader, had been getting such poor grades in her algebra class that she was in danger of being retained. Retention would mean that Lynn would be unable to start high school the following year. Both mother and daughter were panic-stricken, fearing that the letter of retention would arrive in the mail any day.

During this stressful period, the mother described her dilemma to another customer, who, it turned out, also had a daughter. The difference was that the customer's daughter was an undergraduate at a local university, and she loved math. In fact, she loved math so much that the customer was certain that her daughter would be willing to tutor Lynn. After contacting the customer's daughter, the beautician scheduled a tutoring session for Lynn.

One tutoring session transformed Lynn from a math-phobic eighth grader who feared she would be unable to start high school on time into a self-confident student who excelled at algebra. Not only did her grades improve but she actually began to love algebra. Moreover, both mother and daughter were thrilled when Lynn learned by mail that she would definitely be promoted to ninth grade. "I hugged her, and kissed her, and told her how proud I was of her," the beautician told me.

I was intrigued, so I asked her to explain to me why the young college student had been so effective with Lynn after just one tutoring session when the algebra teacher, who had spent nearly an entire academic year with her, had not. The beautician said that after listening to her daughter complain about the algebra teacher's instructional practices, she visited the classroom to see what was going on. During her visit, the teacher had students correct their homework as he called out the answers. Later, however, Lynn told her mother that the whole class had marveled at how differently the teacher behaved when the parent was present. According to Lynn, throughout the entire year he had never gone over the homework but had merely turned on an overhead projector and had students correct each other's work, using the overhead transparency as the answer key. In other words, he routinely failed to explain why certain answers were correct and others were incorrect. Lynn inferred that the teacher not only was impatient but wanted students to learn how to do the textbook work on their own. Furthermore, she believed he was unwilling to offer struggling students, such as herself, extra help when they were confused.

Conversely, Lynn got a different message from the college undergraduate who tutored her. First, she sensed that the tutor loved algebra and wanted her to love it too. She also sensed that the tutor really wanted to make algebra comprehensible to her. In explaining the basic concepts of algebra, the tutor was extremely patient. Moreover, the tutor not only believed that Lynn had the aptitude to excel at algebra but was able to convince Lynn to believe it herself. Consequently, when Lynn left the tutoring session she understood algebraic concepts that she had not previously understood, and her confidence level increased dramatically. When her mother tried to pay the college student for the tutoring session, she refused to accept payment, saying that the tutoring session was fun and she was merely doing what she loved to do.

This story was both heartwarming and perplexing to me. I was pleased to hear the obvious pride in my beautician's voice as she spoke about how her daughter's grades improved and the fact that she would be promoted to ninth grade. On numerous occasions, I had heard her describe various aspects of her children's schooling experiences and related concerns. This milestone was a turning point in her daughter's life. She no longer considered herself to be an underachiever, and her mother did not either.

Even so, the story perplexed me. The teacher, a trained professional, failed to do what an untrained college undergraduate managed to do during one tutoring session, and this teacher was not unique. He was merely one of countless teachers in schools throughout the nation who, for whatever reason, are unsuccessful in improving the academic achievement of African American students. There are numerous reasons why some teachers are effective with African American students and others are not. My personal experiences and research, as well as other scholarly works, have helped me to draw some definitive conclusions about effective and ineffective teaching.

As noted in the previous chapter, teacher qualifications are positively correlated to student achievement. Poor children and children of color, though, are more likely than others to end up with underqualified and ineffective teachers. Ironically, even teachers with the best intentions can become ineffective. For example, in one of my former graduate classes a white public high school teacher remarked, "I am convinced that no white teacher deliberately sets out to hurt African American children." Her strong conviction caused her words to remain with me long after the semester ended. In *Crossing Over to Canaan*, Ladson-Billings contended that having good intentions is not enough. "Most people who go into teaching do so because they really want to teach," she wrote. "They enjoy working with students and want to do it despite the lack of financial reward and occupational prestige. But there is a wide gulf between wanting to be a good teacher and actually becoming one. This gulf is particularly large for teachers who opt to teach in schools serving poor students and students of color."[1] Conversely, Hale argued that teachers "know how to teach and are able to teach effectively the children whose education is of importance to them.

They are willing to teach their own children effectively, as well as the children who are in 'the club.'"[2]

Therefore one of the most obvious ways teachers can increase their efficacy with African American students is to become qualified to teach the subject matter they are assigned to teach. Teachers who are weak in subject matter must do the work that is necessary to strengthen their skills. In addition to having subject matter competency, numerous other factors are linked to effective teaching of African American students. The sections that follow begin with general knowledge and strategies that teachers can use and then present information pertaining specifically to reading, writing, and math instruction for African American students. The professional development plan in the conclusion of this book contains recommended readings that describe additional strategies.

General Information and Strategies

In Learning While Black,[3] Janice Hale, an early childhood specialist, described a comprehensive, multifaceted teaching model that can help teachers increase their efficacy with African American children. "A process of education must be crafted that motivates African American children to regard academic activities as interesting and fun. They must be guided on a journey to a life-long love of learning,"[4] according to Hale. As it currently stands, Hale surmised, the monotonous drill and worksheet-based method of instruction that is common in urban schools prepares African American children for public assistance, unemployment, and incarceration. Thus Hale's model builds on the rich culture and history of African American children with the goal of instilling in them an intrinsic motivation to learn. Her model includes the use of thematic units, the creative arts, small group instruction, the development of social and conflict resolution skills, a balanced approach to literacy that includes phonics in the early grades, and hands-on activities in an "aesthetically pleasing" classroom setting. Moreover, in her model students are given choices that allow them to select topics of interest to study. "The intent is to create a learning environment that complements the culture of the African American community and stimulates higher-order thinking and creativity among African American children,"[5] she wrote.

Data from *What African American Parents Want Educators to Know*[6] and *African American Teens Discuss Their Schooling Experiences*[7] indicated that African American students and parents equate specific strategies and characteristics with outstanding teaching. These were the most frequently cited characteristics:

- They want teachers to make the curriculum comprehensible
- They want teachers to make the curriculum interesting
- They want teachers to give extra help during class, instead of telling struggling students to come before school, after school, or during lunch for help
- They want teachers to be patient in explaining subject matter
- They want a challenging curriculum
- They want beneficial homework that is collected, graded, and related to class work and tests
- They want teachers to encourage students to ask questions, instead of penalizing them for doing so

In my own teaching, I learned some specific ways to improve my efficacy with junior high school and high school students that were related to the very characteristics that later surfaced in my research with African American parents and students. The strategies included the use of the theory of small wins, the writing process, explaining the payoffs, using multiple means of assessment, allowing students to collaborate, connecting the curriculum to the students' personal lives, having high expectations (see Table 2.1, at the end of this chapter), and being on a constant quest to improve my pedagogy. Appendices A through H present examples of how teachers can use several of these strategies. The next three sections describe additional information about reading, writing, and math instructional strategies.

Effective Reading Instruction

In the United States, the "reading wars" have a long history that goes back at least to the 1920s.[8] As researchers, policy makers, and educators have heated debates over reading methods, poor children and students of color get caught in the crossfire. It has been extensively documented, for example, that on average African American students' reading scores, like their scores in other subjects, trail those of their white and Asian grade-level peers (and often, even their Latino peers).[9] This fact is indisputable. What is more controversial is how best to teach African American children to read. Nevertheless, like many other African American researchers, I have strong opinions about how teachers can teach African American children to read. My opinions stem from what I have learned about reading development throughout the years.

Despite always having been an avid reader, I never gave much thought to how reading is taught until I became a teacher. I earned my teaching credential at a time when whole language was adopted in California as the preferred approach to teaching reading. I loved the creativity and literature-based features of whole language and the goal of teaching reading, writing, speaking, and listening skills through the use of literature. Although I heard some of my colleagues complain about whole language, I did not take their concerns too seriously.

One day, however, the mother of one of my African American tenth graders shared a related story with me. "My fifth grade daughter is a much better reader than my tenth grader," she stated. When I asked what she thought the cause was, she said simply, "phonics." Her fifth grader had learned to decode words through a phonics-intensive curriculum, but her tenth grader had learned to read lists of words and then read stories containing the words through the

whole-word method. This method required the student to memorize words. "The problem," her mother remarked, "is that whenever
she sees a word that was never on any of the lists that she memo-
rized, she has no way of pronouncing those words, because she
never learned how to sound words out." Then, the mother gave me
a valuable bit of advice: "When your own daughter starts school,"
she urged, "make sure they teach her phonics first."

Until that point, I knew very little about phonics. Nevertheless,
as I searched for the best preschool for my daughter, each prospective school's approach to teaching reading was among my foremost
concerns. Subsequently, I ended up placing her in a preschool that
had an individualized Montessori-like curriculum. However, after
becoming disillusioned with the differential and negative treatment
that a preschool teacher subjected my daughter to, the following
year I placed her in a predominantly black Christian preschool. Her
new teacher, Sister Reed (not her real name), a middle-aged African
American grandmother, assured me that my daughter and all of her
classmates would be reading before the school year ended. She started
out teaching the students to sound out letters, blends, and eventually short words. This increased their confidence about their reading
ability, and by the end of the year—as Sister Reed had predicted—
my daughter was reading. What was most interesting was that Sister Reed was confident about her ability to teach the children to
read, and she was confident about their ability to learn to read
within that one school year. She did not look for deficits. Consequently, when my daughter entered kindergarten—at a mostly
white Christian school that was closer to my job—she was far ahead
of her classmates academically. On the first day of school, my daughter was shocked that the teacher (a first-year teacher) did not assign
homework, and when she requested homework the teacher was
clearly displeased. Moreover, my daughter believed that the class
work was too easy, for Sister Reed had taught her to expect to be
challenged. The result of Sister Reed's high expectations and strong
academic foundation was that this precocious little African American child unnerved her kindergarten teacher. By the end of the first

week of school, the teacher was strongly recommending that my daughter be promoted to first grade—immediately!

Several years later, my two younger children had a similar experience with learning to read. The school and teacher were different from those during my oldest daughter's initial reading experience, but the method was the same. Their teacher, Mrs. Layne (not her real name), an elderly white woman, started with phonics and quickly had most of the children reading short books. Children who were slower to catch on received extra help; they were not ignored. After my children were much older, I interviewed Mrs. Layne to learn the exact procedure that she used to teach kindergartners to read. I wanted to share her method with my graduate students who were beginning teachers.

Her method consisted of five steps. First she taught consonant sounds to the children. Next, she taught them short vowels. After they mastered the first two steps, she had them read short rhyming books containing common one-syllable words that reinforced these steps. Fourth, she taught them long vowel sounds, followed by having the children read books that reinforced this new information. The final step in her method consisted of teaching the children to pronounce word blends, followed by reading books that would allow them to practice all of their reading skills. After learning each step, the children received a small book to take home and practice reading with a family member. Once they had acquired these foundational skills, they were able to progress to reading more challenging books.

Later, when I became a doctoral student, I read more research about reading and wrote papers about the history of reading instruction in the United States. I also conducted a study to ascertain what teachers knew and believed about topics related to reading.[10] Shortly thereafter, I began to teach graduate reading courses full-time after having taught a similar course part-time at universities while I completed my doctoral studies. At some point during my first year as a full-time university professor, I decided to start "The Literacy Club," an after-school reading incentive program for struggling third and fourth graders. The program was eventually expanded to include fifth graders.

The curriculum model was based on what I had learned from my studies and from Sister Reed and Mrs. Layne. Hence the program rested on a balanced approach to reading development that included phonics exercises and whole language components. Although the children who participated in the program were from racially diverse backgrounds, the lessons I learned from the struggling readers in the program increased my knowledge about effective reading instruction for children, particularly African American children, because one of the participating schools was predominantly black.

The Literacy Club participants taught me that struggling readers know they read poorly. Being forced to read aloud in class is thus a great source of embarrassment for them. The children complained about teachers permitting their classmates to make fun of them as they struggled to read orally, or of teachers permitting their classmates to blurt out words that the children were struggling to decode. One African American fourth grade boy said he did not mind when the teacher corrected his reading mistakes because the teacher was older than he, but he did mind when his classmates did so. One way that this problem could be alleviated is for teachers to set a tone that discourages ridicule and that encourages tolerance for struggling students. The children in the program said that teachers should permit students to take reading materials home to practice reading, instead of forcing them to read unfamiliar material for the first time orally in class. A second lesson the children taught me was that they found the reading materials they were required to read in class to be extremely boring. The children wanted more interesting books to read.

Although I believe that many children, especially African Americans, need a strong phonics curriculum at the beginning of their formal reading instruction, I also believe that phonics can be abused and thus become counterproductive. During the early 1990s, the backlash against whole language resulted in the return to ascendancy of phonics, and eventually a call for a balanced approach to literacy. Even so, many school districts in California and in other states adopted scripted-reading programs that resulted in elementary students being subjected to a phonics-intensive curriculum that has the potential to destroy children's desire to read and their enthusiasm for reading. Those who are most likely to be hurt are African American, Latino, and poor children. Although in my opinion (and that of many other researchers) these children must learn to decode words at the very beginning of their formal reading instruction, at the same time they must be exposed to interesting and culturally relevant literature, and a strong emphasis must be placed on developing their reading comprehension skills.

The Language Experience Approach

During the period in which I ran The Literacy Club, I also served as a mentor at an elementary school that was not affiliated with the club. Thus I learned some additional lessons about improving children's reading skills. Two of the African American boys I mentored were twins from a single-parent home of ten children. Because there were three sets of twins in the family, eight of the children were in elementary school. Since their mother had a limited income, I knew that the twins I mentored (who were in kindergarten at the time) would probably not have access to a wide selection of children's books at home. Therefore, in addition to improving their literacy skills, one of my goals was to assist them in building a home library. I used three strategies to do this. (Each is a variation of the Language Experience Approach that was popular during the 1960s.)

The first strategy was that I made personalized books for each twin, by merely folding several sheets of construction paper and lined paper together, stapling the seam, and writing a colorful and illustrated original story about each boy. For example, one book that

I designed contained each boy's name, age, grade level, the city in which he lived, the name of his family members, and other details that each boy had shared with me, such as hobbies, favorite colors, and what he wanted to become when he grew up.

The second strategy was that I made blank books for each boy and had them dictate their own creative stories to me. As the child created the story, I would write each word he said. I wrote a few sentences on each page and left room for the boy to later draw and color a related picture. I learned that whereas the twins were excited about the personalized books I created for them, they were ecstatic about the stories they were encouraged to dictate. They made up stories about dinosaurs, monsters, their family members, and themselves. Not once did either say, "I don't know" or "I can't think of anything." If time had permitted, it seemed that their storehouse of stories would have been inexhaustible. But when they returned to the classroom, one twin was usually kicked out for failure to cooperate with the teacher's requests.

The third strategy that I used was to let the twins collaborate on a book together. I would start by saying, "Once upon a time" and let the boys take turns adding details to the story, until they created a complete story. This strategy was less effective than the previous two, because an argument would inevitably erupt after one twin attempted to upstage the other. For example, one twin might state, "Once upon a time, there was a dinosaur named Joe." Then the other twin might add, "and a bigger dinosaur came and ate Joe up." The first twin would get upset, because he wanted his character to live until the end of the book.

After all these types of book were completed, I would read each story to the boys after the story and the illustrations were completed. As I read, I would point at each word. Then we would discuss the stories. At the end of our time together, I suggested they take their books home and ask an older sibling or their mother to reread the story to them. The feedback that I received from the boys and an older brother and sister indicated that the books became a catalyst for family reading time.

Improving the Literacy Skills of Older Children

One of the greatest tragedies of the public school system is that many students, particularly those of color, leave the school system with poor reading skills. Even though this finding can be interpreted in different ways, functional illiteracy has been correlated with prison incarceration and poverty during adulthood.[11] Furthermore, studies have shown that for the most part students who have poor reading skills at the end of third grade remain academically behind their peers for the duration of their formal schooling.[12] The problem is compounded by the fact that when they reach junior high school and high school struggling readers are unlikely to receive the assistance they need, since many secondary school teachers have not been trained to teach reading skills.[13] Moreover, while teaching required reading courses for secondary school teachers, I found that many secondary school teachers are resistant, because they do not feel it is their job to teach students to read; in their opinion, the elementary school teachers should have done so. In turn, elementary teachers who fail to teach children to read point the finger at parents or at students. In spite of finger pointing by teachers, the fact remains that many middle school and high school students enter secondary school with poor reading skills. Regardless of how it happened, it is the responsibility of secondary teachers to help students become better readers. In the case where a student cannot decode words, the teacher should request the assistance of a reading specialist. In the case where a student has problems comprehending what is read, the Directed Reading Lesson Model can be effective.

Directed Reading Lessons (DRL), such as those described by Roe, Stoodt, and Burns,[14] are an effective way for teachers to make the curriculum relevant to students' lives and foster development of reading comprehension skills. These lessons usually have "prereading" activities, which activate students' prior knowledge and forge links with the reading assignment and their prior knowledge; "during" reading activities, to ensure that maximum comprehension occurs;

and "post" or "beyond" reading activities, such as formal and informal assessments, writing assignments, and projects. The DRL relies heavily on the use of questioning. Before they begin to read, students are given a list of questions to focus on as they read. These questions can help them identify the main ideas and concepts in the reading selection. According to schema theory (an underlying foundation of the DRL model), all individuals have a mental filing system in which knowledge is stored into categories. Reading comprehension is facilitated when students' prior knowledge is linked to new information. Because many upper elementary school students and secondary students can decode well but have problems comprehending what they read, the three-part DRL is a powerful tool that teachers at all levels can use to improve students' reading comprehension skills.

Improving Writing Skills

One of the saddest realizations that I have come to as a university professor is that many students (not only those of color) have not been taught how to write a decent sentence by their K–12 teachers— or, often, even by their undergraduate and graduate professors. In Chapter Seven, I tell a story about my freshman year in college, when for the first time in my life I was told I had poor writing skills. Because I had never been told this before, or even been given much help with the technical aspects of writing a simple sentence, I projected my problem onto the professor, whom I assumed to be racist. Since then, the chickens have come home to roost for me numerous times, in that students—particularly some African American graduate students—even at the doctoral level have become extremely angry at me when I point out grammatical errors in their writing and hold them to a high writing standard.

I have come to the conclusion that teaching K–12 students how to develop good writing skills is one of the most neglected aspects of teaching. Sadly, just as it is possible for students to graduate from high school with poor reading and poor math skills, it is likely for them to graduate without knowing how to write a simple sentence, much less a simple paragraph or a well-organized essay. A good example pertains to one of my former graduate students.

This third grade teacher had immigrated to the United States from Laos. She considered herself to be an outstanding teacher and often told us about the wonderfully creative assignments that her students were doing. Her entire demeanor toward me changed, however, when I handed back the first paper she wrote for my class. She was outraged at receiving a low grade, because of numerous grammatical errors and incomplete sentences. Although she had the option of revising the paper for a higher grade and taking advantage of an extra credit option, she chose to report me to the dean instead. After seeing a copy of the paper the student had handed in, the dean fully supported my position. Nevertheless, for the duration of the quarter the student continued to be angry at me. She failed to understand my point that in order to teach her students how to write decently, she first needed to work on the weaknesses in her own writing. Moreover, because she had made it all the way to a graduate reading program with instructors excusing her poor writing "because English was not her first language" (as one professor scolded me), she truly believed that I had treated her unfairly.

Throughout my fourteen years as a secondary school teacher, I tried many strategies to make writing a fun, as well as practical, activity for my students. I developed several rubrics, as well as a student handbook on the writing process, and used portfolios; I encouraged students to enter contests, and I showcased their work in award-winning anthologies. Furthermore, several of my students had their essays published in a local newspaper. As a result of these endeavors, trial and error taught me five important lessons.

First, I learned that in order to help students become better writers, I needed to teach them the basic rules of grammar and syntax. This is probably the most neglected aspect of writing instruction. One reason is that many teachers—myself included—were never taught these rules during their own K–12 schooling. Another reason is that when compared to other teaching responsibilities, teaching grammar can appear to be very tedious and boring. Some teachers work in schools where every student receives both a literature textbook and a grammar book. Unfortunately, this is not the norm for many schools. Still, teachers who work in urban schools in which funding is limited and textbooks are scarce should have little difficulty finding a class set of grammar books. Many school district warehouses, school library storerooms, and school and English department offices have unused grammar books that are merely collecting dust.

Once the books have been secured, a simple strategy is for teachers to assign grammar exercises for homework and then have students correct the exercises in class the next day. Another strategy is for teachers to assign grammar exercises as a ten- or fifteen-minute warm-up activity at the beginning of class. A third option is for teachers to give minilectures on grammar and then have students apply this information to a writing assignment.

My oldest daughter, Nafissa, is a good example of what can happen when a student is taught the rules of grammar and is continuously required to apply the information to writing assignments. During eighth grade, she had the toughest English teacher in her private school. This teacher had high expectations and assigned a lot of work from the grammar textbook; she also gave grammar tests throughout the entire school year. Although my daughter complained about this teacher and felt she was too demanding, the skills she learned in that class helped her become an outstanding writer. Today, as a college undergraduate, she has been accepted by three honor societies, earns outstanding grades (particularly on her writing assignments), and is the youngest tutor in the university's writing center.

Another lesson I have learned about helping students develop their writing skills is the importance of using the theory of small wins. This theory can be applied to all aspects of teaching. Many years ago, I was attending a conference at the University of LaVerne when I heard Professor Thomas Harvey describe the theory. The basic premise is that if individuals are permitted to learn new information in small steps, there is a greater likelihood that they will comprehend it, because their stress over learning the new material is greatly reduced. This theory is especially useful in teaching math skills and writing skills. Like scaffolding, it requires teachers to accept students as they are and to move them gradually to the targeted skill level. To do this effectively, teachers must first find out where the students are in their writing (or math skills). Teachers can apply this theory to writing by using several steps.

A good way to start is by conducting an informal writing assessment to identify students' strengths and weaknesses. For example, students can be asked to write a paragraph about how they spent their summer, or a paragraph about a significant event in their lives. This is also a good way for the teacher to set the tone for learning and to show students that their experiences and voices will be valued in the classroom. The "Time Line Project" (which was adapted from the model I learned from Diane Schuster, one of my former professors) in Appendix A and the "All About Me Project" in Appendix B are options that teachers can consider.

Next, the teacher should determine which writing weakness needs to be addressed first by identifying common problems among the students' paragraphs. Third, the teacher should develop an action plan by deciding which problems to address first and what strategies (such as minigrammar lessons) to use in addressing them. The overall goal should be for the teacher to create an action plan that allows students to gradually move from weakness to proficiency. If the majority of the students have extremely weak writing skills, then a good action plan would be to start at the beginning. The teacher would begin by teaching students how to write a basic sentence, consisting of a subject and a predicate. After giving students adequate opportunity to practice mastering writing a basic sentence, the teacher might then instruct students on how to write more complex sentences.

The next step could be to teach students the components of a basic paragraph: topic sentence, supporting details, and a closing statement. After students have mastered basic paragraph writing, they should be taught the components of a basic three-paragraph essay: introduction, body, and conclusion. This step could be followed by teaching them to use transitions to make their paragraphs flow. Subsequent steps could include writing five- and seven-paragraph essays, research papers, observational reports, and comparison-contrast essays.

A third important lesson that I have learned about teaching writing skills is that using a process approach to writing can be beneficial to students and teachers. It teaches students how to write in an organized fashion, and it helps them to accept more responsibility for the quality of their work. For teachers, it reduces the probability of having to correct papers that were written at the last minute. The six-step writing process I required for my junior high school and high school students included prewriting, drafting, sharing (getting written feedback about the rough draft from several individuals), revising (adding, deleting, and reorganizing information), rewriting (writing or typing the final draft that would receive a letter grade), and proofreading a minimum of three times. Students had to show evidence that they used all of the steps.

A fourth lesson I have learned is that to develop strong writing skills, students need detailed and frequent feedback from the teacher. The problem is that many teachers are reluctant to give extensive feedback about student writing. One reason is that they do not want to hurt the students' feelings. Nevertheless, if students do not receive feedback about their writing, mistakes become deeply entrenched bad habits that are difficult to break. The longer the students are permitted to repeatedly write the same errors, the harder it is for the teacher to improve those aspects of students' writing. The four most common mistakes I have seen in student writing samples at all levels—including graduate school—are sentence fragments, run-on sentences, a lack of pronoun-antecedent agreement, and no subject-verb agreement. These problems can be addressed through the grammar exercises that were previously recommended, but they also need to be identified on the actual writing sample.

A colleague once came to my classroom to tell me that one of my tenth grade students had shown him an essay I graded. "My concern," the colleague told me, "is that it looked like the paper was bleeding. Couldn't you have at least used something besides red ink?" I asked him what color he would prefer. He said that research had shown that green ink was less offensive than red ink. So I took his advice and began to correct students' papers with a green ink pen. I do not know if it made them feel any better or not, but I do know that regardless of the color of ink or even pencil the teacher uses, he or she has a professional responsibility to provide students with honest and frequent feedback about their writing. One way to offset some of the hurt feelings that might arise is for the teacher to use both commendations and recommendations when giving feedback.

The fifth lesson I have learned is that students need to engage in various types of writing. In addition to writing formal essays, character analyses, about themes in literature, and research papers, students can also write speeches, poetry, songs, short stories, children's books, and letters (to authors, editors, and politicians).

Effective Mathematics Instruction

Because I never taught math and did not conduct extensive research about specific math strategies during my doctoral studies, I know less about effective math instruction than about reading and writing instruction. However, details about African American students' experiences in math classes and my personal experience have given me strong opinions about some differences between effective and ineffective math teachers.

Although I was an avid reader and bibliophile during childhood, math was my least favorite subject. I do not remember when I first became aware of this fact, but my most negative math-related experience remains clear in my mind today. It happened at the end of the first week of tenth grade. I had been sitting in my algebra class all week, trying to comprehend the information the teacher shared and the problems he wrote on the board. Finally, I remained after class one day to tell him I was lost and confused. Instead of an offer of extra help or suggestions that might enable me to understand the class work and homework, the teacher simply told me that I should transfer out of the algebra class. If I could not understand what was going on, then I was the problem, instead of his instructional methods. As a result, I ended up taking a geometry class. For some reason, geometry was much easier for me to understand. A lot of it had to do with the teacher's approach to teaching. Although his course was rigorous, was loaded with homework, and required numerous tests, the geometry teacher was patient, willing to answer questions, and ready to give extra help to students who requested it. Nevertheless, as a result of my negative experience with algebra I came to believe that I did not have the aptitude to excel at math.

In *What African American Parents Want Educators to Know*[15] and in *African American Teens Discuss Their Schooling Experiences*,[16] complaints about math teachers and how math is taught to African American students surfaced repeatedly. Many of the parents said that during their own schooling, they believed they did not have the aptitude to excel at math. Therefore, many parents felt ill-equipped to assist their children with their math homework. In *African American Teens Discuss Their Schooling Experiences*, middle school and high school math teachers were cited most frequently as "worst teachers" and the students were more likely to fail a math course than any other course.[17] In both studies, participants tended to believe that many math teachers behave in an elitist manner when it comes to math instruction. Similar to the story at the beginning of this chapter, a common belief among the participants in both studies was that some math teachers assign math course work and homework but are unwilling to give extra assistance to students who need it or to offer strategies to parents who want to assist their children with their math homework. Of course, these experiences might also occur among other racial and ethnic groups as well, and they may not be exclusive to African Americans.

Unlike the African American parents in *What African American Parents Want Educators to Know* who continue to feel they do not have the aptitude to excel at math, my whole attitude about math has changed because of the outstanding instruction of one math teacher. There is a well-known saying about this math instructor that illustrates why he has won teaching awards: "David Drew can teach statistics to a rock." When I registered for his quantitative methods course during the second semester of my doctoral program, I was terrified and embarrassed about the fact that I had never taken algebra. A few days before the class was scheduled to begin, I telephoned him to say I did not feel I was capable of passing the class, so I planned to drop the course. Unlike my high school algebra teacher, Professor Drew encouraged me to give the class a chance and said he believed that I would do well. His words were surprising and reassuring. Nevertheless, on the first day of class, I was a nervous wreck.

Instead of plunging right into the curriculum, Professor Drew started the class by asking each student to introduce himself or herself. He also wanted to know how we felt about math. It turned out there were several other math-phobic students in the class—mostly women and students of color, who had probably had negative K–12 math experiences, as I did. When it was my turn to introduce myself, I said, "I hate math and I even get a headache when I have to balance my checkbook!" By the end of the class session, however, my aversion to math started to abate; I also began to develop a bit of confidence about my ability to succeed in the statistics class. This stemmed from three main reasons. First, Professor Drew told the entire class that he believed all of us had the potential to do well in the class. Second, he made the class work so comprehensible on the first day that his actions spoke louder than his words. Third, he told a powerful story about a group of African American college undergraduates who had been earning poor grades when they worked in isolation, but their grades improved dramatically after they began to form study groups. Before the class ended, several of us had formed a study group, and by the time I arrived home later that night I was eager to do the homework for the class.

During each succeeding class session, my confidence increased. Our study group met before class; we reviewed our class notes and homework and—thanks to a member of the group who was a math teacher—did extra problems, just like the students in the study that Professor Drew had described to us. During class, he would begin by reviewing the key points from the previous class session and providing related examples. He wanted to be perfectly sure that we understood the information before he introduced new information. This recursive style of teaching was effective, because it gave us ongoing and repeated exposure to information that we would be quizzed and tested on. Instead of using the textbook as the primary method of imparting information, he merely used it as a supplement to the information he covered in class. When students asked questions, he often prefaced his response by stating "That's a good question." This was extremely effective in encouraging questioning, a strategy that is a hallmark of good teaching.

Although he sought to build our self-esteem related to math, Professor Drew maintained extremely high expectations. Even though his teaching style helped me to become more confident about my math skills, the semester was grueling. In addition to regular homework assignments, we wrote papers for his class and took several difficult quizzes. The midterm for the class was worth a quarter of the course grade, and the three-hour final exam was 50 percent of the grade. Although three-quarters of the course grade was determined by how well we performed on these two challenging tests, Professor Drew also offered several extra-credit options. His teaching practices underscored the fact that he believed all of the support and self-esteem work he did was meaningless if students weren't actually achieving academically.

At the end of the semester, I was overjoyed to earn an A in my first statistics class. More important, I was determined to take the next three statistics courses in the sequence. When I finished my doctoral course work, I was proud that I had taken four statistics classes, and that I felt more confident about my math ability.

Each year, other new doctoral students find themselves in the same predicament that I was in when I took my first statistics class. By the end of the semester, their confidence has increased, and most are excited about continuing to take the rest of Professor Drew's statistics classes, courses that are crucial to their development as effective researchers. Today, many of his former students, including me, have published quantitative work in leading academic journals.

In his book *Aptitude Revisited*[18] and in a *USA Today* article[19] that he wrote, Drew underscored his belief that all students have the aptitude to excel at science and mathematics and that every student (including K–12 children) needs a rigorous math and science background. These fields are important because they are "the key factors that determine who . . . has access to wealth and power in our society and our economy. . . ."[20] Moreover, Drew stated that when parents or teachers assume that certain students do not have the aptitude to excel at math and science, they create a self-fulfilling prophecy— particularly for females, poor students, and students of color, who begin to doubt their capabilities.

As a result of extensive research and his own teaching experiences, in his book Drew made several recommendations that are designed to improve the quality of math and science education in the United States. First and foremost, he argued that the quality of math and science teachers must be improved. Starting in elementary school, students need math teachers who received a good math education and science teachers who received a good science education. They do not need underqualified math and science teachers, in other words teachers who did not major in these subjects. Second, students need math and science teachers who believe that all students, regardless of race or ethnicity, gender, or socioeconomic status, have the aptitude to excel in these subjects. Drew wrote that students "learn more when they are expected to excel, when they are not approached as being in need of remediation. . . ."[21] His third recommendation was that math and science teachers use a "talent development" rather than "mechanical" model of teaching that increases students' self-esteem about their ability to excel in these subjects. The talent development model requires the teacher to connect math and science to students' backgrounds and prior knowledge in an active, engaging manner. Using related stories or metaphors is one way in which teachers can accomplish this. Drew's fourth recommendation was that teachers raise their expectations for students. A fifth recommendation was that teachers permit students to work in cooperative learning groups; "students learn more effectively when they engage in a dialogue with other students (and with their instructors)," he asserted.[22]

Drew's own teaching record and his research illustrate that it is possible to improve the math achievement of African Americans, other students of color, females, and students from impoverished backgrounds. When I was interviewing African American high school students for the study on which *African American Teens Discuss Their Schooling Experiences*[23] is based, an African American male student shared a relevant story.

During the interview, he spoke excitedly about his favorite teacher, an algebra instructor. On the first day of school, the teacher gave every student a red paper flag and a green paper flag. The flags were made of a rectangle of red or green construction paper and then attached to a small Popsicle stick. The teacher told the students that they were to raise the red flag whenever they did not understand any information that she explained. If she saw a red flag, she would try to find an additional way of presenting the information to make it comprehensible. Before introducing new material, she wanted students to raise the green flag if they fully comprehended the previous topic.

When the African American high school student shared this story with me, I was impressed by his enthusiasm in describing this teacher, but also by the teacher's simple but ingenious strategy. By giving students—who were primarily Latino and African Americans—these flags on the first day of school, she conveyed three important messages to them. First, her message told students that she wanted them to succeed in her class by fully comprehending the subject matter. Second, her message told them she was willing to exercise patience in her teaching. Third, her message suggested that if a student did not understand the subject matter, then she assumed the problem was not caused by a deficit in the student; she merely needed to find an additional way of conveying the information to the student. This teacher obviously realized that students have different learning styles. Teachers must be willing to use multiple approaches, instead of the straight lecture style and overreliance on the textbook that is used by many math teachers. In *Learning While Black*, Hale emphasized this point. She said that to become effective math and science teachers, teachers of African American students must permit the students to work in groups, use manipulatives, and engage in hands-on activities. Moreover, the students must be taught the scientific method, which fosters higher-order thinking skills, and that math and science concepts should be interwoven throughout the curriculum.[24]

"The Nation's Report Card Mathematics 2000" revealed some important details about factors associated with higher average National Assessment of Educational Progress (NAEP) scores. The report identified numerous school factors that were linked to higher math scores for fourth, eighth, and twelfth graders. Several related to teacher qualifications, and others pertained to classroom practices.[25]

Eighth graders had higher average scores if their teachers majored in mathematics or mathematics education. Eighth graders whose teachers stated that they had been "very well-prepared" to teach number sense, data analysis, geometry, algebra, and measurement had higher scores than students whose teachers were not. Total years of teaching experience was also correlated with math scores. For example, fourth graders whose teachers had taught for three or more years received higher scores than those whose teachers had taught for fewer years. Eighth graders whose teachers had taught for more than ten years got higher scores than students whose teachers had less teaching experience. Teachers' familiarity with the National Council of Teachers of Mathematics (NCTM) standards was also connected to math scores. Fourth and eighth graders whose teachers were "very knowledgeable" about the NCTM standards had higher average scores than those with teachers having little or no knowledge of the standards.[26]

Four classroom practices had an impact on test scores: the amount of mathematics instruction time, frequency of calculator use, use of a mathematics textbook, and the amount of homework the teacher assigned. Fourth graders whose teachers reported spending four hours or more on mathematics instruction each week had higher scores than students whose teachers spent less time on math instruction. Eighth graders whose teachers reported spending "more than two and one half hours but less than four hours" each week on mathematics instruction had higher average scores than students whose teachers spent two and a half hours or less, or four or more hours per week on math instruction. These results suggest that elementary students need more math instruction time per week than eighth graders do. However, homework practices revealed different findings. For fourth graders, less homework was associated with higher grades, but for older students the converse was true. For example, fourth graders whose teachers did not assign daily math homework and those whose teachers assigned only fifteen minutes of daily math homework had higher average scores than students whose teachers assigned more than fifteen minutes of daily math homework. By contrast, eighth graders whose teachers assigned forty-five minutes of daily math homework had higher average scores than students whose teachers assigned less homework.[27]

Two other classroom practices that affected math scores were the frequency with which teachers permitted students to use calculators and whether or not students did math problems from a textbook. Although the frequency of calculator use did not have an impact on fourth graders' scores, it was significantly linked to higher average scores for eighth graders. Eighth graders whose teachers reported allowing them to use calculators daily, whose teachers taught students how to actually use calculators, whose teachers placed no restrictions on calculator use, and whose teachers permitted them to use calculators on tests had higher scores. Finally, fourth and eighth graders who reported never doing math problems from a textbook had lower scores than students who used a math textbook daily, weekly, or monthly.[28]

The report also found that students' attitudes about math had an impact on their scores. Fourth, eighth, and twelfth graders who liked math and who believed that math was useful for solving problems had higher average scores than those who disagreed.[29] Similarly, Drew's research[30] (as noted previously) and a seminal study that was published by the American Association of University Women (AAUW) uncovered important details about the link between students' attitudes about math (as well as science) and math achievement.

In the AAUW report, "Shortchanging Girls, Shortchanging America: Executive Summary," researchers studied a random sample of three thousand preadolescent and adolescent students on issues pertaining to self-esteem (see Chapter Three for more information). Several of the findings pertained specifically to math and science. For example, boys were more confident than girls about their math abilities, and were more likely than girls to place their math difficulties outside of themselves. Girls tended to blame themselves. Moreover, although boys were more likely than girls to like math and science, girls who liked these subjects had higher self-esteem and more tenacity about their career aspirations than those who did not. The researchers concluded that such common school practices as tracking, certain instructional techniques, less praise for girls by teachers, and less effective feedback from teachers result in a gender bias that sends girls negative messages about their math and science aptitude.[31]

Summary

One of the ongoing problems with education reforms in the United States is that we tend to go from one extreme to another and then back to a previous extreme. A common result is that teachers are given conflicting messages and students end up suffering. African American, Latino, and poor children usually bear the brunt of the effects of failed reforms.

The No Child Left Behind Act (NCLB)[32] is a good example. NCLB's overall objective of closing the achievement gap is a great and much-needed goal. Every child deserves a quality education that will empower the child and improve his or her future. However, NCLB's overemphasis on standardized test scores and the lack of adequate federal and state funding to support the act could doom it to failure, like most other education reforms. In spite of this, effective teachers know that no test can truly measure the depth and breadth of students' knowledge, since many students suffer from test anxiety and have poor test-taking skills. Therefore, they understand that multiple ways of assessing what students know through projects, writing assignments, individual and group presentations, portfolios, quizzes, and tests should be used. Because NCLB has given teachers and administrators the message that a standardized test score is the best judge of teaching efficacy and of children's learning, in the long run it may succeed in harming the children who have traditionally been hurt by the education system and who continue to be hurt by it today.

I have met many teachers who are exhausted and feel confused or even demoralized by the education system's history of moving from one reform to another and then back to previous reforms in rapid succession. However, some soon learn that to become effective teachers of African American students and other students, teachers must develop the ability to differentiate between nonsense and good teaching practices. Teachers who want to become good find ways to rise to the challenge, regardless of politics, the students' backgrounds, and so on. Chapter Four offers a detailed look at a teacher who chose to do so. Teachers who do not will continue to look for excuses. They blame the "system," the parents, and the students, but they never engage in any self-reflection that would suggest they themselves—through their negative attitudes, beliefs, expectations, and poor instructional practices—might actually be the biggest deterrent to African American student achievement.

Table 2.1 contains a list of strategies that I found to be effective with students of color and white students during my years as a junior high school and high school teacher. Most of the strategies can also be used with elementary school students. As noted previously, the professional development plan in the concluding chapter contains an extensive reading list. Many of these books include more instructional strategies.

TABLE 2.1. Eighteen Effective Strategies with Students of Color.

Strategy	*Comments*
1. Let students know you care.	Make it clear to them that you truly care about their welfare.
2. Share the real you, by letting them see you are a real human being.	Share your hopes, dreams, and background with students. Too many of them think that teachers have never walked a mile in their shoes or that teachers did not have to struggle to attain their own goals.
3. Have high expectations.	Do not lower standards or shortchange students, but be willing to take them where they are and gradually bring them up to your expectation level. The theory of small wins advocates leading individuals to a big goal through baby steps.
4. Keep reminding them of the big picture and why what they are doing in class is important.	Tell them constantly what the short-term and long-term benefits are.
5. Get to know students on a personal level.	Do so as early in the school year as possible; you will never look at them in the same way again. After you get to know them, you will not only understand them better but also be able to see their potential for academic success and creativity. Exercises requiring them to complete questionnaires about their likes, dislikes, goals, and dreams; autobiographical writing; partner interviews; the Time

TABLE 2.1. Eighteen Effective Strategies with Students of Color, Cont'd.

Strategy	*Comments*
	Line Project (see Appendix A), the All About Me Project (Appendix B), and the Cultural Awareness Project (Appendix C) will give you insights into students' academic skills and other important information.
6. Make the classroom experience relevant to the real world.	In particular, emphasize relevance to their communities. The Community Problem-Solving Project (Appendix D) is one way to do this.
7. Use schema theory.	Find out what they already know about the topics that will be covered, and help students link their prior knowledge to the new information.
8. Use storytelling to arouse their interest.	Tell them what you are currently reading. Tie storytelling to their lives and the curriculum. Find out what they have read and what they would like to read. Encourage students to write original stories, and give them opportunities to share them.
9. Showcase their talent.	Give students opportunities through mock trials that pertain to literature, history, and current events; student teaching (allow volunteers to create their own lesson plans about pre-

TABLE 2.1. Eighteen Effective Strategies with Students of Color, Cont'd.

Strategy	Comments
	approved topics, and to actually teach their lessons to the class for extra credit); posters; and group projects.
10. Give students multiple ways to succeed academically.	
11. Encourage them to synthesize.	Have them synthesize what they have learned from the reading assignments into group projects, such as songs, children's books, videos, puppet shows, T-shirts, and debates.
12. Use questioning to spark discussion.	"How would you feel if you . . .? Well, that's how the main character felt."
13. Encourage students to write letters to authors of books they have read.	
14. Stress core vocabulary.	Before students begin to read, have them complete multiple vocabulary exercises based on the most difficult words and important concepts in the literature and textbooks that they will read. Appendix H includes numerous vocabulary-building strategies.
15. Use the old and the new.	Make use of postmodern literature, multicultural literature, and the classics.

TABLE 2.1. Eighteen Effective Strategies with Students of Color, Cont'd.

Strategy	Comments
16. Assign regular, beneficial homework.	Assign worthwhile homework regularly (a minimum of three nights per week) to teach discipline and responsibility, as well as to reinforce class work and improve skills. However, be aware that for elementary students too much homework can be counterproductive.
17. Offer multiple extra-credit opportunities.	
18. Assess their skills and knowledge in advance.	Find out if students have the prerequisite skills and knowledge to be successful in your class. If not, it is your professional responsibility to fill in as many gaps in their education as you can.

3

Effective Classroom Management

Of all the topics I discuss with teachers during trainings that I conduct in schools, classroom management is probably the most problematic. Although there is a great chance that teachers might infer the wrong message from any training topic, the risk appears greatest when the topic of classroom management surfaces. At the outset, to decrease the likelihood of misunderstanding and misinterpretation, I want to make four definitive statements that readers should keep in mind as they read the rest of the chapter.

My Four Underlying Beliefs About Classroom Management

First, I do not believe that any teacher should tolerate disrespect or abuse from any student. Second, I believe that all teachers have the right to teach in a nonthreatening environment, and all students should be able to learn in a safe and orderly classroom. No student should be permitted to prevent the teacher from teaching or other students from learning. Third, when I taught junior high school and high school I strongly believed that these were my rights as an educator and that my students' learning should not be disrupted by other students. Fourth, I believe that every teacher deserves to teach in a school that is led by supportive administrators.

As a result of these underlying beliefs, during my years as a secondary school teacher my classroom management style was categorized as strict and authoritative. This style did not stem from theories or models I learned from my teacher training courses. It resulted from my personality, my upbringing, and the school of hard knocks during the period in which I worked as a substitute teacher, and eventually as a first-year teacher in urban fringe schools. With time and through trial and error, I developed a system that worked for me. The system was not perfect, of course, because when it comes to human behavior no system is. Throughout the remainder of this chapter, I synthesize research and share personal stories that are designed to help teachers develop a classroom management system that might enable them to increase their efficacy with African American students.

A Widespread Problem

During an interview I conducted for *What African American Parents Want Educators to Know*,[1] Francine, a thirty-five-year-old African American mother of four, made an interesting observation: throughout most of her son's years in school, he was labeled a "discipline problem," sent to the office repeatedly, and suspended from school. In fifth grade, things changed. His grades improved, and so did his behavior. Francine attributed these improvements to her son's teacher, who happened to be his first African American teacher. But the fact that his teacher was African American was not the reason for the improvement, in Francine's opinion. Instead, she believed that the teacher's classroom management style and her ability to gain Francine's son's respect were the reasons. Nevertheless, cultural differences clearly played an important role. According to Francine: "With white female teachers, he thought that he could do anything that he wanted to do in their classes. I think they weren't strict enough. He ran over the teachers. . . . With his fifth grade teacher, he met his match! She's done an excellent job, because she has changed my son's life."[2]

Francine's story is not unique. In fact, it is indicative of a pervasive problem in schools: classroom management is a major source of consternation for many teachers. This is particularly true of new teachers.[3] Although teachers are the most important in-school factor affecting student achievement, most new teachers are unprepared to meet the needs of students from diverse backgrounds.[4] As noted previously, teachers rarely find that teacher training institutions have adequately equipped them with strong classroom management skills. Consequently, in many classrooms a considerable amount of instructional time is lost each day as a result of poor classroom management by teachers. The fact that African American children are disproportionately represented among the students who are suspended and expelled from school[5] indicates that teachers often find their classroom management skills are ineffective with them.

A CNN article underscored this point. According to the article, "White Teachers Fleeing Black Schools,"[6] white teachers throughout the nation were leaving predominantly black schools for two primary reasons: they felt out of place, or they felt overwhelmed by the students' problems. Even so, some white educators and some African Americans believed these teachers were merely looking for an excuse not to teach in black schools. Regardless of the criticism leveled against these teachers, the fact remains that they felt so strongly about these issues that they chose to teach elsewhere. Two other stories are related.

One story pertained to a controversy that erupted at a school in Pasadena, California, after a white teacher circulated a letter to his colleagues stating that the African American students were not only the lowest academic achievers but also the worst-behaved students at the school. Although many educators and local residents, including some African Americans, agreed with the teacher, others accused him of merely making excuses and shirking his professional duty to teach all students.[7]

The second story, which aired on our local television news stations, concerned a predominantly black school in Los Angeles. In November 2002, several white teachers at the school told reporters that their classrooms were out of control and the entire school was chaotic. According to the teachers, students were gambling, fighting, and even engaging in prostitution at school regularly. The students were controlling the school, and the teachers were afraid for their own personal safety. Consequently, they lost faith in the school administration's leadership.

Although these stories received a lot of public attention because of media coverage, undoubtedly there are countless other teachers who feel just as overwhelmed by students' misbehavior but who never go to the media to express these concerns. A case in point involves a former teacher whom I met. This young white woman had taught in a predominantly black elementary school in Richmond, California, for one year before quitting. Although she succeeded in raising her second graders' reading scores, she became so disheartened by the students' personal problems and the lack of support from school administrators that she decided to leave the teaching profession completely.[8] Despite the fact that this teacher eventually decided to return to the teaching profession, her case (like those in the aforementioned examples) is illustrative of some of the problems facing teachers in predominantly black and urban schools. These examples are also indicative of the fact that many nonblack teachers, as well as some black teachers who may have the very best intentions often fail in urban schools. According to the U.S. Department of Education, 22 percent of new teachers leave during the first three years.[9]

In my opinion, classroom management is one of the main areas of teaching in which the cultural mismatch and cultural misunderstandings between nonblack teachers and African American students become most apparent. Unbeknownst to many teachers from mainstream backgrounds—particularly young white women—standard socialization practices and their upbringing can actually set them up for failure in urban schools.

How Socialization Can Contribute to Classroom Management Problems

African Americans in urban communities are socialized very differently from whites from middle-class communities; this difference, in my opinion, contributes to the culturally polarized battlefield that often arises in classrooms. This issue came up in a course for new teachers that I taught several years ago. The students and I discussed Cattani's description in *A Classroom of Her Own*[10] of how many middle-class white women are socialized and how their upbringing can lead to discipline problems and weak classroom management skills. Many of these women are socialized to speak softly and in a nondirect manner, and to adopt a nonassertive persona; they "are more likely to be experienced in submitting to authority than in exercising it."[11] According to Cattani, these factors, plus the women's young age, compound their classroom management problems. During the ensuing class discussion, the white women in the class agreed with Cattani's description of how they had been socialized. What was most interesting to me, however, were the comments by the white males in the class. In essence, they collectively stated that they had been reared to equate assertiveness and outspokenness from women with a term that is synonymous with a female dog—a term they did not hesitate to use in emphasizing their point.

Conversely, African American children in urban environments tend to be socialized very differently. There are numerous reasons why students might misbehave in class or be perceived as behavioral problems. Besides the fact that some kids are "spoiled brats" who are used to having their way (see Chapter Seven) and will do anything to get attention, some of these reasons pertain to socialization differences between students and teachers, and others do not. For example:

- Students might be sending a message to the teacher about the teacher's instructional style or negative messages that students might infer from the teacher's attitudes and behaviors.

- Students might be attempting to hide an academic weakness.

- Students might be confused by conflicting messages they get from home and school.

- Students might not respect the teacher.

- Personal problems might manifest themselves through inappropriate behavior at school.

- Students might have low self-esteem.
- Another theory is that there is a high degree of aggression in urban communities that surfaces in schools.

The sections that follow offer detailed explanations. But since this is not a child psychology book, this chapter is not intended to explain all of the possible reasons for students' misbehavior. Moreover, although I share my interpretation of the causes of the student behavior described in this and other chapters, I am aware that these interpretations are subjective and that other explanations are possible.

Aggression and Misbehavior at School

As I said in Chapter Two, several years ago I served as a mentor to four elementary school children—(three African American boys and a white girl), all of whom educators had labeled as at-risk. This school had no African American teachers and only one African American employee, an instructional aide. The school was located in a predominantly white community, and many of the African American students were bused in from a lower-socioeconomic-status community.

During several visits to the school, I witnessed incidents that made me very angry. One incident upset me so much that I reported it to the assistant superintendent and other school district officials. The incident occurred as I was waiting for one of the children I was mentoring to be summoned from class. As I waited, I noticed that a white woman was clutching a young black boy by the arm. The child was obviously fighting tears, and he clearly was refusing to budge from his spot. The woman, a secretary, who had been rude to me on several occasions when I was in the school office, was trying to force him to go to the office against his will. Apparently, his teacher had become upset with him for some reason and telephoned the secretary to remove him from the classroom. Although the boy was not verbalizing his resistance, his legs spoke volumes, for he refused to budge, and the more he resisted, the more she clutched his arm. At some point, the secretary looked up and saw the horrified look on my face. She released the boy's arm and gave me a nervous smile. Without smiling back, I went looking for the principal. When I found her, I told her that I did not think that secretaries should be grabbing children's arms in the manner in which I had witnessed. In fact, it seemed to me that the secretary was actually trying to provoke the child to act out.

The principal told me she would investigate the incident and get back to me. When I left the school that day, I had to do deep breathing exercises in my car to calm myself down. What transpired between the secretary and the boy was not an easy scene for me to forget, because the boy resembled my own son. The next day, when the principal and I spoke by telephone, she told me that she understood my anger, but I needed to also understand the realities of her school. "The fact of the matter is," she declared, "we have a lot of violent children at this school and most of them happen to be black boys." I was stunned by her statement and wondered why I had never witnessed any of this violence during my weekly visits to the school. Furthermore, a white vice principal at the school had often told me that adults at the school would overreact to the behavior of the African American students, because there was a widespread belief that black kids did not belong at his school. Today, I remain unnerved by the principal's statement, for it reflects a view that is widespread in American society—that of the violent, predatory black male.

Much has been written about this topic. In *Rock My Soul: Black People and Self-Esteem*[12] bell hooks traced the legacy of violence among some African Americans to the slavery era, and later to the black resistance movement. She stated, "When we study the psychohistory of African Americans it becomes apparent that the foundation of the shaky self-esteem that assaults our sensibilities is rooted in the experience of traumatic violence. . . ."[13]

Several researchers have found that children in urban communities are socialized to learn self-defense mechanisms early in life, because of a high incidence of violence in their communities.[14] For example, one researcher, Canada, who studied school violence in America found that African American single mothers routinely teach their children survival skills to prevent the children from being victimized. Instead of teaching their children to be nonassertive, they teach their children to stand up for themselves.[15] However, at school, as a result of zero-tolerance policies, both victim and perpetrator are penalized.[16] In *What African American Parents Want Educators to Know*, several of the parents who were interviewed for the study discussed this issue. One mother whose daughter was bullied frequently at school said the girl was afraid to go anywhere alone and had actually resorted to carrying mace.[17]

Majors and Mancini-Billson said that for African American males who adopt the cool pose or cool mask to cope with the marginalization they experience in American society, violence and aggression become part of the adopted persona: "Toughness, violence, and disregard of death and danger become the hallmark of survival in a world that does not respond to reasonable efforts to belong and achieve."[18] They also wrote: ". . . America has not provided many black males with legitimate channels or resources for developing a strong sense of masculinity, status, and respect. Violence has become a readily available and seemingly realistic tool for achieving these critical social rewards; it is in this sense that violence can even become a form of achievement when everything else has failed."[19]

The results of the Centers for Disease Control's Youth Risk Behavior survey for 2001 reveal some interesting details about violence among youths. For example, whereas 33 percent of the youths reported that they had been in a "physical fight one or more times during the past twelve months," only 13 percent had actually fought on school property. A higher percentage of black students reported that they had been in fights in general (37 percent) and at school (17 percent) than other racial or ethnic groups. Conversely, a higher percentage of whites than black and Latino students reported that they had carried a weapon, such as a club, gun, or knife, during the past thirty days off campus. There was little difference among the percentages of whites, blacks, and Latinos who reported bringing a weapon to school. A third finding was that a higher proportion of Latino students (10 percent) and black students (10 percent) than whites (5 percent) reported that during the past thirty days they were absent from school because they felt too unsafe to go.[20]

A review of research about violence and aggression among African Americans, especially African American males shows that the origins can be traced to slavery, as hooks asserted, and then passed on as a cool-pose coping strategy—and of course, also through family and community violence. However, the role of the media and teachers' and administrators' expectations should not be discounted. When African American boys are presumed to be violent and aggressive merely because they are African American males, a self-fulfilling prophecy may occur.

Although aggression and violence have traditionally been associated with males, there is growing evidence that females can be as aggressive and as violent as males. *Odd Girl Out: The Hidden Culture of Aggression in Girls* is the result of group and individual interviews that Rachel Simmons conducted with preadolescent and adolescent girls in ten schools, and interviews with their parents and other adult women. According to Simmons, the book "tells stories of perpetrators and victims."[21] Simmons dispelled many myths about females and aggression and contrasted the differences between how males and females display anger and aggression. Despite her discovery that girls are taught to "be nice" and not to display their anger openly, she found that "there is a hidden culture of girls' aggression in which bullying is epidemic, distinctive, and destructive."[22] However, unlike the direct and open forms of aggression that are typically associated with males, she reported that females tend to display aggression nonphysically, indirectly, and covertly, which makes it difficult for teachers and other adults to detect the aggression.[23] "Girls use backbiting, exclusion, rumors, name-calling, and manipulation to inflict psychological pain on targeted victims,"[24] she wrote. Moreover, whereas males usually bully strangers or acquaintances, females "frequently attack within tightly knit networks of friends, making aggression harder to identify and intensifying the damage to the victims."[25]

In addition to learning that females tend to show anger differently from males, Simmons also found that sociocultural and racial or ethnic differences existed in how females display anger and aggression. One difference she noted is that girls "whose lives were marked by oppression" were more likely than others to view "silence and indirection" as "signs of weakness."[26] Moreover, the African American participants in Simmons's study were more likely to voice their anger and deal with conflict openly than most of the white girls who participated. In fact, Simmons stated, "At times, I was positively floored by some girls' courage and outspokenness, which felt so different from my own."[27] Like Canada,[28] Simmons also learned that many of the girls of color in her study from urban backgrounds said their parents had taught them to defend themselves and to not permit themselves to be victimized. According to Simmons, "I was struck by the extent to which many of them were socialized to defend themselves physically when provoked. In some instances, girls reported being struck by their parents for returning home beaten."[29]

One of Simmons's main conclusions was that although there were noticeable differences between how most white girls and girls of color displayed anger and aggression, there were exceptions. For example, some African American middle-class girls were socialized to speak indirectly and nonassertively in order to appear nice in an attempt to be accepted by whites. Furthermore, some white girls were just as likely to use overt acts of physical aggression and outspokenness as many urban girls of color were. Therefore, Simmons stated, "Girls from all walks of life have different experiences. Not all white, middle-class girls avoid conflict, and not all other girls embrace it. Every child is her own person with her own unique set of life circumstances. Indeed, dominant middle-class notions of femininity are foreign to the experience of many white girls."[30]

Like Hale,[31] Simmons suggested that teachers incorporate conflict-resolution training into the curriculum. She recommended that teachers provide students with alternatives to handling anger, starting in preschool. Classroom discussions about anger and the many faces of aggression, as well as rewarding students for "truth telling and assertiveness," are additional suggestions for teachers from Simmons.

Low Self-Esteem and Misbehavior

A white woman who was reared in a middle-class home once asked me, "Do black women have higher self-esteem than white women?" I was surprised by the question and asked why she had asked it. I was even more surprised when she answered, "I believe that black women have higher self-esteem." Since then, I have given a lot of thought to this topic. Research and my own personal observations suggest that self-esteem among African Americans is a complex issue. In short, like all other groups, African Americans wrestle with issues related to self-esteem, and many factors are related, including negative messages from the media and common schooling practices. In spite of this ongoing barrage of negativity that African Americans must contend with throughout their lives, some researchers have found that outside of school African American boys have high self-esteem, and overall African American girls have higher self-esteem than white and Hispanic girls.

We live in a world in which no one wants to be on the bottom. Throughout the world, in every country and in every society with which I am familiar, some groups are disparaged and relegated to the lowest socioeconomic levels. In America, although many groups have been oppressed, Native Americans, Latinos, and African Americans tend to be looked down upon more than other groups. But in an effort to separate themselves and deem themselves as superior, even other members of oppressed groups consider themselves to be "better than the blacks." A good example is that it does not take long for some newly arrived Southeast Asian and Latino immigrants to the United States to begin to refer to African Americans by the "N word"—and they do not mean it as a term of endearment. I have personally heard people who could barely speak English use the N

word; in fact, one woman with a heavy Southeast Asian accent actually used it in reference to me—to my face! Moreover, some of my
Latino and Asian American former high school students told me
that their parents, grandparents, or other relatives would not permit them to have African American friends, invite them to their
homes, or date African Americans. Child psychiatrist Dr. James
Comer summarizes this situation well: "For many reasons . . . America has always resorted to scapegoating. . . . The descendants of
African slaves have been particularly vulnerable. This caste group
would become for the nation what the 'problem child' is to a family that is not functioning well—a permanent scapegoat."[32]

Consequently, African American children learn at an early age
that most Americans look down upon them. This negative message
is promoted by the media, in literature, in daily relations, and through
school curricula. One result can be low self-esteem, and just as other
groups feel better about themselves and their "subordinate" status
in the United States by looking down on African Americans, some
African Americans must find validation by finding others to dis-
parage. As a result, some African American children and adults become extremely cruel and inhumane in their relations with other
individuals. A story shared with me by a Nigerian mother illustrates
this point.

Our sons attended the same middle school, and we met during
a school assembly at which our sons were receiving "Principal's
Honor Roll Certificates" in early 2003. As we waited for the assembly to begin, this woman and I began to chat. She told me that although her son, an eighth grader, earned outstanding grades, she
was concerned about his social skills. "He has no friends and he
doesn't want to be bothered with people," his mother remarked. "I
tell him that he will have to learn to deal with people, because one
day he will join the work force," she added. As she continued to describe her son, the reasons for his seemingly antisocial behavior
soon became very clear to me.

It turned out that although her son was born in the United
States, he was rejected by his African American peers very early in

his schooling. "They said all kinds of horrible things to him," his mother told me. "They called him 'monkey,' and asked him if he climbed trees."

When the eighth graders began to enter the auditorium, the mother proudly pointed out her son to me. He was one of the tallest boys in his class, but his expression was what was most noticeable to me. It was a combination of seriousness, sadness, and defensiveness. It almost appeared that his expression was a protective measure against would-be tormenters. The mother caught her son's attention and began to wave frantically to him. When his name was called to receive his award, he lumbered to the podium as if he would have preferred to be elsewhere. His mother stood in the aisle, snapping pictures. When he returned to his seat, his teacher informed his mother that she could take her son to the back of the auditorium for close-up pictures, if she liked. Because I had been watching the son's African American peers' behavior, I knew that this was a bad idea. Several African American students who were sitting near her son had been nudging each other, pointing at the mother's hair (which was unstraightened and brushed away from her forehead in no particular style) and her outfit (a pair of casual slacks, a shirt, and slide-in shoes), and giggling in disparagement. However, the mother appeared to be oblivious to what was going on. Conversely, her son, who was obviously used to this behavior, was well aware of what was going on. Consequently, when his mother summoned him to go to the back of the auditorium to take more pictures, he became angry. When she returned to her seat, she said, "He told me to stop taking pictures. He doesn't want any pictures." Her feelings appeared to be hurt.

This story bothered me then and it still bothers me today. In my opinion (of course, other explanations and interpretations of the students' behavior are possible), it speaks volumes about many issues related to low self-esteem and self-hatred among some African Americans. It illustrates how African American students who have heard only negative messages about Africa from their social studies and history classes, from the media, and from their parents, and who are undoubtedly a product of the same negative messages, have been taught to perceive Africa and Africans. It also illustrates the need of some African Americans to find someone to look down upon in order to make themselves feel better. Although the incident occurred outside of the classroom, similar manifestations of self-hatred and low self-esteem can surface in classrooms or other places at school.

In *What African American Parents Want Educators to Know*,[33] several parents talked about how other students' behavior had affected their children's self-esteem. For example, a single parent said that his daughter, a fifth grader, was suffering from low self-esteem as a result of being teased by other African American children about her dark skin. According to her father, ". . . she hears a lot of jokes, like 'You're black, like an African,' or 'You're black, like a skillet.' She hears this from other kids, mostly black kids. I guess that is what hurts her the most."[34] Two mothers who were interviewed for the book said that their daughters—who were perceived to be very attractive—were singled out by jealous African American girls. One mother said that another girl even threatened to cut her daughter with a knife and shoot her with a gun. A stepmother said that she had to walk her biracial stepchildren to school to prevent other students from attacking them. Another mother said that her daughter had resorted to carrying mace to school; this is a message that also surfaced in *African American Teens Discuss Their Schooling Experiences*.[35] During one interview an African American high school senior said that "ugly girls" were always looking for excuses to fight her, which led to her decision to carry mace to school.

In his research regarding African American boys, Kunjufu found that African American boys exhibited a high degree of self-esteem outside of school, but the opposite was true in school. He wrote, ". . . our boys came into the classroom at kindergarten with a very high level of self-esteem and the teacher's low expectations and the lack of understanding [of] the male child and his learning styles destroyed it."[36] Kunjufu also cited the role of tracking and negative labeling of African American boys as contributing to their low self-esteem in school. He wrote: "It is very significant that African American boys who may have been destroyed in the classroom, have insulated themselves with Black culture in the Black community and have found a way to feel good about themselves irrespective of the schools. Gangs and rap records are expressions of this phenomenon."[37]

The AAUW report "Shortchanging Girls, Shortchanging America: Executive Summary" presents more information about self-esteem. The report found that self-esteem was linked to gender, race, family relations, and schooling factors such as teachers' attitudes and beliefs about student aptitude. At all three schooling levels (elementary, middle school, and high school), a higher percentage of boys had high self-esteem than girls. For both groups, the percentage reporting high self-esteem dropped significantly after elementary school, but particularly during middle school. The decrease for girls was much higher than for boys. For example, whereas nearly 60 percent of the middle school boys had high self-esteem, only 37 percent of the girls did. The AAUW report indicated that for girls the "declining sense of themselves" had a greater impact on their aspirations, academic achievement, attitudes about math and science, and classroom behavior than what boys experienced. The researchers found that boys were more likely than girls to "speak up in class" and "argue with my teachers when I think I'm right."[38] The study also found that "girls are much more likely than boys to say they are 'not smart enough' or 'not good enough' for their dream careers."[39]

Another finding was that since many girls view teachers as role models, "feelings about academic performance correlated strongly with relationships with teachers."[40] Positive relationships with teachers were linked to high self-esteem. Teachers' negative beliefs about girls' aptitude were linked to low self-esteem. Therefore, the researchers concluded, "Teachers have a special opportunity to affect the self-esteem of their female students, and by instilling confidence to shape their interests and aspirations."[41]

The researchers also found differences in self-esteem among racial and ethnic groups. A higher percentage of Hispanic elementary girls than black and white girls respectively demonstrated high self-esteem. Conversely, among middle school girls a higher percentage of black girls had high self-esteem than Hispanic and white girls respectively. Among the high school girls, black girls were nearly twice as likely as Hispanic girls and more than twice as likely as white girls to have high self-esteem.[42] Yet the researchers emphasized that, like the other groups of girls, black girls' self-esteem was adversely affected by common schooling practices.

In *Rock My Soul: Black People and Self-Esteem*, bell hooks also described the negative effect of school on the self-esteem of African Americans. She explained that when schools were totally segregated African American children had limited contact with whites. The most influential individuals in their lives were therefore other African Americans. Hence, ". . . away from white supremacist control black folks could invent themselves."[43] However, this situation changed as a result of integration, when African Americans were forced to become more "obsessed with race" and to experience more "racist assaults." Hooks concluded, "Even the well-meaning and kind white teachers often believed racist stereotypes. We were never away from the surveillance of white supremacy. . . . And it was this constant reality that began to undermine the foundation of self-esteem in the lives of black folks."[44] As a result, hooks argued that low self-esteem is common among many African Americans from all socioeconomic levels and regardless of the labels that are placed on African American students at school. For example, she said that even "smart" African American students in predominantly white schools "often began a journey into the abyss of self-doubt" that stems from being "set apart" from other African American students and from never being "fully accepted by white students."[45]

Personal Problems

Many students arrive at school with personal problems (a topic that is revisited in Chapter Four). Sometimes these problems make it difficult for students to concentrate on their school work, and in some cases personal problems become a catalyst for disruptive behavior at school. Throughout my years as a secondary school teacher, I often saw minor examples of how students' personal problems can lead to misbehavior at school. Two major examples, though, had a great impact on me. Although the examples do not pertain specifically to African American students (the first case involved a Puerto Rican student, and the second involved a Mexican American student), they taught me important lessons about why some students misbehave, how teachers should react, and the importance of administrative support. Although I attribute the incidents to the students' personal problems, I am aware that other explanations are possible.

The first incident occurred when I was a substitute teacher and had not yet taken any teacher training courses. In 1984, I received an assignment to substitute in a middle school classroom for three days, while the regular teacher attended a funeral in another state. The trouble started on the first day during first period.

The students were so overjoyed to have a sub that most refused to take their seats when the bell rang. They made it clear that they did not plan to do any class work or listen to anything I had to say. After all, I was a sub, not their real teacher, and I could not tell them what to do. Nevertheless, through my no-nonsense, stern demeanor I somehow succeeded in getting most of the students to take their seats and quiet down. However, a small group of boys who were huddled in the back of the classroom continued to ignore my requests. Out of exasperation, I gave them an ultimatum: they would have to take their seats immediately, or I would send them to the vice principal's office. This worked for all but one of the boys. After all of the students were in their seats, he stood in the back of the room reading. Upon approaching him, I saw that he had a pornographic magazine. When I told him that I was going to write a referral for him to go to the vice principal's office, all of a sudden, I had his attention.

When I returned to the teacher's desk, the student followed me. Although he proudly stated his name when I asked, as I wrote the referral he stood menacingly close to me, glaring his displeasure. When he noticed that I had written, "Pedro [not his real name] has been a pest since the class period started," the student unleashed a torrent of anger at me. "So, I've been a pest, huh?" he jeered. He was clenching his fists, as if he actually planned to hit me.

At this point, the rest of the class was totally silent, obviously enjoying the show. They wanted to see action, and I am sure that I had few, if any, supporters among the crowd. I also knew that I had few options. The telephone was too far away for me to reach nonchalantly. Moreover, if I showed fear then I would never be able to return to that school again, because none of the students would respect me. The problem was that I was not only fearful, I was terrified. My hand shook as I continued to write the referral and my knees were knocking beneath my long skirt. But I also remembered a fundamental lesson from my urban upbringing: bullies thrive on fear. So—wisely or unwisely—I attempted to hide my terror and finish writing the referral, in spite of the student's proximity, as I wrote.

When I finished writing, he said, "I ought to hit you in your ole ugly face," and his clenched fists and scowl indicated that he was probably serious. At this point, I mustered up all the courage that I could find from the soles of my paralyzed feet, and gave him an equally menacing look that said, "If you hit me, I'm going to hit you back." Then, I replied, "Well hit me then." For what seemed like eternity, the student glared at me. His fists were clenched, but I glared back. He did not know it, but in spite of my false bravado, I was secretly praying for mercy and for protection. The class watched this scene in eager but silent anticipation. Then, to my great relief, the student unclenched his fists, snatched the referral from the desk, and said. "Naw. I'm not gonna hit you, 'cause you too ugly!" As soon as he left the classroom, I rushed to the telephone and called the vice principal. "Pedro _____ just threatened to hit me," I said, as I gasped for breath. Today, two decades after the incident occurred, the vice principal's answer disturbs me just as much as it did when he uttered it: "Oh yes, Pedro, has a problem with authoritative women," he replied calmly. "He's in a foster home for beating his mother. She's in a wheelchair, you know."

I was totally flabbergasted. Of course, I did not "know"! I had walked into that classroom naïvely assuming that this would be a typical subbing day, and that after a few minor power plays and tests the students would eventually settle down and get to work. I had not assumed that there would be a student with a serious psychological problem in the class. Moreover, I had no idea that if such a student were in the class the administrators would not have the professional courtesy to warn me. If I had known, I would have handled the situation much differently. I would never ever have placed myself in such a dangerous situation by possibly "provoking" the student to violence or by causing the situation to escalate in order to save face. In fact, if I had known that the student had a problem with authoritative women, I would have called security or the vice principal immediately. But back then, I was naïve, untrained, and unprepared for this level of behavioral problem at school.

The second incident occurred a decade later. The circumstances were different, but the message was the same: some students have personal problems that are so severe that these problems manifest themselves in inappropriate behavior at school.

The 1994–95 school year had an auspicious beginning for me. In addition to my regular teaching duties, as an official district-selected "mentor teacher" I would continue to work with new teachers for a second consecutive year. Moreover, I had developed a monthly newsletter that would allow teachers to share their innovative lesson plans and teaching strategies with other educators and had created a small pamphlet of suggestions for new teachers. Although I did not know it at the time, that year would become my very worst year of teaching.

It started in September. The day so far was going great. All five of my classes had gone well, and I was almost finished teaching my last class for the day, when my classroom telephone rang. I was totally unprepared for the caller's words. After spewing a barrage of expletives, a male voice said, "I'm going to kill you." In a daze I hung up the telephone. I did not know whether the call was merely a joke or something serious, but the look on my face alarmed my students. Several asked if everything was OK. The dismissal bell saved me. After all of the students left, I telephoned the school principal and explained what had happened. The principal sounded genuinely concerned and said he would be right over. When he came to my classroom, he expressed regret over the incident and seemed supportive. Then, he stated, "I don't know how to say this, but try not to make too much out of it." So, like the principal, I decided it was probably a mere prank, nothing I should take too seriously. Therefore, aside from telling my husband and several colleagues about the incident, I decided to try to forget about it.

A week later, however, during the same class period and almost at the exact same time as the previous call, the classroom telephone rang. Once again, the caller spewed profanity and stated that he was going to kill me. I slammed down the telephone, but before I could react, it rang again. This time, I asked my student assistant to answer it. After she hung up, she stated, "I can't repeat the things that he said, because they're really bad, but I can tell you that the calls are coming from the Little Theatre on campus." When I asked how she could tell where the calls had originated, she said that the acoustics in the Little Theatre were different from those of all the other rooms at the school.

By this time, my shock had turned into outrage. I telephoned the principal, relayed what had happened, and told him that I was going to the Little Theatre. He tried to dissuade me, but I ignored his request. I asked another teacher to watch my class, and I hurried over to the Little Theatre. I was in the process of explaining what had happened to the drama teacher, and asking him who had just used his telephone, when the principal arrived and ordered me to return to class and let him handle the matter. Before I left, the drama teacher pointed to a large male student and asked me if I knew him. The student looked totally unfamiliar to me, but the drama teacher said that before I arrived the student had been near the telephone.

Unfortunately, the principal was unsuccessful in his attempts to resolve the matter. Although many students in the Little Theatre had actually witnessed the caller—the same student whom the drama teacher pointed out to me—in the act of telephoning my classroom, they were fearful of sharing what they knew with school officials or campus security. I soon learned that for some reason, which is still unclear to me today, this eighteen-year-old, emotionally disturbed student with gang ties had singled me out for death threats (and, later, other frightening behavior). A year earlier, he had been hit in the head with a hammer and behaved erratically from that point on. Because he had never been enrolled in any of my classes, the only explanation I was given for why he might have targeted me was that he hated black people and used the N word regularly in reference to African Americans. The problem I had with this explanation was that there were other African American teachers on campus, yet he was fixated on me. Because so many people knew that this student was the "guilty party," in the beginning I was still hopeful that school officials would take appropriate action. However, I soon began to lose hope, as other strange incidents started to occur.

Before long, I noticed that the student seemed to be ubiquitous. When I arrived at work in the morning, I would notice him standing in one of the teachers' parking lots—the one in which I always parked. I started to wonder if he was going to place a bomb under my van. When I noticed him in the parking lot during lunch, I stopped sitting in my van and listening to the radio during lunchtime, as I often did. One day, during third period, someone opened my classroom door and threw a wad of burning paper inside. After that, I started locking my classroom door during class time. On another day, my teaching was interrupted by a male voice standing outside my classroom door bellowing expletives that were clearly directed at me. During this time, I had gotten word that the student was angry that school officials were investigating him, but because the witnesses refused to speak against the "suspect," the investigations continued to prove futile.

The stress started to affect my health. My hair began to fall out, and I experienced chest pains. Then, in November, in the midst of all of this, there was an unexpected rainstorm. The roof of the building that housed my classroom was damaged and, one by one, sixteen tiles gradually fell from the ceiling. As a result, I had to keep moving students' desks to keep them from getting hit in the head by falling tiles. When I complained to the president of the teachers' union, he warned me that *I* could be sued if any student was actually hit by a falling tile. The stress accumulated, and I ended up in urgent care on two occasions, fearing that my chest pains were actually a heart attack.

By the time January arrived, I had become so depressed and fearful that the student would eventually kill me that I decided to start looking for a job at another school. The principal had not made any progress in his investigation and the student continued to exhibit menacing behavior whenever I saw him. During this time, numerous students came to me and expressed sympathy, and several stated that "everyone" knew the student was indeed guilty, but they also feared him as a result of his mental instability and his ties to one of the most notorious gangs in the city.

By spring, I was counting the days until the school year would end. At least the student would graduate at the end of the year. Then, in March, I got a call from my hometown, indicating that one of my younger sisters was ill and had been hospitalized. This compounded my stress. After surgery, however, she appeared to be getting better, but six weeks later she took a turn for the worse. I was in her hospital room visiting her when she died. Returning to work after the funeral was extremely difficult. Nevertheless, I returned and tried to do my best, in spite of the stress, my fear, and my despondency.

Shortly after I returned, I was walking toward the Media Center on campus during my planning period when someone called my name. I turned around. A Latino student with a shaved head and wearing a white T-shirt, the uniform of the gang in question, was approaching me. He looked unfamiliar, so I expected more trouble. Upon closer inspection, I noticed that his neck was covered with hickies. He said, "Excuse me. Are you Mrs. Thompson?" Assuming that he must be connected to the death threats in some way, I looked for an escape route. When I reluctantly affirmed that I was indeed

Mrs. Thompson, to my surprise he remarked: "You don't know me, but I heard that you are looking for another job. I heard about what's been happening to you and a lot of us think that it's wrong. I never had you for a teacher, but I heard that people learn a lot in your class. I just want you to know that from now on, I'm going to look after you. I'll be checking on you to see how you are doing and I guarantee that you will not have any more problems from the person who has been bothering you."

Although it may seem amazing, this student, a stranger to me, was true to his word. He started visiting my classroom for a few minutes several days each week to ask how I was doing and whether or not I had had any more problems with the "suspect." Each time, I was happy to report that I had not had any more problems. Today, I remain grateful that this student did what administrators and school police refused to do. He used his influence at school and in the local community to pressure the disturbed student so that the death threats and other harassing behaviors ceased immediately. As a result, my hair began to grow back and the anxiety-related chest pains that had twice sent me to urgent care subsided (but have never totally disappeared). Moreover, I was able to survive that horrible school year. One of the lessons I learned from this experience is that after the school principal and school police repeatedly failed to resolve the matter, I should have contacted the city police department. Undoubtedly, they would have taken the situation more seriously.

Misbehavior as a Cover-Up for Academic Problems

Another cause of misbehavior is the fact that the student is attempting to hide an academic weakness. In *African American Teens Discuss Their Schooling Experiences*,[46] a dyslexic African American teen who was terrified that her classmates and teachers would realize she could not read said she slept in class or left without permission when teachers asked her to read orally. "In fifth grade," she said, "a teacher forced me to read and I felt bad. I was trying to read and kids were laughing at me. So, I just got up and left."[47]

In "I Ain't Writin' Nuttin': Permissions to Fail and Demands to Succeed in Urban Classrooms,"[48] Ladson-Billings described an African American student, Shannon, who refused to complete a writing assignment in class. During her observation of Shannon's combination kindergarten-first grade class, Ladson-Billings realized two important points related to Shannon's defiance: "Her refusal to write was not just stubbornness, but a ploy to cover up her inability to read, or more specifically, her lack of phonemic awareness."[49] However, Ladson-Billings also noticed that Shannon's teachers colluded with the girl. Because they did not equip her with the skills she needed to complete the writing assignment but merely permitted the six-year-old to make a decision not to do the work, they had given her "permission to fail." According to Ladson-Billings, "Although most students were encouraged to write each day, Shannon was regularly permitted to fail. . . . I cannot help but wonder if the permission to fail was granted Shannon so easily, in part, because her cultural style, form of language, and attitudes deemed her unworthy of teaching in her teacher's eyes."[50]

In *Our America: Life and Death on the South Side of Chicago*,[51] teenage authors LeAlan Jones and Lloyd Newman (with David Isay) depict their Southside Chicago housing project community in vivid detail. One of the most poignant stories in the book was shared by an African American teacher, Dr. Osentowski. During the 1994–95 school year, she found herself in a confrontation with an extremely problematic fifth grader. On the first day of school, Johnny refused to take his assigned seat; the more the teacher insisted that he do so, the more he resisted. In open defiance, Johnny selected a seat in the back of the classroom instead. Again, Osentowski asked him to move to his assigned seat. He refused. When she insisted, he attempted to hit her. At this point, Osentowski could have exercised any number of options, including retaliating in self-defense, calling security, or banishing Johnny from her class. Instead, she grabbed his arm and insisted that he take his assigned seat. Subsequently, when Johnny saw that she was not going to back down, he finally took his seat. To his surprise, this teacher had passed the all-important "first day of school test." She had not allowed him to intimidate her, and she clearly demonstrated that she—not he—was in charge of the class. This incident marked the beginning of a strong bond between the teacher and the student, because she had earned his respect. Moreover, Osentowski soon discovered that one of the reasons why Johnny had behaved so defiantly was that he was hiding a secret: he could not read.

In addition to academic problems, Johnny also had numerous personal problems, among them that his mother, a single parent, was addicted to drugs. Consequently, Johnny was not well supervised at home. After a young neighbor tattled on Johnny and his best friend Tyrone for attempting to coerce him into stealing candy for them, Johnny and Tyrone decided to teach the little boy a lesson. They forced him to accompany them into an abandoned high-rise apartment. Then, they dangled him out of a window, head first. When the little boy's brother bit one of the culprits, they accidentally dropped the child.

As a result, Johnny and Tyrone were convicted of murder and sentenced to be incarcerated until they reached adulthood. In spite of these tragic circumstances, his teacher lamented the role that his academic problems played in his misbehavior. As Osentowski stated: "The schools failed Johnny. They had not met his needs. When he came to me he had not learned to read, and yet he was ten years old. But after I had been with him for a while, he was one of the most docile and nicest-acting persons that I have ever had any encounter with. And he tried to do his work. The child was actually trying to do this work. So he was fitting in just fine as far as I was concerned."[52]

Misbehavior as a Message to the Teacher

A recurring theme in *What African American Parents Want Educators to Know*[53] and *African American Teens Discuss Their Schooling Experiences*[54] is that when African American students "act out" in class, they often do so because they are sending messages to the teacher. One message is "The curriculum is boring." In both studies, parents and students complained about a boring curriculum, a boring style of instructional delivery, and low standards. In fact, several parents attributed their children's behavioral problems at school to the fact that their children were bored; the children in turn rushed through their class work and had idle time on their hands that caused them to get into trouble. In fact, in both studies some participants complained about teachers assigning busy work that was designed merely to keep students occupied, though it was not meaningful work.

In *What African American Parents Want Educators to Know*,[55] a mother described in detail how the curriculum contributed to her son's behavioral problems at school. Although her son, a fifth grader, earned high scores on standardized tests and good grades, he was a discipline problem at school. According to his mother, "I think he's probably bored to death, because he'll do his work and once he's done, he's off. He'll go help [other students] without being asked to help, and the teachers don't want him to help. They think he's disrupting the class."[56] Another parent, a mother of a third grader, shared a similar story. Because of her son's academic performance, he was promoted from kindergarten to first grade during the first month of school. Although he was socially immature as a result of being younger than his classmates, his school work continued to be nonchallenging for him. He too earned high standardized test scores and good grades but rushed through his work. His mother reflected, "I think he's bored. . . . I don't think he's challenged."[57] In both of these cases, instead of offering the two boys a more challenging curriculum, enrichment activities, extra credit assignments, or the option of assisting struggling classmates with their work, the teachers assumed that the boys had attention deficit disorder (ADD).

In *Learning While Black*,[58] the eminent African American scholar Janice Hale used her son's educational experiences at an elite private school to illustrate the myriad problems African American students, particularly males, face in public and private schools. She said, "If my son, an African American male in an exclusive school, receives racialized treatment, how much worse is it for a boy in the inner city with no advocate to keep him from falling through the cracks?"[59] One of her conclusions was that "the Black male child is most at risk for feeling uncomfortable in the classroom."[60] Like the two mothers in the previous examples, Hale found that instead of searching for other sources of her son's problems in the classroom his second grade teacher assumed he had ADD. Two of the real causes of her son's problems were his white classmates' unfair math advantage over him and the seating arrangement in the classroom.

The math advantage stemmed from the fact that many of his classmates had older siblings who had been in the class. At home, these children had access to math workbooks and materials long before the teacher assigned them to the rest of the class. Moreover, the white parents who had been members of the elite private school "club" setting for several years tutored their children in math topics that would later be covered in class. Subsequently, these students were able to perform well in these math areas because they had a head start in gaining practice and becoming familiar with the material before Hale's son did.

Hale also realized that the seating arrangements contributed to her son's problems. In kindergarten, her son's teacher often complained about his behavior. Upon careful observation, Hale noticed that her son was usually grouped with two students whom "he was having friction with." When she suggested that the teacher rearrange the groups, the situation improved. It turned out that in his previous group, her son had felt uncomfortable. However, after the groups were changed, Hale said that her son "found more comfort in the classroom, and the behavior problems stopped. No more critical notes, no more complaining phone calls."[61]

Hale's research, classroom observations, and her son's experiences led her to underscore the importance of teachers' understanding the "social context" for misbehavior. She also said that teachers must understand that students' learning styles can lead to misbehavior or the perception that they are behavioral problems.

Because many African American children are kinesthetic learners who learn by doing rather than sitting passively in class, certain teaching styles can contribute to the perception that they are misbehaving in class.[62] For example, when a child such as an African American boy who is a kinesthetic learner is forced to sit in a classroom in which lecturing and an overreliance on the textbook are the primary ways in which the teacher presents the subject matter, the kinesthetic learner's boredom might surface through inappropriate classroom behavior (passing notes, whispering to other students, fidgeting, and so forth). According to Gay, "The energy and exuberance with which highly culturally affiliated African Americans invest their interactions . . . is troublesome to many teachers. They may view this behavior as impulsive, overemotional, and out of control. Consequently, much of their classroom interaction with these students is of a disciplinary and controlling manner. . . ."[63]

My own research also revealed that another cause of misbehavior is that "the student does not respect the teacher," because he or she believes the teacher has been disrespectful, is unworthy of respect as a result of a failure to establish authority in the classroom, or has engaged in racist or other unfair behavior on the basis of stereotypes or a distorted view of the student's background.[64] In the parent study I conducted, several parents were appalled at how some teachers permitted students to behave in class, especially by allowing them to eat candy, chew gum, and use profanity and other disrespectful language when addressing their peers or teachers.[65] As one mother put it, "A lot of things can be avoided by teachers stepping in and simply saying, 'I'm not gonna have it.'"[66] Delpit's work presented important information about how a nonauthoritative classroom management style can result in a lack of respect for the teacher on the part of African American students.[67]

In the parent and student studies I conducted, some parents and students also described how a combination of weak classroom management skills and negative beliefs about African American children can result in racial profiling by teachers and administrators. They reported that teachers' biases and weak classroom management skills cause certain teachers to stigmatize and single out African American children as "behavioral problems," or accuse them of suffering from ADD. The result can be that negative labels are placed on African American children that follow them throughout their school years. If teachers and administrators assume that an African American child is problematic, the label and related assumptions can become a self-fulfilling prophecy, as I have noted repeatedly throughout this book. For example, during her interview an African American grandmother compared her young grandson's schooling experiences to the life of an ex-con who had "paid his debt to society" but was still being penalized. However, after observing her grandson's class, she noticed that one of his white classmates could misbehave in class with impunity.[68] In another interview, a mother of two school-age children said that although her son earned outstanding grades, he was being treated like a criminal by school officials, a pattern that started in second grade. "I feel he's been blackballed pretty much and feel that he doesn't even want to go back to school anymore," she said.[69]

Mixed Messages from Home and School

Another theme that surfaced in my own studies was that African American students can get conflicting messages from school and home in at least three ways: talking loudly, asking certain questions, and using self-defense to protect themselves (which was discussed earlier in this chapter). These messages can result in discipline problems at school.

First, African American children are often penalized at school for "talking loudly," because many teachers equate loudness with defiance. However, teachers fail to realize that in some cultures, including African American, talking loudly is considered to be normal behavior. Furthermore, what constitutes loudness or normal speech is subjective. When children are permitted to talk loudly at home and in their community but are punished for doing so at school, they get mixed messages. One mother stated that her daughter, an eighth grader, was just starting to be labeled as a discipline problem at school for this very reason. She remarked, "She's a loud person. My husband is a loud person, and when they get to explain themselves, they get loud. Their voices go up. Then, the teachers think she's being disrespectful. She's gotten a referral for that once. Actually, she's just starting to have problems."[70] Chapter Nine gives more details about this topic.

Another mixed message between school and home environments concerns outspokenness and asking certain questions. In both studies, students and parents said that although some African American students may be permitted to question why they have to do certain tasks at home, at school this can be problematic. One father, for example, said that his son, an eighth grader, constantly got into trouble at school for "questioning the teacher's authority" and for verbalizing his belief that certain assignments were pointless. However, an English teacher, who gave him opportunities to express himself verbally and in writing, had a better rapport with him than his other teachers.[71] In African American culture, outspokenness and lively verbal exchanges are so common that even in traditional black churches parishioners are permitted to "talk back" to the minister during sermons and to the choir.

Effective Classroom Management

In the parent and student studies that I conducted, seven practices that African American students and parents equate with good classroom management (and thereby good teaching) surfaced. Some of the practices and characteristics of effective classroom management have also been cited by numerous other researchers, most of whom have been cited frequently throughout this book.

The studies revealed that, first, an effective classroom management system is built on fairness. Unfair and biased behavior inevitably leads to discipline problems. Teachers who single out African American students for engaging in minor childish behavior while ignoring children of other racial groups who engage in the same behaviors are asking for trouble. The same is true of teachers who have negative beliefs about African American students that result in racial profiling, leading to an inordinate number of referrals to the office, suspension, and expulsion; or to reprimanding African American students in class for the same behaviors that are tolerated in other students.

Second, an effective classroom management system is built on an open mind and a positive attitude about students. Teachers who expect African American students to be problematic will find that their beliefs may become a self-fulfilling prophecy. Those who believe that African American students arrive at school with cultural capital that can be used to strengthen their academic skills may also find what they are looking for.

Third, explicitness and consistency are crucial components of an effective classroom management system. Teachers must explain their class rules on the first day of school, to students and to parents, verbally and in writing; they must then remind students of the rules on an ongoing basis. The rules must make sense, and they should emphasize the need for students to treat each other and the teacher respectfully. However, the teacher must model the rules by treating students respectfully as well. When a rule is broken, the teacher can use it as a teachable moment opportunity, by explaining why the behavior is inappropriate (see Payne[72] for specific examples).

Fourth, more than anything, the foundation of a good classroom management system is a curriculum that is comprehensible, interesting, challenging, and culturally relevant, and a qualified teacher who has an engaging style of delivery. Teachers who are successful in creating an exciting and effective classroom environment use multiple instructional strategies to address different learning styles. Additionally, they often permit African American students to work in partnerships and small groups, to participate in class discussions, and to create individual and group projects. These teachers find that they have fewer discipline problems with African American students than teachers who rely primarily on lecture and the "open your textbook" method of instruction.

Fifth, to create an effective classroom management system, teachers must be preoccupied with teaching, instead of with discipline. Too many teachers, according to the parent and student studies I conducted, are looking for an excuse to send African American students out of class. Consequently, in these classes very little teaching or learning occurs. Instead, teachers and students become locked in a battle of wills. Moreover, Hale recommended that teachers include teaching good social skills and conflict resolution strategies in their pedagogy.[73]

Sixth, to have an effective classroom management system, teachers must be firm but not mean. As Delpit noted, African American students are unlikely to respect teachers who appear to be weak.[74] Teachers must speak clearly and declaratively, and mean what they say. If students appear not to take a teacher's directions seriously, the teacher must be willing to take action. For example, when students continue to engage in whispering or side conversation after the teacher has asked them to be quiet, the teacher can use several strategies to convey the message that this behavior will not be tolerated. One strategy is for the teacher to stop speaking and stare intently, but not rudely, at the students who are talking. Most likely, those who are talking out of turn will notice that not only is the teacher watching them but the rest of the class is watching as well. Usually, at this point the talkers become uncomfortable enough to give the teacher their undivided attention. Another strategy is for the teacher to walk over and stand right next to the students who are talking. Often, the teacher's proximity to the misbehaving students is enough to make them cease from talking. A third option is for the teacher to move one of the talkers to a "special" seat that is right next to the teacher's desk.

Finally, patience is another key component of an effective classroom management system. Too often, African American parents and students find that teachers are impatient and unwilling to give struggling students in-class assistance. If an African American student fails to comprehend the lesson and infers that the teacher is unwilling to help, misbehavior becomes an option to either hide the student's confusion or send the teacher the message that the student is angry or lost academically.

Summary

One of the biggest failures of many teacher training institutions is the failure to equip teachers with strong classroom management skills. Subsequently, teachers must learn through trial and error, professional development, and reading on their own how to develop these skills. The ability to differentiate among normal childish behaviors, minor infractions, and more serious or even dangerous behaviors must be included in this work. Moreover, teachers must become hypervigilant to avoid engaging in racial profiling and early negative labeling of African American children that might create a self-fulfilling prophecy and propel African American children on a long-term trajectory of chronic misbehavior at school.

In my opinion, one of the most bittersweet aspects of being a teacher is that on a spectrum from genius to sociopath one never knows who is really sitting in the classroom seats. Furthermore, it is sometimes extremely difficult to know which behaviors are minor and worth ignoring and which are major signs that all is not well. Even more frightening is the fact that some students can behave like model citizens in class and commit heinous crimes outside of class. For example, during the period when I taught junior high school the six-year-old sister of one of the eighth graders at the school disappeared one day. This little girl, who was biracial (half-white and half-black), had been missing for several days before her body was discovered in a field not far from the junior high school. The child had been murdered.

Shortly thereafter, a former playmate of the victim, a diminutive white tenth grader, was arrested for the crime. He had killed her after the girl's mother forbade her to play with him—upon learning that the boy was actually a teenager rather than a little kid, as his stature implied. The public was shocked, for the boy had not appeared to be violent.

Later, I learned from his high school English teacher that on the actual day of the murder he had come to class late and behaved as if nothing had happened. The teacher stressed that she never saw any signs of antisocial behavior in this student. Although it is true that this might occur, in other cases there are clear signs that must not be overlooked. Consequently, when a teacher is certain that a student is acting antisocially or dangerously, the teacher must know what recourse to follow and be willing to act swiftly. A final story illustrates this point.

During my first year as a full-time junior high school teacher, I befriended another African American first-year teacher at the school. One day, she told me about an incident that had occurred the previous day. As a result of misbehavior, she had assigned detention to an African American student. After school, he reported to her classroom and was well-behaved and congenial during the detention. The teacher was surprised, so after he had served a portion of the detention time she told him that she needed to make a quick trip to the school office, but when she returned his detention would be over. The student appeared to have no problem with this plan. As promised, the teacher went to the office for a short time and returned to her classroom. Because the student appeared to have remained in his seat, patiently awaiting her return, she told him he was free to leave. Soon, thereafter, the teacher also left school for the day.

The next morning, when she arrived, the janitor was waiting for her. To her dismay, he told her that when he had gone to clean the tiny workroom in the back of her classroom, he found feces smeared all over the floor and walls.

After recounting this story to me, the teacher told me that she was not only embarrassed but, because of the sensitive nature of the incident, she was unsure of how to proceed. Later that day, when the student arrived for her class, she asked him if he had "left anything in the back room." To my recollection, she said he smiled sheepishly but never replied. Hence, the teacher was even more confused about what action to take. Therefore she did nothing.

Several years later, after I had become a high school teacher, this incident came to mind when I learned that the same student had been arrested for raping a three-year-old relative.

My point in recounting this story is to emphasize the fact that teachers must be able to differentiate between minor childish behavior and serious or even dangerous behavior. Moreover, they must be aware of how to handle serious situations and proceed quickly. Whereas it is unfair for teachers to assume that every "loud," active, talkative, or noncompliant African American student needs to be kicked out of class or is dangerous, it is foolish for them to ignore clear indicators of sociopathology in any student, regardless of race or ethnicity. In this last case, at the very least the teacher should have involved the school psychologist and the assistant principal, because every adult knows that it is totally abnormal for an eighth grader to defecate in a classroom and spread it around as if it were finger paint. Hence, common sense must become an important component of decisions relating to student behavior. A related point is that teachers who assign detention should leave the classroom door open. This decreases the likelihood of the teacher being accused of inappropriate behavior.

Another lesson I have learned about classroom management was captured in a phrase I heard former "national teacher of the year" Guy Doud state on a radio broadcast. He said, "Obnoxious qualities in people are merely cries for help." This statement is a reminder that many misbehaving students are crying out for help from their teachers. The problem is that teachers who are compassionate and who truly care about their students' physical, emotional, and academic well-being can become consumed by students' problems if they are not careful. Therefore, finding a way to help those who have personal problems without developing a self-defeating "savior complex" requires balance and wisdom. In other words, teachers must do what they can to help troubled students, but at the same time they must try not to take these problems home with them. They must also use available resources—the school psychologist, school nurse, the Department of Social Services, and others—when necessary. Teachers must do their very best but realize they cannot save the world. They can, however, choose to have a powerful impact on the lives of their students, a theme that is revisited in the next chapter.

Another important point is that teachers who have low self-esteem must work on this issue if they are going to be able to develop strong classroom management skills. When teachers with low self-esteem have students (particularly African American students) with high self-esteem, problems are inevitable. The outspokenness and assertiveness of many African American students might unnerve a teacher to the point that he or she ends up engaging in discriminatory behavior. Another possibility is that the students might perceive the teacher as weak and take advantage. The result can be that the students end up controlling the classroom. Moreover, female teachers with low self-esteem can become victims of blatant disrespect and misogynist behavior from male students. Consequently, it is crucial that teachers with low self-esteem do the personal growth work needed to improve it.

Furthermore, teachers, staff, and administrators must be willing to take students' concerns and complaints seriously. The prevalence of bullying and other types of victimization at school has received much media attention. In many of the high-profile school shootings that have occurred in recent years, the perpetrator was victimized repeatedly by peers before resorting to violence. When students and parents infer that teachers and other school personnel are unwilling to protect students from being victimized and are unwilling to take students' complaints seriously, negative outcomes are likely. Starting in elementary school, teachers must stop assuming that the child who complains about mistreatment by peers is merely a wimp or a tattletale. When teachers blame the student who is victimized by peers for his or her own victimization, they are in effect colluding with the peers who are responsible for the victimization.

In conclusion, one of the national education goals of Pres. George W. Bush's administration is the eradication of the black-white achievement gap.[75] For this goal to be met, the classroom must be a safe and orderly place that is conducive to optimal learning. That is, it must be a community in which students can thrive academically. Too often, however, school policies and practices, cultural misunderstandings, teachers' instructional practices, and weak classroom management skills create a climate that is not conducive to learning. I strongly believe that regardless of race or ethnicity teachers who truly want to increase their efficacy with African American students can do so. Teachers who are willing to listen to the messages students send, who educate themselves about cultural differences, who practice the essential components of an effective classroom management system, who use good teaching practices, and who use common sense increase the likelihood that no child—African American or other—will be left behind academically.

PART TWO

What Teachers Want to Know But Are Afraid to Ask

4

How Can Teachers Reach African American Students from Challenging Backgrounds?

One evening, as I was reading the *Los Angeles Times*, two articles made me cry. Both pertained to promising African American fourteen-year-old boys. One of the boys, a highly respected and much-beloved student, was determined to attend UCLA after he graduated from high school. The other boy, an only child who was also highly esteemed by his family and friends, had recently joined the church choir and was looking forward to singing publicly with the choir for the first time the following Sunday. Neither boy lived to see his dream materialize. During the same week in December 2002, in separate incidents in California cities sixty miles apart, each boy was murdered by a gang member—even though neither was affiliated with any gang. In fact, the choir member was on his way to choir rehearsal at the time when he was gunned down, merely for wearing a red hat.

As a mother of three African American children—(one a thirteen-year-old son), the sister of a gang member who was murdered in 1998, and a scholar specializing in research to improve the schooling experiences of African American children and other students of color, I found these stories overwhelming. For a short time, they made me feel hopeless and helpless about the plight of African American urban youth, who have so many forces working against them.

From my teacher trainings in schools, I learned that many teachers often feel the same way. I found that although many administrators and teachers are interested in learning about effective instructional practices and classroom management strategies for students of color, they are often preoccupied with a more pressing issue: in many urban schools, there is a widespread, though often unspoken, sense of helplessness and hopelessness among educators regarding their ability to truly have a positive impact on students who come from troubled homes. When these educators become aware of some of the adverse circumstances, such as poverty, abuse, and neglect, that certain students regularly experience, they develop a sense of despair. Some continue to teach to the best of their ability in spite of this despair, while others become so overwhelmed that they actually quit teaching and go into other professions. A third group uses their despair and hopelessness as an excuse to shortchange students academically through low standards and low expectations, assuming that the students will not amount to much in life anyway. During trainings, in addressing the question "How can teachers reach African American students from challenging backgrounds?" I shared examples from the biographies and autobiographies of African Americans who overcame adversity. I also shared a synopsis of my dissertation work on resiliency, and I described my own difficult childhood and Mrs. Tessem, the teacher who changed the direction of my life. This chapter contains a brief synopsis of my dissertation research on resiliency, which is followed by the story of my childhood and its implications for teachers.

A Study on Resiliency

In *Predictors of Resilience Among African American Adults*,[1] my dissertation research, I attempted to uncover the factors explaining or predicting the resiliency of African American adults who had experienced adversity during childhood or adolescence. I conducted interviews with successful African American adults and collected questionnaire data from African American college undergraduates.

I learned about the main obstacles the participants had encountered and the factors—including the role of teachers—that were linked to their resiliency.

Racism or discrimination was the most frequently cited obstacle that many participants experienced during childhood. Others said that having an unemployed parent, their parents' divorce, or having a substance-abusing parent were the main obstacles they experienced. A smaller number experienced homelessness, physical abuse, having an incarcerated parent, having a physical disability, or having a learning disability during childhood. Age ten to fourteen was the period when the average participant experienced the adverse circumstance; older children were more likely than younger children to be affected negatively by the problem(s).

Four similarities surfaced among the participants, particularly those who participated in the interview phase of the study: during childhood, most had good grades, most dreamed of having a better life, most had a strong work ethic, and most had at least one positive role model. Parents were the most frequently cited role models, followed by another relative. Teachers, the third group of role models for the participants in this study, preceded ministers in popularity.

As indicated by this resiliency study, teachers play an extremely important role—either positively or negatively—in their students' lives. A lesson I have learned from conducting trainings is that whereas the scholarly research I shared was of great interest to the audiences, my own personal story of resiliency and the powerful sixth grade teacher who changed my attitude about my aptitude was of greater interest to them. This lesson was stressed to me repeatedly. For this reason, I believe the autobiographical story I share during teacher trainings might be useful to other educators who are questioning whether or not they can reach African American children from difficult backgrounds. With this in mind, I present a personal memoir and suggest related implications for educators. As during the trainings, my goal is to convince educators who are wrestling with despair and hopelessness about their ability to reach children from challenging background of three points:

1. One outstanding teacher can have a positive impact on students, even when it appears that the teacher's efforts are in vain.

2. Every educator can make a personal commitment to become a powerful and influential teacher.

3. When teachers view their students—regardless of students' backgrounds—they should not overlook their potential for great success.

Carrying Baggage to School

When I started school, two months short of my fifth birthday, I was a four-year-old crybaby who needed to be at home. On an emotional level, I was not ready for school, but on a practical level it was prudent—for my mother's sake—that I start school at age four, instead of a year later when I would be older and at least developmentally more mature.

My mother said that I was born a crybaby, and throughout the years I have heard two explanations for the hypersensitivity that manifested itself in my crying at the drop of a hat. The first explanation is that one of my mother's sisters lived with my parents while my mother was pregnant with me. This aunt was very sensitive and cried easily, two traits that constantly irritated my mother throughout her pregnancy. As a result, my mother's constant frustration with this aunt "marked me" while still in utero. I was destined to inherit the same unnerving traits.

The other theory that has been used to explain my hypersensitivity is attributed solely to my mother herself. She once told me that she cried throughout her entire pregnancy with me, and she had plenty of reasons to cry. She cried because she was married to her high school sweetheart, who, like her, was very young and physically attractive. But he was also unfaithful and often physically abusive—even during her pregnancies, she claimed. As the mother of a two-month-old newborn, when she found herself not only unhappily married but pregnant with child number two (me) she had a lot more to cry about. She was ashamed of this pregnancy, knowing that people would look at her disparagingly and whisper about the two children's closeness in age. To make matters worse, when the new baby arrived, unlike her eleven-month-old sister, she was considered to be an ugly child in a family of beauties.

So, less than five years later, I started kindergarten with my nearly six-year-old sister. By that time, I had two younger siblings. My parents had separated and my mother was pregnant with child number five. We lived in a two-bedroom house in a poor black neighborhood in what was once called "America's Finest City." My mother had gone from being a married housewife to a single mother on welfare. This occurred during the humiliating era when welfare investigators would actually come in and search the homes of welfare recipients to ensure that no husband or boyfriend lived in the home and that the recipient did not have "too much" food or too many material belongings, which could be signs of an additional source of income. Thus the fear that our family could be cut off welfare at any point constantly loomed over us. I have vivid memories of having to hide boxes of cereal and other food items before the welfare investigator's arrival. On these occasions, we were scrubbed clean, dressed immaculately in our thrift shop or rummage sale outfits, and then required to sit in silence while we and our home were inspected for evidence of wrongdoing. Because of the great amount of stress in her life at that point, I have always suspected that my mother sent me to school a year before I was ready, to get a mental health break from so many kids. After all, by sending my older sister and me to school together for several hours a day, she reduced the number of children in the household by half.

For some reason, my sister and I were placed in the same kindergarten classroom. Almost immediately, our teacher began to compare us. I was short, pudgy, and already felt ugly in comparison to my sister's tallness, thinness, and beauty. More important, my sister was less sensitive than I, and she definitely was not a crybaby. She was ready for kindergarten and I was not, so it was easier for her to adapt to the school environment.

Whenever I cried, my exasperated teacher, who happened to be the only African American elementary teacher my older sister and I would ever have, sent me to the restroom that was connected to the classroom, for the equivalent of a "time out." My memories may be exaggerated, but it seems that I spent most of my kindergarten year in that cold, bleak restroom. Often I could hear the rest of the class obviously enjoying some activity. The only positive memory that I have of kindergarten is that once we made ice cream sandwiches out of graham crackers and I got to participate in this activity.

The Family Tragedy

In January of my kindergarten year, the most tragic event of my childhood occurred. It gave me more to cry about and affected each of my family members (including the child that my mother was carrying—the child who as an adult would be murdered) in a different way. On that fateful night, while my mother was still pregnant with child number five (my brother Calvin), I remember that she put me and my two sisters (that is, the one who was eleven months older and the one who was fourteen months younger than me) to bed early. In the bedroom that we shared, we whispered until we fell asleep. In retrospect, I remember that the house was very dark. My mother and my two-and-a-half-year-old brother slept in the other bedroom. Although the house was small, their room seemed far away.

At some point, my sisters and I were awakened. The bedroom light was on. There were strangers, white men in uniforms, in our room. They were police officers, who began to ask us questions. Throughout the course of their questioning, it became clear to us that something terrible had happened. Someone had entered our house through a damaged window and had disfigured my pregnant mother. The assailant had cut her face, slicing through her left eye, left nostril, and the left side of her mouth. Many years would pass before my siblings and I learned that from that point on our mother was blind in her left eye.

The house was full of blood. Mama had been rushed to the hospital. While the police officers pondered what to do with four small children (our father had moved to another city and we had no other relatives in California), two neighbors whom we did not know volunteered to take care of us in their house until my mother was released from the hospital. Although their offer seemed to be motivated by kindness and altruism, my older sister and I soon learned that these neighbors had an ulterior motive, and each day we longed for our mother to return.

The day she finally returned is imprinted indelibly in my mind. She was wearing a long, gray, woolen coat, and she appeared to be wearing a white headband. I remember thinking that she looked very beautiful. However, when I approached her, I realized that instead of a headband, she was wearing a huge white gauze patch over her eye. When reality set in, I felt very sad and sorry for my poor mother. From that point on, I decided I would do everything I possibly could to make her happy. The assault destroyed one of her beautiful almond shaped eyes and left a permanent diagonal gash across one side of her face. It also made her paranoid and fearful that her assailant—who was never identified or arrested—would return one day and kill her.

My mother's terror and fear permeated my existence. Like her, I became preoccupied with the thought that the attacker would return. However, shortly after her return from the hospital, my mother needed some items from the old house (in which she refused to set foot), so I volunteered to go back and get them for her. At that point, our entire family was living with the two neighbors. In spite of my fear, I volunteered because I wanted to make her happy, at a time when her world had fallen apart. I was a terrified little five-year-old, but I went back into that blood-stained house, leading the way for our sinister neighbor to help me collect the things my mother needed. From the time the neighbor and I entered the house, until the moment we left, I expected my mother's assailant to jump from behind the bathroom shower curtain or out of a closet and harm me. When I returned to our neighbors' house and proudly gave my mother the items she had requested, I felt that for one small moment I had succeeded in bringing joy into her life.

A New School and Another Defining Experience

As soon as my mother could make arrangements, we moved from the neighbors' house to another poor black neighborhood in America's former finest city. Moving meant living in secrecy. We were not allowed to tell anyone from the old neighborhood anything about our new neighborhood, and we were forbidden to give out our new address. The message that anybody could be the assailant and that we should not trust anyone became implanted in our young minds. Moreover, we were forced to become proactive. After the assault, the police had advised my mother to always leave a light burning during the night, and from that point on she heeded the advice. We also created a ritual that required us to build a homemade alarm system. Each night, we would take all of the canned foods out of the cupboards and stack them against the front door and on the windowsills. If anyone tried to break in, we would hear the commotion caused by the falling cans and have time to yell for help, as well as get brooms, mops, and other weapons. Each morning, however, before my sister and I could leave for kindergarten, we had to dismantle the alarm system—a task made more arduous by the fact that I could not sleep well anymore, fearing that every little noise presaged danger.

In June of the same year, two momentous events occurred. My younger brother Calvin, sibling number five, was born—a beautiful dark-chocolate-toned baby who was always extremely nervous (and later extremely violent). The second event was that my sister and I were both promoted to first grade. We had both been deeply affected by the family tragedy and were undoubtedly suffering from posttraumatic stress disorder and in need of counseling, but we were promoted nonetheless. In my case, the fact that the teacher knew the personal circumstances of our family during that year may have had some bearing on her decision to promote me.

In September, my older sister and I started first grade. Before the academic year ended, we moved to another neighborhood and transferred to another predominantly black elementary school. The two of us would complete the duration of our elementary schooling at this school, though with quite different experiences. In retrospect, my older sister and I would look back and perceive most of these experiences through an extremely negative lens.

My first memory of my new school is the image of myself standing in a corner of my new first grade classroom, crying. I do not remember why I was crying. I could have been crying about a problem at home. By this time, it had become dangerous to cry at home, unless the crying occurred during one of the frequent beatings to which we were subjected—in which event not crying would make the beating more brutal and last a lot longer. A wise child learned to howl immediately and loudly as soon as a beating began. But with the exception of beatings, after the family tragedy crying was no longer tolerated, at least not from the older children in the family. I learned this lesson after one of my father's visits.

During his visit, the closer it came to the time when he would leave to return to his home in another city, the sadder I became. I could not put my feelings into words. As the time for his departure got closer, all of my pent-up sadness erupted in a trickle of tears. No one could hear me crying, but my parents noticed my tears. When they asked what was wrong, I could not explain that I did not want my father to leave. One reason was that I felt it would be disloyal to my mother, who struggled every day to feed us, clothe us, keep a decent roof over our heads, and to instill positive moral values in us, whereas my father just swept into our lives occasionally. The next day, my father was going to visit us a final time before he left town. I started crying even before he appeared. My mother was combing my hair when she noticed the tears trickling down my cheeks. She gave me a full-fledged slap across the face and told me that she had no time for my nonsense.

But another possibility for my crying at school could have been that I disliked my first grade teacher. Miss Erickson had sharp fingers, and she was always pinching me about something and then sending me to stand in a corner for punishment. At the end of first grade, I was relieved to get out of this woman's classroom. Like kindergarten, the experience was overwhelmingly negative. My relief, however, was short-lived. All of my crying at school had caught up with me. I was shocked to learn from my mother that I would not be promoted to second grade. Miss Erickson told her that I was "emotionally immature" and needed another year in first grade. Today, it is difficult for me to articulate the degree to which being retained in first grade affected my life.

At home, it changed how my mother and siblings viewed me. From that point on, whenever my sisters became angry with me they would hurl the embarrassing but true mantra at me: "At least I'm not so dumb that I flunked first grade!" Their words never failed to make me recoil in shame. The words were all the more painful because soon my younger sister would be labeled as "gifted." She was the family star who was so brilliant that she actually studied the dictionary when she was very young, primarily to erase any lingering doubts that we might have about her brilliance. On many occasions, she would say smugly, "I'll bet you're so dumb that you don't even know what _____ [fill in the blank with any multisyllabic, unheard-of word] means." We would be amazed that she not only could pronounce these words we had never heard of but actually knew their definitions as well. Teachers loved my younger sister and tried to convince my mother that she should actually skip a grade. To my mother's credit, she had compassion for me and realized that if she permitted my brilliant younger sister to skip a grade, it would destroy any remaining vestiges of self-esteem I might have.

In my mother's case, my retention lowered her expectations of me. The school system had said that I had a problem, and she equated this problem with a lack of aptitude. As a result, whenever we brought our report cards home she would always tell my younger sister that she was proud of her straight A's. She would tell my older sister (who had become an angry, defiant, behavioral problem at school) that she could do better. Yet when she reviewed

my report card, she always said, "Gail, all I expect from *you* is a C."
Unlike most of my teachers, at least she thought I was capable of
average work.

Like my mother, after I was retained in first grade my elementary teachers believed that I did not have much, if any, academic
potential. Still, before I returned to school the following September to repeat first grade I spent the entire summer pondering my
dilemma. I prayed that a miracle would occur, and I hatched a plan.
On the first day of school, as I stood in the long line to pick up my
room and grade assignment, I noticed my friends standing in line.
This made me more uneasy, yet I decided to forge ahead with my
plan. When I reached the front of the line and was told the name
of my new first grade teacher and the classroom number, I said,
loudly, "Oh, you must have made a mistake. I'm a second grader."
Soon, I was begging, but my pleading and protests were in vain.
While my friends and older sister marched proudly off to second
grade, I was forced to trudge back to first grade.

I was upset. Although my new first grade teacher was much
nicer than the mean, sharp-fingered Miss Erickson whom I had the
previous year, I decided I would behave differently in her class than
I had in Miss Erickson's. I would never resort to crying and risk
being labeled as emotionally too immature to go on to the next
grade. I would swallow my pain and humiliation and adopt another
persona: that of "expert." As a retainee, I had been there and done
that. I knew everything about first grade, including the old, boring
Dick and Jane stories that we were forced to digest. So I began
telling the other children what to expect and what the rules were.
I talked and talked and talked, competing with the teacher for authority status.

To some degree, I won. I became the leader of a group of gullible
little girls who would walk home with me, seeking my advice about
many issues. During this time, I earned the reputation of being an
excessive talker at school. Unlike my previous teachers, who had
punished me for crying in class, this first grade teacher would scold
me for excessive talking, without resorting to damaging methods.

Although she probably did not think much of my aptitude, she was a humane individual. Somehow, we were able to co-exist that year, and in June, to my great relief, she recommended that I be promoted to second grade.

Teachers Who Chose Not to Make a Positive Difference

For some reason, I have no memories whatsoever of second grade. I do not remember the teacher or any positive or negative experiences. Third grade is a different story. Although I had several negative and abusive teachers during elementary school, the worst was my third grade teacher, Miss Root. Today, when I look back on my third grade year, I am convinced that this teacher and some others at that school truly hated black children. I also believe many of the teachers at that elementary school were dismissed from suburban schools and sent to our mainly poor black school to do penance for their poor teaching or some other infraction that they had committed in suburbia.

Before I even entered her classroom on the first day of third grade, Miss Root was ready for me. She had "taught" my older sister the previous year and knew all about our family. She disliked my sister so much that she actually told the class to stay away from her, because she was "a very bad girl." Miss Root also tried to convince my mother that my sister had a serious psychological problem and required psychotropic drugs. However, nothing that I had heard about Miss Root could prepare me for her.

She was an imperious looking woman, with white hair that she always wore in a bun at the crown of her head, and she wore high heels and dresses that stood out, as if she had crinolines or a can-can underneath. This was in the sixties, when other women wore mini-dresses or tailored outfits like Jackie Kennedy's. But Miss Root was stuck in the fifties, not only in her manner of dressing but also in her perspective of black children. Although educators, psychologists, and researchers viewed black children as "culturally disadvantaged" at that time, I believe Miss Root and many other teachers at that school actually viewed us as subhuman.

The fact that she truly detested us became evident through her actions. We were only third graders, but we were not permitted to go to the restroom during class time, so children often urinated in their clothes and sat in a puddle out of fear of Miss Root's wrath. One girl routinely whined in class about being hungry. One day, when she had not engaged in her routine whining, Miss Root walked over to her and said, "Why haven't you cried today like you usually do?" As if on cue, the girl contorted her face, but instead of crying as she normally did she fought the urge. Then Miss Root began to goad her. "Come on," she urged. "Go on and squeeze those tears out; squeeze them out." Soon, she was crying as usual, and Miss Root's sadism appeared to be satiated for the moment.

One of my most unnerving memories of third grade concerns a girl in my class who had an identical twin sister in another class. Their names even rhymed. One day, their father, a Baptist preacher, stormed into our classroom and announced, "Miss Root, I'm here to make an example of my daughter." Miss Root seemed to be the only person in the class who was not surprised. (We later learned that she had telephoned Reverend M. to complain about his daughter's incessant talking in class.) Carrying a switch in his hand, Reverend. M. rushed over to his frightened daughter, yanked her out of her seat, and proceeded to hit her. "Didn't I tell you to behave in class?" he yelled, striking her legs repeatedly with the switch. "Yes Daddy! Yes Daddy!" she cried repeatedly, as she danced on one leg and then the other, attempting to miss his blows. The questions, replies, and hitting continued until, after what appeared to be an interminable period, the switch broke. Finally, the horrible ordeal was over. Yet before I could sigh with relief, I realized that the beating had not ended. Reverend M. was not finished. He was just warming up! When the switch broke, he asked Miss Root for a ruler. For some reason, she gave him a yardstick, and the beating, questioning, and tearful replies resumed, until Reverend M. was satisfied that he had made an example out of his daughter, or until he was too exhausted to continue.

I was traumatized. I had gotten many beatings in my young life, mostly as a result of my inability to clean the kitchen spotlessly, and had even gone to school regularly with welts from switches and purplish-green belt marks all over my body. Two of the most painful beatings resulted from a telephone cord and an extension cord. Blows from switches and belts are painful, but nothing compares to the pain or bruises caused by cords, because they tend to have small metal wires inside. During these two beatings, the pain was so great that I actually longed for death. Once I was beaten in our tiny bathroom, in which there was no room to run or hide, and very little room to even jump in an attempt to dodge blows. That night, I feared that my mother was going to beat me to death, simply because I had mumbled under my breath, "Why do I have to always do it?" when she told me to give my baby sister—child number six—a bath. So I was quite used to beatings. In fact, what my classmate got at school did not really qualify as a beating. Since her father had struck only her legs, it actually constituted a "whipping," which was milder than a beating. But I had never gotten a public beating or whipping (except from my older sister, who once attacked me on a bus, and from peers) and definitely not in front of a room full of my classmates. I wondered how this girl could ever live down the humiliation that would soon spread throughout the entire school and eventually follow her all the way through high school.

Although I was no longer a crybaby in front of other people, I was still a highly sensitive child, and for a long time I could not get this incident out of my mind. After school on that day, when my friend L. and I arrived at our apartment complex, we hurried to tell her mother what had happened. Her mother, who often used corporal punishment to discipline her own children, was appalled. She could not believe that Reverend M. had beaten his child in front of her classmates. When I went home and told my own mother about the whipping, she laughed and jokingly said, "I should have thought of that myself. That's a good idea."

In spite of her comments, however, for some reason my mother never followed Reverend M.'s example. With all of Miss Root's complaints about me, my mother had plenty of reasons to whip me at school. Once, for example, Miss Root caught me cheating on a spelling test. She was dictating the spelling words when she passed me and noticed that I had left the spelling list in plain view on my desk. The tongue-lashing that she gave me was almost equal to any public whipping that I could have received. However, Miss Root's greatest pet peeves with me were my handwriting, which she criticized frequently, and my excessive talking. After realizing that my mother, unlike Reverend M., was not going to nip my problems in the bud by making a public example of me, Miss Root found another solution.

One day, she called me to the front of the room and told me that from that point on, whenever I talked in class without permission, I would have to stand in front of the class with a wedge of cardboard in my mouth. The punishment started that very day. I stood in front of my classmates, feeling ugly, stupid, and ashamed with cardboard protruding from my mouth. Miss Root's plan was cruel and ingenious, yet it was destined to fail. Not only did I continue to talk in class, but I even outsmarted her by acquiring a taste for cardboard. Each time she shoved a neatly cut wedge in my mouth, I would eat half of the cardboard, so that only the part that was visible to her and my classmates was left. Until she pulled what was left of the soggy, half-eaten mess out of my mouth, she could not tell that I had eaten a sizable portion of it. Then she would look at me with contempt and fling it into the trashcan—probably wishing she could fling me there instead. Miss Root hated me, as she had hated my sister the previous year, and I hated her.

However, she and other teachers failed to realize that one reason for my talking was that the curriculum and instructional practices were extremely boring. Another obvious reason is that I am naturally a talkative person, and being forced to sit in silence with no opportunity to interact with my peers clashed with my personality. A third reason is that I was legally blind and needed glasses. I literally could not see the chalkboard or bulletin boards from my seat, so I found other ways to occupy myself. By the time I eventually got eyeglasses, Miss Root and I had reached the point of no return. By mutual consent, our relationship could not be salvaged.

At the end of third grade, I was promoted to fourth grade, possibly because Miss Root feared that if she retained me I would end up spending a second year with her. But a more plausible reason is that I had become an extremely good reader during elementary school (with no thanks whatsoever to my teachers). In fact, the school system almost turned me off to reading by forcing me to "read" the Dick and Jane basal series. They were to me terribly boring, bland stories about children whose world was totally unrelated to my own. In the real, interesting, nonschool-related world in which I lived, I sang and danced to the great music of Motown— even though my church said it was a sin—and entertained my siblings with original scary stories at night. I organized and starred in talent shows for the kids in our apartment complex and designed elaborate wardrobes for my homemade paper dolls; I was a tether ball champion, and a great softball player. I also attended the Pentecostal church, in which I sang in the choir, witnessed exorcisms, and saw faith healers making people's legs grow before my very eyes.

Although my teachers assumed that my home life and culture were deficient and that our parents did not care about our education, they failed to realize that the credit for my strong reading skills belonged to my mother, not the school system. Though inadvertently, at home my mother modeled the importance of reading to us and stressed the value of education. She routinely asked if we had completed our homework, and she expected the older children to assist the younger ones with theirs. Even after she was blinded in her left eye, she continued to read magazines voraciously. The only other reading materials at home were the Bible, the little cards we received from Sunday School, and bills. But our mother warned us not to touch her magazines. This, of course, sparked our curiosity. Before long, my older sister and I were hiding in dark closets, struggling in secret to comprehend our mother's *True Confession* and *True Romance* magazines. We soon learned that these magazines were a lot more interesting than reading about Dick and Jane. So behind my mother's back we honed our reading skills (eventually became outstanding readers) and ruined our eyesight.

Like Miss Root, my fourth grade teacher, Mr. McCarthy, knew about my reputation before I arrived. He expected me to be a discipline problem through my outspokenness and excessive talking, and his expectations were fulfilled. Mr. McCarthy was very grumpy and desperately in need of a retirement incentive, but he did not resort to cruelty. Instead, he banished me to a coat closet in the back of the classroom. However, he was also capable of kindness. Once, he took the class on a field trip to his home in suburbia and let us swim in his pool.

In most ways, fifth grade was similar to my previous years in school. Mr. Jangaard, my fifth grade teacher, had my sister the year before and already expected me to be a discipline problem. He was tall, stout, and had a head full of red hair. Unlike Mr. McCarthy, he kept me after school for excessive talking. What he failed to realize is that if a teacher assigns detention to a student for talking, then the teacher must share the punishment. So, day after day, when Mr. Jangaard kept me for detention, I talked and talked. Because of my nonstop talking, he could not do any of his work. Finally, he decided that if I were not going to shut up, then the best solution would be to listen to me. Before long, he was asking me questions about my culture and other topics.

One day, to my utter amazement, he declared, "You know, you're not dumb like they said. You're really very smart." Instead of feeling grateful, I was offended. I thought that he was making fun of me. When I looked at him, my eyes shouted "Liar!" I was very angry that after years of being told I was dumb, at home and at school, this teacher was mocking me. Mr. Jangaard did not care about my opinion. My nonstop chattering during detention convinced him that I had potential, and he wanted others to know it. Soon, I was required to be tested at school. The only part I remember was an oral question-and-answer session through which I talked as if I were an expert on topics that were foreign to me. One question was about *Romeo and Juliet*. Despite the fact that I had never heard of Shakespeare or any of his plays, I talked about Romeo and Juliet as if I had met them personally. The next thing I knew, other people at school started telling me that I was smart, but I refused to believe them. The negative messages I had internalized about my aptitude over the years were too deeply ingrained in my psyche.

The Power of One Influential Teacher

My sixth grade year was probably the most important of my life. During this time, I was blessed with a remarkable teacher, Mrs. Susan Tessem, the feistiest and most down-to-earth white woman I had ever met. She appeared to be in her late twenties or early thirties, had short and stylishly-cut blonde hair, and often wore the sleeveless above-the-knee colorful shifts that were popular during the late sixties. Like several of my other teachers, Mrs. Tessem had had my older sister the previous year. Sometimes my sister would tell me about the exciting activities that occurred in Mrs. Tessem's classroom. She was the first teacher who managed to penetrate my sister's anger, defiance, and hatred. With the exception of her second grade teacher, I believe that Mrs. Tessem was the only elementary teacher my sister actually liked. When I learned that I was assigned to her class, I felt honored.

There were many differences between Mrs. Tessem and my previous teachers. Her actions and treatment of us indicated that she taught at our school by choice. She wanted to work at this school, and she truly loved her job. She had definitely not been dismissed from suburban schools. Realizing that music was an important part of our culture, she started a choir and took us on singing trips throughout the city. In the classroom, she created a community that was based on mutual respect. Instead of viewing excessive talking as a problem, she encouraged us to engage in lively class discussions on any number of issues, such as racism, current events, and moral dilemmas. She valued our opinions, and we valued hers. She taught us to think critically through problem-solving exercises. For example, she often wrote famous quotes on the chalkboard and asked us to interpret them—a practice that I would later incorporate into my own teaching (see Appendix G). Once she wrote, "To err is human;

to forgive, divine" and asked us what it meant. She refused to accept "I don't know" as an answer and encouraged us to use context clues to figure out what the word *err* meant.

Mrs. Tessem's class was fun, and she made the curriculum relevant to our lives. She had extremely high expectations for us, and she was very strict. On several occasions, she got directly in my face to give me a lecture about my behavior. One of these incidents occurred after the choir returned from a field trip. During the bus ride back to our school, one of my classmates and I began to tease each other through a popular cultural tradition that we called "basing" at that time. (In some predominantly black regions, terms such as "playing the dozens," "capping," or "signifying" are used to describe the same routine.) The purpose of this verbal exchange is for the participants to outtalk each other by trading "harmless" insults with the goal of making the audience laugh.

When the verbal fight started, my opponent and I were both doing a fairly decent job of raking up invisible points by our audience: schoolmates who were sitting near us on the bus and whose comments, cheers, and laughter let us know when one of us had scored an invisible point. Before long, however, I had the lead. Encouraged by my schoolmates' cheers, I became ruthless, saying every insulting thing that I could possibly say about this girl. Soon she began to cry and I felt sorry for her, but I was also a little miffed that she had not bothered to cry when the crowd was cheering in her favor, at my expense. When we arrived at school, it was lunchtime, and Mrs. Tessem, who had been on a different bus, came looking for me. The look on her face told me I was in trouble. "I just heard what you did," she stated, "and I'm very angry and disappointed in you." Now it was my turn to cry. I cried because I respected Mrs. Tessem so much that I did not want to disappoint her in any way. But she refused to feel sorry for me. She wanted me to realize that words can be damaging, and that I should use them wisely.

In addition to using more effective instructional practices than all of my previous teachers, another factor that differentiated Mrs. Tessem from them was that she truly cared about us as individuals.

She took a personal interest in our lives both inside and outside of school. She actually gave clothes to two overweight girls in our class. When I became jealous of the attention she gave them, she replied that if I were not so skinny she would give me some of her clothes too. When my youngest sister, child number six, a kindergartner, was hit by a car, paralyzed on her left side, and left in a coma, Mrs. Tessem took a personal interest in her welfare and the effect of the accident on me. Throughout the school day, she would let me go to the front office to telephone the hospital to find out if my sister had emerged from the coma. When I would return to class looking dejected, Mrs. Tessem offered words of comfort. On the ninth day of this ordeal, when my sister emerged from the coma, Mrs. Tessem rejoiced with me as if she were celebrating the miraculous recovery of her own child.

The most important difference between Mrs. Tessem and my previous teachers was that she did not view me or my classmates as deficient, and if she viewed us as culturally deprived she certainly fooled us. She was also well aware of the baggage that I carried to school. She knew a lot about my family but did not waste time criticizing my home life or feeling sorry for me. She was clearly on a mission, and she only had one academic year to fulfill it. Throughout that year, she was unrelenting in her efforts to convince me I had more academic potential than I had been led to believe. She also stressed that it was imperative that I use education to improve the quality of my life. When she took us to her house for homemade hamburgers and french fries and permitted us to frolic in her swimming pool, she let me know that I could one day own a nice house, if I used the educational opportunities that were available to me.

On the last day of school, Mrs. Tessem and I had our final heart-to-heart talk. "Can you keep a secret?" she asked excitedly. Although I was known for having a big mouth, I vowed to keep any secret that Mrs. Tessem told me, even if it killed me. "Next year," she said, "your younger sister, T., is going to be in my class." Then I learned that Mrs. Tessem had actually requested that I be placed in her class. The fact that I had been assigned to her was no accident.

She was committed to helping as many members of my family as she could.

The second part of our talk concerned my future. Mrs. Tessem emphasized that I must strive to do my best in junior high school and high school. The most surprising thing she said, though, was "And you'd better go to college!" She stated it as a command, and I felt I had no choice. No one had ever mentioned college to me, but I felt that after all of the time and effort she had invested in me during that one phenomenal year, going to college would be the least I could do to repay her.

During the summer, we moved from the neighborhood, so my younger sister never had the privilege of having Mrs. Tessem for a teacher. The worst part of moving was that I lost contact with Mrs. Tessem. By this time, my mother had completed a training program, found a job, gotten us off of welfare, and purchased a brand new four-bedroom home in a much nicer neighborhood. Many years later, I tried to contact Mrs. Tessem to give her an update on my life. I learned that she and her husband were divorced and that a health problem had caused her to quit teaching and move to Costa Rica.

Years later, I contacted the school district for which she had taught, to see if they could help me locate her. My efforts proved futile. On several other occasions, I attempted to reach her ex-husband, a prominent attorney. When I finally spoke to him by telephone, I told him that I wanted to tell Mrs. Tessem that I had turned out OK and wanted to thank her for the positive messages about my potential that she had instilled in me. She had convinced me that I possessed the ability to use education to improve the quality of my life. I also wanted her to know that I had become a junior high school teacher, and then later a high school teacher; moreover, I modeled my teaching style after her example. I will never forget his reply; "Susan still lives in Costa Rica," he stated, "but if she ever returns to the U.S., I'll tell her that you called. In fact, I'm going to add your name to the long list of her other former students who are also trying to find her."

A few years ago, I resumed my search for Mrs. Tessem. I wanted her to know that I had returned to school, earned a doctorate, and become a university professor. I was able to speak with her former mother-in-law, only to learn that she was still probably living in Costa Rica. I also conducted an Internet search and wrote to Oprah Winfrey, asking her if she could try to locate Mrs. Tessem.

Today, I do not know if Mrs. Tessem is dead or alive. I do know, however, that even though she never knew I turned out OK, I became successful nonetheless. Mrs. Tessem never saw the fruits of her labor, but her hard work paid off. The positive seeds that she planted grew and are still growing, because she made a personal commitment to become a powerful and influential teacher of an African American child who had been written off by the educational system. When she viewed me, she chose to look beyond my "deficits" and painful personal circumstances. Instead, she chose to focus on my potential for success and to convince me I had the aptitude to use education to improve the quality of my life.

Lessons for Educators

The challenging circumstances of my childhood may appear to be extraordinary, but they are not unique. Today, classrooms throughout the United States are filled with children who come from difficult homes. According to the U.S. Census Bureau, in 1990 there were 690,658 substantiated cases of child abuse in the United States, but in 1998 the number reached 861,602. More than half of these cases involved neglect; 23 percent involved physical abuse, and 13 percent involved sexual abuse. Girls made up 51 percent of the child abuse cases in 1998, and the majority of the victims were school-aged children. Moreover, although 18 percent of the children in the United States lived in poverty during 1998, Latino (34 percent) and African American (36 percent) children were disproportionately represented among poor children.[2]

When educators hear such dire statistics or see the evidence among their own students, some become overwhelmed and adopt a sense of helplessness. Others—the Mrs. Tessems—accept the fact that many aspects of their students' lives are outside of their control. They also realize that during the school day they have numerous opportunities to plant positive messages and foster seeds of resiliency in their students. Like Mrs. Tessem, these teachers make choices every day to offer their students both academic and personal tools for success. Instead of watering down the curriculum and shortchanging their students academically, they have high expectations and assist students in rising to the level of those expectations.[3] Instead of assuming their students will not amount to much in life, they strive to convince students they can use education to improve the quality of their lives. They also choose not to view students as deficient, regardless of their background. Instead, they recognize that their students arrive at school with valuable cultural capital (no matter how much it differs from the values of mainstream society) that can be put to use in the classroom. Furthermore, they look for assets on which to build.

Every classroom teacher makes a choice, consciously or subconsciously, every day. Each teacher makes a choice to strive to become an outstanding and influential teacher who has a long-term impact on students and to see students' potential for success, or the teacher makes a choice to use students' problems as an excuse to shortchange them academically.

Any decent teacher can become successful with well-behaved and high-achieving students. Only the phenomenal teachers who possess the Mrs. Tessem mind-set can succeed with underachievers, students from challenging backgrounds, and those who are perceived as discipline problems. Becoming a phenomenal teacher is not easy, but it is an option that is available to all teachers.

5

Standard English or Ebonics: Should We Force Them to Speak "Correctly"?

As I related in the previous chapter, during my childhood the world I inhabited was almost exclusively African American. I saw whites on television, and with the exception of my kindergarten teacher all of my elementary school teachers were white; the owners of the local grocery store were white. Even so, my "real world"—the world that mattered to me—was populated by people who looked similar to me and who spoke like me. Like myself, most of these individuals spoke Ebonics, or Black English. We did not speak "The King's English," and we did not speak Standard English. But from preachers who used vivid stories of hellfire and damnation to convince us that we were sinners in need of salvation, to my closest friends with whom I was able to share my dreams and secrets, we were all able to communicate with each other in a manner that was mutually comprehensible and acceptable. Therefore I had no problem with how I spoke. In fact, it did not become an issue until junior high school, when I began venturing into a mainly white environment.

After attending a predominantly black elementary school, during the academic year following sixth grade I rode a school bus full of African American kids across town to attend junior high school. We were participants in a voluntary busing program that was designed to integrate the primarily white junior high school that was in a more affluent section of the city. Because my older sister had already attended this junior high school for a year, I had some idea of what to expect. Most of my classmates were white, but there were enough African American students at the school for me to feel comfortable, at least outside of class. My friends were other African Americans who were bused in and a few African Americans who lived near the school. Like my friends during elementary school, my junior high school friends and I felt comfortable speaking Ebonics. I knew that our white classmates spoke differently from us, but since they were not my friends and my interactions with them were extremely limited—probably by mutual agreement—the differences between how we spoke and how they spoke was not important to me. This changed, however, at some point during seventh grade.

One day, I was sitting in my English class when the teacher summoned me to her desk. An elderly white man had been discussing something with her. The teacher told me that, starting that day, I would be working with this man twice a week. I do not recall if the man told me or if the teacher told me, but sometime between my being summoned to the teacher's desk, led out of the classroom by this man, and ending up in his office, I learned two surprising details: the man was a speech therapist, and I had a speech impediment.

When I heard this news, I did not know whether I should laugh or scream. It was totally ludicrous to me—a person who talked practically nonstop at home, school, and church—to be told that I could not speak well. Instead of screaming, I laughed inwardly, deciding that the man, not I, had the real problem. I thought of telling him that since none of my previous teachers (most of whom would have loved to find another deficit to attribute to me) or the significant people in my life said I had a speech impediment after all of these years, there was absolutely no way I would believe him. Instead, I decided to play his little game.

So each time he would summon me to his office, I would go compliantly. When he told me that we needed to continue to work on my "lisp," especially the way in which I pronounced words containing *th* or *s,* I complied. When he pronounced words and told me to copy how he pronounced them, I did so. When he rewarded me with a chocolate-covered pecan cluster for each correct imitation of his speech, I accepted each piece of candy with feigned gratitude. But in my heart I thought I was playing him for the fool I suspected that he was. In my opinion, this man was crazy if he really thought I was going to go around enunciating words in the manner in which he insisted. To do so, I believed, would make me an object of ridicule to my family and friends.

I made a valiant attempt to resist the speech therapist's gentle but unrelenting attempts to change the way in which I spoke, but unbeknownst to me at the time his efforts were having a long-term effect on me. Each "therapy" session gradually began to erode my confidence in my speaking ability. By the time the sessions officially concluded at the end of the school term, the damage was done. I had developed a huge complex about how I spoke. Years later, when I eventually went away to college, I was totally self-conscious about speaking in front of my white classmates. Although I had much to say, the fear that I did not speak correctly or would stumble over my words, or lisp them, often became overwhelming. The result was usually silence.

Today, some African American school-age children react to the message they infer at school about their language and their speaking ability in a similarly passive way, but others resist more overtly. When I conduct trainings in schools to show teachers how they can increase their efficacy with African American students, classroom management is usually the topic most likely to lead to misunderstanding. Conversely, Ebonics or Black English is the topic that appears to be most difficult for them to understand. The two themes that arise most often are (1) many teachers do not understand what Ebonics actually is, and (2) many teachers do not understand why African Americans continue to speak Ebonics. The remainder of this chapter addresses these two points and includes suggestions for teachers.

What Is Ebonics?

Although Standard English has been referred to as the language of the middle class[1] or the language that educated people use,[2] Haskins and Butts said that classifying languages or dialects as "standard" or "nonstandard" is based on arbitrary measures. They also said that one dialect being considered more socially prestigious than another "has nothing to do with that particular dialect's linguistic merits."[3] Gilman said that *standard* is an elitist term.[4]

Although defining Black English is easy, classifying it is more challenging.[5] Regional and class differences, plus the fact that many blacks who live outside of Africa speak some form of Black English, exacerbates the situation. For example, in Louisiana, Creole, a French-based dialect that has been influenced by several languages is spoken in many black communities.[6] In the Caribbean, there are other black dialects. Moreover, the psychological, class, political, and racial ramifications as well as historical biases that are associated with the topic add to the confusion.

For example, one of my former graduate students, an elderly white high school teacher, once remarked in class, "My problem with kids speaking Ebonics is that it is so vulgar and offensive." His statement reflected the extent of the ignorance and confusion that exists about Black English. The statement also served as a perfect teachable moment opportunity for me to share what I knew about Ebonics. During my training sessions in schools, I have found that most nonblack teachers are just as confused as this graduate student was. Some think that Ebonics and profanity are synonymous; others believe that Ebonics and slang are the same.

Unlike Ebonics, *slang* refers solely to words that have a colloquial or informal meaning. Although it may be, slang is not necessarily governed by rules, and it changes on an ongoing basis. Therefore slang words can be in vogue one day and obsolete after a short period of time. In August 2000, *Ebony* magazine published a list of slang terms that included "knuckle up," which means to fight; "bout-it-bout-it," which means "in support of;" "Betty," an attractive female; "chickenhead," an unattractive female; and "flossing," to show off, as examples of the most popular slang words and slang terms of the new generation.[7]

Conversely, there are two schools of thought about Ebonics. One argument posits that it is merely a bad form of English; the other claims that Ebonics is actually a derivative of West African languages. Earlier white theorists believed that speakers of Black English could not speak Standard English because of physical and cognitive deficiencies. Other theorists posited that Black English was not necessarily a sign of deficiency, but merely a cultural difference. Prior to the 1960s, the pervasive viewpoint about African Americans was that they no longer retained any vestiges of African culture; therefore the language that most of them spoke was merely a "bad" form of Standard English. The overarching assumption was that Black English had its sole origin in English.

During the 1970s, many researchers began to challenge the existing beliefs about Black English. In 1972, for example, both Dillard and Labov published seminal works on Black English. Dillard's work was widely used by black writers to "prove" that although Black English did stem from Standard English, it also included many words that originated in Africa as well. Dillard theorized that Black English evolved from pidgin into Creole and then into Black English. [8] Other researchers disagreed and insisted that Black English was basically a nonstandard form of English. Africanists, however, maintained that Ebonics is the proper term for how most African Americans speak; their theory rests on the notion that Ebonics is fundamentally different from English in its deep structure. Although the terms have been used interchangeably in this book, Black English and Ebonics are not synonymous. Instead, they indicate a political way of viewing this topic. One viewpoint, according to Smith, is Eurocentric in that it defines Black English as being basically English in origin; the other is Afrocentric in that it views Ebonics as being a language that is based on the phonology, morphology, and syntax of West African languages. [9]

Specific Features of Ebonics

There are numerous differences between Ebonics and Standard English, among them tense, orthographic, and phonological differences; the omission of certain beginning and ending syllables; and, most notably, the use of or absence of the copula *be* and how negative statements are formed.[10] Carroll[11] and Smitherman[12] said that there are also certain words used exclusively by speakers of Ebonics. Traugott[13] noted that many words originating with Ebonics speakers have been incorporated into Standard English but may have lost their original meaning. Furthermore, in Ebonics active sentences are used more frequently than passive sentences,[14] and Ebonics tends to be more direct than Standard English.[15] This directness can also create conflicts between some teachers—especially those who were socialized to use indirect speech—and African American students whose direct manner of speaking may be viewed as rudeness.[16]

Tense

The rules and style of Ebonics are often different from those of Standard English.[17] Dillard[18] and Traugott[19] said that one of the fundamental differences is that Ebonics speakers have an option of whether or not to indicate tense. When using the present tense, for example, many speakers of Ebonics omit the -s at the end of the verb. Therefore *She helps* becomes *She help*; *She goes* becomes *She go*.[20] Smitherman also noted that the -ed suffix in past tense verbs is often omitted in Ebonics.[21]

Phonology

One of the main phonological differences between Ebonics and Standard English is that speakers of Ebonics simplify certain consonant clusters, such as -sk, -sp, -st, and those ending in -s, -z, -l, -r, -t, -d, and -x. In some clusters, the sound of the first letter may be lost, and in others the second sound may be lost. In the case of plurals, the -s is usually omitted.[22]

Johnson also observed that certain sounds, particularly the *th-* at the beginning of words, are nonexistent in Ebonics. The result is that speakers of Ebonics often use *d-* in lieu of *th-*. He also found that -d- or -v- is used as a substitute for words that have -th- in the middle and -f is substituted for the -th sound at the end of words.[23]

Smitherman, however, found that the *th-* sound does exist for words such as *thought* or *thing*. In other words, if the initial *th-* is silent, no substitution is used.[24] Concerning phonology, she also noted that Ebonics speakers often emphasize the initial syllables of words. For example, *Detroit* might be pronounced as *DEE-troit* and *police* might be pronounced *PO-lice*.[25]

Invariant "Be"

The most notable feature of Ebonics is the use or absence of the copula and auxiliary forms of *be*.[26] Fasold and Wolfram said the way in which *to be* is used in Ebonics is very different from how it is used in Standard English. They wrote: "When the verb *to be* is used as a main verb in Standard English, it appears as one of the five variant inflected forms *is*, *are*, *am*, *was*, or *were* depending on the verb tense and the person and number of the subject. In [Ebonics], the form *be* can be used as a main verb, regardless of the subject of the sentence, as in *I be here this afternoon* and *Sometime he be busy. . . .*"[27]

The second use of invariant *be* is quite different. According to Fasold and Wolfram, "This type of invariant *be* occurs because *to be* is possible in [Ebonics] without tense specification with a meaning something like 'object or event distributed intermittently in time.' This use of *be* as in *Sometime he be here and sometime he don't* occurs only in [Ebonics] and is usually misunderstood by Standard English speakers."[28]

Smitherman concurred that the use of *be* indicates a habitual condition and the absence of *be* signifies a temporary condition. She also mentioned that *be* can refer to the future.[29] Labov on the other hand, focused not so much on the meaning of *be* as used by speakers of Ebonics but on the underlying rules that determined when and if the copula or auxiliary *be* would be used. He observed that although the copula and auxiliary *be* are usually nonexistent in Ebonics, they do appear under certain conditions; he concluded that the rules governing when the copula or auxiliary would be omitted or used, however, did not depend on which form of *be* was required but whether or not a contraction could be used. He wrote: "We find the following general principle holds without exception: Whenever [Standard English] can contract, [Ebonics] can delete *is* and *are*, and vice versa; whenever [Standard English] cannot contract, [Ebonics] cannot delete *is* and *are* and vice versa."[30]

Negatives

The use of double or multiple negatives is another common feature of Ebonics. Haskins and Butts said that whereas white speakers may use double negatives periodically, in the case of Black English "what is generally meant by the term is multiple, cumulative negation as in 'I did not see nobody.'"[31] Haskins and Butts also explained that this common occurrence is based on grammatical rules: "The Black English rule of negation is that a negative is attached to all negatable elements within the same simple sentence. That is, for a negative sentence to be grammatical according to the rules of Black English, all indefinite pronouns, all indefinite articles, all indefinite adverbials, and the verbal auxiliary must be made negative: "Nobody ain't never met no ghost nowhere."[32]

Although this explanation of some of the rules and features of Ebonics may appear to have been detailed and a bit too "academic," it is crucial to any discussion pertaining to this topic. It offers teachers rudimentary knowledge about how to differentiate Ebonics from slang, and it may assist teachers in forming their own opinion about whether Ebonics is merely "bad English," a dialect, or a language that combines some West African words and English words.

During fall 2002, I presented these details to my graduate students in my Closing the Achievement Gap course. At the end of the lecture, one of the African American men in the class said, "This is making me mad." When I asked why, he stated that he was angry that all of his life he had been ridiculed and disparaged for speaking Ebonics; "Nobody told me any of this stuff about rules or anything." The average African American K–12 student who speaks Ebonics may never articulate such anger. However, students' anger over disparagement at how they speak can surface in other ways, as the next sections illustrate.

Why Many African Americans Continue to Speak Ebonics

I used to believe that African American children from urban and other nonmiddle-class backgrounds did not start speaking Standard English after they entered school because they had limited contact with it. In other words, if the children lived in a home in which Ebonics was spoken, interacted with peers who spoke Ebonics, and attended churches or other organizations in which Ebonics was spoken, then the only time they really heard Standard English spoken was when their teachers and other school personnel spoke it, or when they heard it spoken on television or radio. Therefore, they had limited opportunities to hear and practice using Standard English. This is similar to the experiences of some first-generation Mexican American students who participated in a study that I conducted. Although the majority of the Latino students were actually born in the United States, when they started kindergarten Spanish was their only language, because it was the language in which the significant individuals in their lives had communicated with them from birth. Once they arrived at school, the students tended to socialize with those with whom they felt most comfortable: other children who spoke their language. When they returned home, to communicate with family members they had to use Spanish. Consequently, they had few opportunities to hear and practice Standard English throughout the school day.[33] However, as a result of my own children's experiences, my theory about the reasons many African American children do not speak Standard English has changed.

After attending a predominantly white Christian school for most of her life, my oldest daughter rebelled at the end of her junior year of high school. It started with her request to enroll in summer school at the local public high school. For the first time since preschool and attending Sunday school, she found herself in class-rooms in which there were more than a handful of African American students, and she loved it. Consequently, when summer school ended, she announced that she did not want to return to the private school. She was tired of constantly being told by her white class-mates that although she "had a big butt" she did not "act black," and tired of being excluded from social activities. In case my hus-band and I had any reservations about permitting her to complete her senior year at the public high school, she warned us that as our two younger children got older, they would eventually rebel against the racism and ignorance that were common among many of their white classmates at the private school.

After long discussions and weighing the pros and cons, against our two younger children's wishes my husband and I enrolled all three of our children in public schools. Because the racial composi-tion of my son's fifth grade classroom was similar to that of his old school, he adapted easily to his new environment and experienced few problems. But my daughters' experiences were different from his, and language was one main reason. Although both of them were constantly accused by their African American schoolmates of sounding white or acting white, they handled the situations differ-ently. The high school senior asked a friend to give her "Ebonics lessons." The seventh grader's hurt feelings over being rejected by most of her African American peers at the new school led to many tears, which soon developed into anger. Over time, the anger gave way to a fortitude that made her extremely selective in choosing friends. Today, as a tenth grader, although she remains bitter about her negative experiences during her first year of public school she is proactive when her African American peers ridicule her for speak-ing Standard English. Her retorts are designed to force them to con-sider the messages they convey when they make judgments about people on the basis of ignorance. Recently my son, who is now an eighth grader and who for the first time was accused of acting white by two of his African American classmates, used his sister's method. Three of the questions he asked his classmates were "So, are you saying that I have to sound a certain way to be black?" "Are you saying that it's wrong for black people to use Standard English?" and "What does it mean to be 'black,' in your opinion?" According to my son, the girls' tone changed and the three of them ended up having a meaningful discussion. At the end of the conversation, one of the girls told him, "I guess we were guilty of stereotyping."

As a result of my own children's experiences as middle-class African American children who were socialized at predominantly white schools to speak Standard English, my new theory is that many African Americans refuse to speak Standard English for self-preservation. Although African American students in urban environments may realize that Ebonics is disparaged by "educated people" as merely a dialect or form of bad English, many African American students are unwilling to give up their language. It ties them to family, community, their peers, and African American history. It can also connote insider versus outsider status. As my children learned when they enrolled in public school, many African Americans judge other African Americans by how they speak. For some African American students from lower socioeconomic backgrounds, the use of Standard English by an African American peer creates the assumption of difference that is often equated with "You think you're better than us," "You must think that you're white," or "Your family must have more money than ours." After all, Standard English is usually spoken by teachers, including those who have given some African American children the message that they are deficient, starting in their earliest years of school. Some of these teachers have also given African American children the message that the students' own language is bad. Consequently, it is logical that some African American students would resist the language of individuals who appear to be oppressive. As Delpit stated, "To speak out against the language that children bring to school means that we are speaking out against their mothers, that their mothers are not good enough to be a part of the school world. And in the African American community, talking about someone's mother is the worst form of insult."[34]

One of my former graduate students, a white middle school teacher, fell into this category. In our university class, she would often brag about her stance on language. "I tell the black kids that they can speak it [Ebonics] outside on the playground with their friends, but in my classroom, it's not allowed," she stated emphatically. "They can only speak Standard English in my classroom." To me, it was interesting to note that this woman, by her own admission, was unpopular with her African American students, who frequently accused her of being racist. Moreover, she often complained about acts of resistance from her African American students. She attributed these problems to their bad attitude, but I believe her own attitude had a lot to do with the students' attitudes and behaviors. Like many teachers, she failed to realize a fundamental point: if teachers tell students they cannot speak the only way they know how, then the teachers are destroying any opportunity the students might have to engage in discussion and meaningful dialogue in the class. If students are required to censor every word they utter in an effort to speak in some correct way, they will feel that too much effort is required and choose not to participate since they are prohibited from using their natural style of discourse and the language with which they feel most comfortable. In *Other People's Children*, Delpit said that when children of color reject literacy in the classroom, it is often because they feel their own styles of discourse have been rejected. For example, children who speak Ebonics or Black English are overcorrected by teachers to the point that their "affective filter" becomes blocked. Consequently, attempting to read becomes an unpleasant experience because they are constantly being corrected as they do so.[35]

The middle school teacher's attitude and stance about how her African American students spoke is common. The disparagement of all things black that has a long history in the United States continues to surface when it comes to how speakers of Ebonics are viewed by educators and many members of the public. For some, Ebonics is equated with ignorance, backwardness, and a lower socioeconomic status, instead of a crucial tie that connects speakers to the African American community, particularly urban and rural communities. But many educators are hypocrites; they are much more sympathetic and compassionate in their treatment and views of nonblacks who speak non-Standard English.

I have witnessed this numerous times, especially while serving on committees. One committee required me and other educators to read the school's district-mandated student writing exams. At least two teachers had to read and assign a score to each exam. In the event that a great disparity arose between two raters' scores, a third teacher would be required to read and assign a score to the writing exam. During this time, I noticed that some teachers were willing to excuse the grammatical errors of Vietnamese, Cambodian, and Laotian students by attributing their errors to second language interference. In the case of African American students whose exams contained grammatical errors, low ratings were assigned. When I mentioned that it was not fair to excuse the errors of some students in the name of second language interference, but not the errors of all students who did not speak Standard English, the teachers acted as if they could not understand what I meant. The problem was solved by an African American educator who was serving as one of the trainers on that day. She agreed that exceptions should not be made for any group, because the goal of the exam was to ensure that each student could write a decent paragraph. To assign a passing score to those who needed more writing practice would be counterproductive.

In the edited volume *The Skin That We Speak: Thoughts on Language and Culture in the Classroom*, several scholars and educators stressed the need for teachers to understand why so many African American students speak Ebonics, and for teachers to realize the damage they do when they do not value students' styles of discourse and their primary language.[36] One of the contributors, Wynne, surveyed teacher education students and found that most believed students should only be permitted to speak Standard English in class. She stated, "I believe the abuses of linguistic oppression toward children of color are horrendous; the consequences are severe; and the damage to the self-esteem of youths is unconscionable."[37] Nevertheless, Wynne, like many educators, believed that in order to advance in the United States students must learn to speak Standard English. The key is for teachers to create a "psychological sanctuary" in the classroom that is predicated on teaching them to use Standard English in a way that does not devalue or denigrate their home language. She also said that white students need to learn "about the beauty and richness of the language of Black America," and that universities must do a better job of teaching prospective educators to honor students' language.[38] In another chapter, Purcell-Gates described how teachers' insistence on the use of Standard English can only have a negative effect on children's literacy development; "If you are forbidden to use your language to learn to read and write, if you are forced to speak differently when reading and writing, then you are in effect being closed off, or at least seriously impeded from accessing the world of print."[39]

Summary

Good communication skills are important at every level of society. Even infants have innate communication skills that allow them to express their desires and moods. Ineffective communication skills can cause many problems, from a "simple" misunderstanding to a full-blown war. In the classroom, communication (both verbal and nonverbal) is the vehicle through which teachers and students interact and make judgments about each other. Because it is linked to teachers' ability to convey instructional and behavioral objectives and subject matter clearly and to students' ability to comprehend, classroom communication is extremely important. Additionally, students must use communication skills to demonstrate whether or not they have mastered subject matter.

Today, many urban schools nationwide are primarily African American. Since most urban and lower-income African American children, as well as many middle-class African Americans, speak some form of Ebonics and most teachers do not, communication problems are inevitable. These communication problems may be one of the causal factors of the underachievement of many African American children. As Kohl put it, "Teacher talk and student talk are essential components that determine the quality of learning in the classroom. When there is dissonance between them, other kinds of strife develop."[40] Hilliard concurred with this idea: "If an African American child is seen as language deficient, we can show that the behavior of the teacher actually changes toward that child as compared to 'normal' children. He or she will engage the child in communication less and pay less attention to the child. . . . It is this teaching behavior and not the language of the child, no matter how different, that creates the problem for learners."[41]

Several recently published works indicate there is still disagreement over many key issues relating to Ebonics. This ongoing dissension has undoubtedly affected how teachers interact with speakers of Ebonics. Teacher uncertainty and prejudice toward Ebonics have far-reaching consequences. Several writers, including Delpit, have noted that teachers tend to overcorrect students who speak Black English.[42] Others have asserted that teachers tend to give higher ratings to children who speak as they do. Therefore a powerful bias against children who speak Ebonics continues to exist. This bias might be one of the causal factors of the poor scores, high dropout rate, and discipline problems of African American students. It is also linked to special education referrals, as linguist Ernie Smith illustrated in his work. After his elementary school teachers labeled him "a verbal cripple," he was placed in language remediation classes during junior high school and special education during high school. Teasing by other students resulted in fights. However, at the same time that his language skills were being criticized by teachers, Smith found that his "linguistic competence" was valued on the streets.[43]

To increase their efficacy with African American students, teachers must understand the role of language in students' schooling experiences, and the impact of teachers' attitudes and beliefs about language and styles of discourse. Teachers who equate speaking Ebonics with ignorance and deficiency covertly or overtly transmit a negative message to African American students. As Delpit wrote, "The negative responses to children's home language on the part of adults around them insures that they will reject the school's knowledge and everything else the school has to offer."[44] Teachers who "honor" students' primary language while at the same time teaching them the importance of learning to speak Standard English—the language of the culture of power[45]—will empower African American students.

Effective language instruction must therefore begin with an improvement in teachers' belief systems. The first belief that must be eradicated is that African American students who speak Ebonics are deficient. Baker,[46] Purcell-Gates,[47] and Delpit[48] said that to teach African American students to speak Standard English, teachers must use an additive pedagogy that is built on a legitimate (not feigned) respect for their home language. Baker said, "I see no reason why students have to be convinced that the way they talk is wrong [in order] to master formal English grammar and speech."[49] Second, teachers have to believe that African American children are capable of learning. They must also make the curriculum relevant to students' culture and personal lives. In the chapter "Trilingualism," Baker, a teacher at a Boston public high school, described the system she developed to improve her students' language skills. The system rested on a foundation of respect for the students' home languages and a culturally relevant curriculum. The students were required to become experts about their home language and to share their expertise with their classmates. In class the students studied each home language by examining "patterns of speech, rules of grammar, vocabulary, tonal features, and emotional characteristics of language which we note, label, discuss, and eventually compare to the features of what we call 'formal' English," Baker said.[50] One of her conclusions was, "For my students, the validation of their home language which comes from studying it allows them to feel comfortable with language study in general. It becomes just as acceptable to ask 'How would you say this in formal English?' as it is to ask 'How do you say this with your friends . . . ?'"[51]

Some of the most recent theories about language acquisition may change educators' attitudes toward speakers of Ebonics and improve the quality of education for lower-income and urban African American children. Postmodernist theorists agree that teachers should respect the languages their students speak. According to Nieto, "No child should have to make the painful choice between family and school which inevitably becomes the choice between belonging or succeeding. The costs of such a choice are too high, from becoming a 'cultural schizophrenic' to developing doubts about one's worth and dignity."[52] Baker's work in using an additive pedagogy, one that starts with a respect for the home language that students bring to school, and the work of other researchers indicate that teachers who are willing to do the work can effectively teach African American students to speak Standard English. These teachers can help students understand why they need to learn to speak Standard English, and to realize that the ability and willingness to use Standard English when necessary can empower them. Moreover, they can convince students they do not have to give up their home language to become empowered.

6

Can They Call Each Other the "N" Word?

Near the end of 2002, a maelstrom erupted in Congress that quickly spread to the general public. During a birthday party for Sen. Strom Thurmond, Senate Majority Leader Trent Lott proclaimed that if Thurmond had won the presidential election years earlier, the United States would not be experiencing the problems it was experiencing. Because Thurmond had run on a segregationist platform, many Americans—both white and nonwhite—inferred that Lott was condoning segregation. The result was that Lott was characterized as a racist who was unworthy of retaining his position. Although he apologized numerous times, even on Black Entertainment Television (BET), political and public pressure soon forced him to resign as Senate majority leader.[1]

As I read and listened to the news reports, one of the questions that was foremost in my mind was, "What would have happened if Lott had used the N word publicly?" If praising a prosegregationist's political views cost him his coveted position in the Senate, perhaps using the N word would have cost him his entire senatorship. After all, during the O. J. Simpson trial the revelation that former police officer Mark Furman had routinely used the N word was a pivotal factor in Simpson's acquittal.

In the twenty-first century, most Americans in public office know it is politically incorrect and totally unacceptable to use certain words or make certain statements that were acceptable in previous eras. The N word is an example of a term that has been politically incorrect for public utterance by nonblacks since the post-civil rights era. According to Harvard law professor Randall Kennedy, who wrote an informative book about the word, "It is impossible to declare with confidence that when hurled as an insult [the N word] necessarily inflicts more distress than other racial epithets. . . . In the aggregate, though, [the N word] is and has long been the most socially consequential racial insult."[2]

Today, the use of the N word has become a source of consternation for numerous teachers. Because the term is commonly used by many African American students and even by some nonblack students, many teachers do not know if they should allow students, particularly African Americans, to use it in class. The problem is compounded by the fact that, just as the use of the word is offensive to many African Americans, it is also offensive to some whites. For example, during a training that I conducted for three high schools, a white high school teacher told me that he and his wife (another high school teacher) retained negative memories that were associated with the use of the word during civil rights era activism. Thus when African American students use it in class, these teachers become extremely uncomfortable but are unsure of how to proceed. Undoubtedly, other whites who consider themselves to be progressive and nonracist, or who have actively fought to improve social and economic conditions for African Americans and others, might feel the same way; in fact, Kennedy found that the word was often applied to such whites as "[N word] lovers."[3]

To give teachers information about whether or not to permit African American students to use the N word in class, during training for the three high schools and a middle school I devoted a segment of my presentations to the use of the word. This chapter presents background information about the word, controversies associated with the term, and reasons why I strongly believe teachers should not permit students, including African Americans, to use it in class.

A Brief History of the "N" Word

In *Mommie What Is a [the N Word]? The Case of the Centuries*, Mia Isaac, a veteran African American teacher, wrote that her parents taught her that the N word was applied to blacks prior to the fifteenth century.[4] In his thorough examination of the origins, uses, and controversies associated with the word, Kennedy explained that "the [N word] is derived from the Latin word for the color black. . . ."[5] Various forms of the word appeared in print as early as the 1600s. Although it did not begin as a derogatory term, it eventually took on negative connotations. In Kennedy's words, "We do know, however, that by the end of the first third of the nineteenth century, [the word] had already become a familiar and influential insult."[6]

In fact, the use of the word became such a popular insult that it was used at all levels of American society. Kennedy wrote: "[The N Word] first appears in the reports of the United States Supreme Court in a decision announced in 1871. . . . In the years since, federal and state courts have heard hundreds of cases in which [the word] figured in episodes of racially motivated violence, threats, and arson."[7]

Use of the word was so prevalent in newspapers and American literature, as well as by white organizations such as the White Citizens Council, and among upper-class and lower-class whites, politicians, and even Supreme Court justices that, "for many whites in positions of authority . . . referring to blacks as [the N word] was once a safe indulgence."[8] Among the prominent whites who used it publicly were Sen. Benjamin Tilman of South Carolina, Gov. Coleman Livingston Blease of South Carolina, Sen. James Byrnes of South Carolina, Sen. Huey P. Long of Louisiana, Gov. Eugene Talmadge of Georgia, Supreme Court Justice James Clark McReynolds, Pres. Harry S. Truman, Pres. Lyndon B. Johnson, and Pres. Richard M. Nixon. Kennedy therefore concluded, "A complete list of prominent whites who have referred at some point or other to blacks demeaningly as [the N word] would be lengthy indeed."[9] Of course, a list that included whites and members of other racial and ethnic groups who use the word privately would be inexhaustible.

African Americans and the "N" Word

On the Saturday following Thanksgiving Day 2002, I walked to a local middle school for my regular jog. Before I could run my third lap around the track, my ears were assaulted by the N word. On the grass in the middle of the track, twelve teenage boys were playing an informal game of football. As they tossed the ball and ran to and fro, one of them yelled the word twice. All of the boys were black, and the speaker's use of the word did not appear to phase them. Although it troubled me, I had enough sense to realize that sharing my thoughts with them would be futile.

There are numerous reasons why many African Americans like these teens have chosen and continue to use a word that has historically been used to demean them; just as the use of the word has a long history among whites, it also has a lengthy history among African Americans. As Kennedy wrote, "Given Whites' use of [the word], it should come as no surprise that for many Blacks the N Word has constituted a major and menacing presence that has sometimes shifted the course of their lives."[10]

The use of the word by African Americans dates at least as far back as the slavery era in the United States. It appeared in slave narratives in which black slaves used it in reference to themselves and to other African Americans. It also appeared in black folklore and in comedy routines. According to Kennedy, although the word "has long been featured in black folk humor . . . . Before the 1970s, however, [the word] seldom figured in the routines of professional comedians. It was especially rare in the acts of those who performed for racially mixed audiences."[11] Richard Pryor is the comedian who is credited with changing the status quo. Pryor used it in his live performances and albums, and he even won a Grammy Award for an album that featured the word in its title. "Since then," Kennedy wrote, "the N Word has become a staple in the routine of many Black comedians."[12] Today the word can routinely be heard in black films, comedy routines, gangsta rap, black literature,[13] and even in classrooms. Moreover, in 2002 actor Bernie Mac used it in his television sitcom.

The fact that the N word is commonly used by many African Americans is indisputable. The reasons why are more complex. As Kennedy stated, "Unsurprisingly, Blacks have often used [the word] for different purposes than racist Whites."[14] In fact, Kennedy described at least seven reasons why African Americans might use the word.

The most obvious reason stems from self-hatred. A second is to belittle someone else. A third is that it can be used as a sign of defiance in which the users, according to Kennedy, throw "the slur right back in their oppressors' faces." Another reason is that African Americans might use it to illustrate "a pessimistic view of the African American predicament." A fifth is that some African Americans use the word to distinguish themselves from other African Americans whom they perceive to be less authentically "black" than themselves; in other words, according to Kennedy, by using the word they perceive themselves to be identifying with the black masses by "keeping it [their speech] real." A sixth reason why African Americans might use the word is to "rope off cultural turf," so that nonblacks cannot appropriate its use in order to profit from it commercially. A seventh, and possibly more perplexing reason, is that some African Americans actually use the N word as a term of endearment.[15] In summarizing the myriad reasons why African Americans might use the word, Kennedy wrote, "Traditionally an insult [the N word] can also be a compliment. . . . Historically a signal of hostility, it can also be a salutation announcing affection. . . . A word that can bring forth bitter tears in certain circumstances, [the N word] can prompt joyful laughter in others."[16]

Although many African Americans use the N word publicly, the African American community has not reached a consensus on this point. In my opinion, the black community can be divided into three groups regarding the use of the N word.

One group consists of individuals, such as myself, who do not believe that the N word should be used by anyone, including African Americans. Kennedy wrote, "Some people—I call them eradicationists—seek to drive [the N word] out of rap, comedy, and all other categories of entertainment even when (perhaps especially when) Blacks themselves are the ones using the N Word. They see this usage as bestowing legitimacy on [it] and misleading those Whites who have little direct interaction with African Americans."[17]

The second group, in my opinion, consists of African Americans who believe it is OK for African Americans to use the word as long as they do so privately. When I was an undergraduate at the University of Southern California, I witnessed a falling out between friends as a result of the violation of this long unspoken but well-known rule among African Americans. A group of African American students, including myself, were socializing in a large public quad. Two friends were joking with each other when one young woman referred to her male friend by the N word. All of a sudden, his demeanor changed. He became visibly angry and tense. It turned out that at the moment when the woman jokingly used the word a group of white students were passing by. In the offended student's opinion, his friend had violated a well-known, and at that time widely held, cultural taboo among so-called educated African Americans. The rule was to never divulge cultural secrets to non-blacks, and by all means to refrain from using the N word in the presence of whites, especially at an elitist school such as USC.

A huge argument ensued as both students presented their cases to the rest of the African Americans who were there. The young woman kept insisting that not only did she mean no harm but she had repeatedly used the N word in reference to her friend in the past, and it had never been a problem. Moreover, it was not her fault that whites were passing by at the very moment she used the word. For some time, the male student refused to be mollified; his friend had disrespected him in the presence of whites. Her behavior was thus inexcusable. The two students eventually resolved the disagreement, but that incident was also one of the factors that contributed to my stance as a hard-line eradicationist when it comes to the N word.

The third group, in my opinion, consists of African Americans who believe the word can be used with reckless abandon. Many popular African American comedians, musicians, writers, and athletes fall into this category. Consequently, because of the prevalent public and private use of the N word by some high-profile African Americans, many nonblack youths have also begun to use the word publicly to emulate popular figures they admire. They often use it to appear cool, and as a term of endearment for their nonblack friends. For example, there is now even a version of the word that applies solely to whites. However, according to Kennedy, "Even Whites who immerse themselves in Black hip-hop culture typically refrain from openly and unabashedly saying [the word] like their Black heroes or colleagues, for fear that it might be perceived as a sign of disrespect rather than one of solidarity."[18]

Last year, the African American comedian Cedric "The Entertainer" devoted a portion of one of his television shows to illustrate this point. In the TV clip, a group of African American men decided that one of their white friends had proven he was cool enough to be given permission to use the N word. When they told their white friend, he felt honored but also unsure about whether or not it was OK to do so. His friends kept telling him it was, and he finally uttered the N word. Before he realized what had happened, his friends began to physically attack him. The beating landed him in the hospital. Later, while visiting him there, the friends apologized profusely, said it would never happen again, and once more granted him the insider status of permission to use the N word. It took much coaxing, but the white guy eventually believed them and again uttered the N word. All of a sudden, an African American doctor who had been working in another section of the room and had heard the preceding conversation ran to his bed and began to beat him. The moral of the story was that it is still unwise for any white man—cool or otherwise—to use the N word in the presence of African Americans.

Although the third group has been instrumental in increasing the frequency with which the word has been used publicly by African Americans, they have not succeeded in completely destroying the long-standing cultural taboos in the African American community regarding use of the word. Today it remains controversial for

African Americans to use the term publicly, and—as the Cedric story illustrates—it is totally unacceptable by most African Americans for nonblacks to use the term. These very same issues, of course, often surface in the classroom.

The "N" Word in the Classroom

During one of my earliest years as a high school teacher, two of my tenth grade students—an African American boy and a Latina—started teasing each other. From their previous classroom interactions, I suspected they had a crush on each other. One day, for some reason, their teasing became argumentative. Neither student wanted to lose face in front of his or her peers, so when the African American student said to the girl, "Why don't you go back to Mexico?" she retorted "Why don't you go back to Africa?" The African American student (who had probably never learned one positive detail about Africa from the media or from his social studies or history teachers) became visibly enraged. He refused to calm down or listen to my advice. In fact, he clearly wanted to strike the girl. Because I was unable to calm him down, I felt it best to send him to speak with his school counselor. Later (as I did in the Trent Lott case), I wondered how much worse the situation would have gotten if the Latina had called him the N word. However, eventually the word did surface in my classroom, and when it did it happened in two ways: in literature and among students.

Many literary works that are routinely used in schools throughout the United States contain the N word as well as other racist, sexist, and offensive terms. This often creates a dilemma for teachers. As a high school teacher, I found myself in a similar predicament, because one of the books that I most enjoyed reading and discussing with my tenth graders, *Black Boy*,[19] Richard Wright's autobiography, contains numerous instances of the N word. Because I am an eradicationist, I decided not to permit my students to use the actual N word on the occasions when we read sections of the book orally in class. Therefore, before we began reading, I simply instructed students to skip the word when it was their turn to read orally. Since I had already taken the time to explain to students that I found the word to be offensive and refrained from using it myself, they accepted my decision without any complaints.

I know of two other cases, however, in which teachers chose to handle the situation differently. In both cases, the teachers were white and the book containing the N word was *The Adventures of Huckleberry Finn*.[20] One of the individuals was a first-year teacher. This middle-aged woman, who had left another career to become a teacher, was enrolled in one of my teacher education courses several years ago. When the topic of the N word came up in the graduate course, she said she permitted her high school students to vote on how they wanted to deal with the N word when it surfaced in literature that the class would be reading orally. "The students decided that it was not a big deal," she said, "so they decided to go ahead and use" the word.

I had three problems with her strategy. My main concern with her method was that because this woman taught at a predominantly Latino school (where there had previously been riots between blacks and Latinos), African American students would usually be outnumbered in her classes. Therefore, if there were only three or four African Americans in each class that was reading the book, even if they objected to hearing the word read orally or to reading it aloud themselves, their vote would be nullified. A second reason why her voting solution concerned me was that because the majority of the students in her classes were Latino, they could not relate to how an African American might feel when the N word was uttered by a nonblack publicly in a mixed setting. It would thus be unlikely that Latino students would find the word offensive enough to vote against its use. My third concern about the teacher's voting practice was related to the second. Many youths, including African Americans, are extremely ignorant about the painful history, origins, and uses of the N word by nonblacks as a tool to subjugate and demean. Consequently, it is quite understandable for them to decide that reading the word orally in class was "no big deal," especially since they constantly hear it used in music and by some celebrities.

The second case involved a Portland, Oregon, teacher who permitted his students to use the N word while reading *The Adventures of Huckleberry Finn* orally. In November 2002, an African American freshman in one of the teacher's classes told the teacher he was offended by the way in which the N word was being used in the classroom. According to a related article that appeared in the local newspaper, the student "was offended by the repeated use of racial slurs"[21] in the book. The teacher decided to send the student to the library to read another book. This upset the student even more. Soon, the student became a *cause célèbre*. An African American junior at another Portland high school took up his cause. This student, Charles McGee, got more than 250 students to sign a petition calling for "cultural sensitivity training for teachers." He presented the petition to the school board, which agreed to take the students' concerns seriously. Interestingly, McGee's actions were also rooted in his own personal experiences with reading *The Adventures of Huckleberry Finn*. Unlike the upset freshman student's teacher, McGee's own teacher had handled the situation in a culturally sensitive manner. Before the class actually read the book, the teacher educated them about the history and uses of the N word and other offensive language. A tone was thus set that prepared all students to be culturally sensitive and to behave appropriately when they actually read the book.[22]

The second way in which the N word surfaced in my high school classroom involved the very issue that teachers brought up during the trainings I conducted at the middle school and the three high schools, described in Appendix I. A few African American students wanted to use the N word in class in reference to other African American students. They were usually "playful" about it and clearly meant no harm. However, their use of the word still posed a problem in class.

Once, when it happened, a white male student asked why a double standard existed. He wanted to know why he often heard African Americans using the word, yet they would get angry when someone of another race or ethnicity used it. When I asked the African American student who had just used the word how he would feel if a white, Asian, or Latino student called him the N word, the student said he would respond with physical violence.

This reply was the perfect segue into my explanation of why no offensive language was permitted in my classroom. In addition to the N word, "wetback," "honky," and other racially offensive terms were off-limits. In most cases, when I explained my eradicationist stance on the use of the N word students were receptive. However, for a few of my African American students, the N word was so ingrained in their vocabulary that they had difficulty refraining from using it in class. One student even challenged me and indicated he had no plans to stop using it in class. In his opinion, as long as African Americans were using the term, there was no problem. I disagreed, yet he continued to use it occasionally. Consequently, for the occasional student who needed more than a teachable-moment talk about my "no N word in class" policy, I had to implement a simple five-step plan (see Table 6.1 at the end of this chapter), which other teachers might find useful.

Why I Am an Eradicationist

Whenever teachers ask me whether or not they should allow African American students to use the N word, especially the form that ends with an *-a* instead of *-er*, I always say no. I do this for several reasons:

- As noted previously, I am an eradicationist.
- I do not believe the N word is ever a term of endearment.
- I believe that permitting students to use it in class can become extremely problematic for teachers.

These beliefs are not grounded in research; they are based on personal experiences. At the core of my stance as an eradicationist is my strong conviction that the N word has never been a term of endearment for me. Hence, I believe that no one—African American or other—should use the term. Furthermore, I am not hypocritical about my stance. Just as I do not believe that anyone else should use the term, I also practice what I preach and refrain from using the term myself. My position on the N word originated from pertinent childhood, adolescent, and young adulthood experiences.

During childhood, from as far back as I can remember, I was routinely referred to by the word by one of my parents. It was often prefaced by "black . . ." or "stupid. . . ." In each case, the word was hurled from hateful lips as a weapon to demean and inflict pain. The word always made me cringe, and it often made me cry. Each time it was used, the end result was that I felt devalued and very small.

My childhood playmates also did not view the N word as a term of endearment. For most of us, being called by the N word was the ultimate insult. Two of the ditties that were popular with the children in the apartment complex in which I spent many of my formative years reveal this fact. The first was created as a warning to any whites who might decide to use the N word to refer to us. Ironically, at the time we were totally unaware that the term *white Paddy* was also racially offensive to whites, particularly to those of Irish descent:

> White Paddy,
> White Paddy,
> You don't shine.
> Call me a [the N word]
> And I'll beat your behind.

The second was solely for other African Americans who might use the N word to refer to us:

Don't call me a [the N word],
I'm a Negro.
When I become a [the N word]
I'll let you know.

My strong dislike of the N word also surfaced during junior high school when I was a participant in a voluntary busing program, in which African Americans from the "hood" (our neighborhood's nickname) were bused to a predominantly white suburban school. When I was in seventh grade, an African American friend and I were in the girls' restroom one day when we heard a white student using the N word. She was standing at the mirror bragging to another white girl about her tan. "Now, I look just like a [the N word]," she said, proudly. I balled up my fist, planning to sock the girl in the head. Before I could do so, my friend saw the angry look on my face, heard me mumbling an act of revenge, and pulled me out of the restroom. When we were outside, she told me, "Don't even bother to respond to her. She's not worth getting into trouble over." I knew she was right, but I still thought it would have felt quite good to knock some cultural sensitivity into the racist girl's head. I had already socked one white girl in the head for calling me an expletive that was prefaced with "black" and ended with the female equivalent of dog, and I had almost gotten suspended for doing so. In fact, the only reason I was not suspended was that, fearing my older sister's wrath, the white girl accepted full responsibility when the vice principal (a blatant racist) questioned us. My friend's advice was truly in my best interest.

Many years later, during my college undergraduate years, I spent a summer working as an intern for a newspaper in another state. The city in which the office was located housed the state penitentiary. Although there were few people of color residing in the actual city, the penitentiary was full of African Americans and Native Americans. During the summer that my roommate, who was biracial (half-black and half-white) and I spent in this city, we experienced numerous

incidents of cultural insensitivity and overt racism. We had difficulty finding an apartment manager who was willing to rent an
apartment to us, even for the summer. The middle-aged white couple who finally rented an apartment to us would snoop through our
apartment while we were at work and leave us menacing notes.

At work, our colleagues often made culturally insensitive
remarks—about our hair, for instance, which one woman asked to
touch and said felt "just like Brillo." One day, when we were walking to work, a car screeched to a halt within inches of us. The dri-
ver, an angry-looking white man, yelled the N word at us and told
us that the next time he would run us over!

More recently, a nonblack friend of mine, who is also a woman
of color, and I were discussing another African American on the
telephone. To my dismay, she used the N word to refer to him. Immediately, I told her that I do not use the N word, I do not like for
others to use it in my presence, and I find the word to be extremely
offensive. She apologized and explained what she had meant and
why she had used the term. I accepted her apology, but the conversation was noticeably strained thereafter.

What was most troubling to me was that she is highly educated,
progressive, and extremely humane. I often went to her for advice
about academia and found her to be wise and full of great suggestions. In fact, I was always impressed by her discernment about people, her insights about the politics of academia, and her perception
regarding the role of scholars of color in the academy. Nonetheless,
in a split second the N word had glided off her tongue effortlessly.

For a long time after the conversation ended, I pondered what
her use of the word meant. Did it mean she used the N word regularly to refer to African Americans, including myself? Did it mean
she felt so comfortable in my presence that she thought that we
were cool like that—that she had insider status? Did it mean she
was permitted to use the word by her other African American
friends and thereby assumed it would also be acceptable to me? Did
it mean she was as confused about the word as many other nonblacks are? Or did it mean the ultimate—the question on which

most interracial dynamics hinge—that she was a closet racist hiding behind the façade of liberalism, progressivism, and a social justice agenda, like so many other educators and researchers whom I have met?

Nearly two years later, I still am unsure of what her use of the word meant. I do know, however, that after she used the term, apologized, and even apologized again several months later, my perspective of her was altered. This led to a change in my attitude toward her. I no longer feel comfortable in her presence and continue to wonder if she is a closet racist who regularly uses the N word in private. As a result, at the present time we remain estranged. The fact remains that whereas I cannot prevent other African Americans (unless they are my children or my students) from choosing to use the N word in my presence, I can definitely choose not to maintain friendships with nonblacks who do so.

My Recommendations to Teachers

During the trainings that I conduct, I strongly urge teachers not to permit students to use the N word in class. In addition to my position as an eradicationist, some of the reasons have been presented in this chapter. Two final examples are illustrative of the point that I am trying to make.

In 2003, one of my African American doctoral students was excited about an opportunity to hear a well-known South American educator speak at another university. The next time I saw her, she told me she was totally disgusted with the speaker. I was surprised because I had heard him speak at another event prior to the presentation that she attended, and I thought he had made several powerful points about racial injustice in America. However, when the student told me why her enthusiasm turned into disgust, I understood completely. Unlike the presentation that I attended, during the one that she was at the speaker used the N word. When the student, one of only two African Americans in the audience, raised her hand to protest and tell him that she was offended, the speaker refused to permit her to speak. Later, although she had been able to voice her displeasure to the professor who invited the speaker, she was still upset. Nevertheless, when I suggested that she e-mail the speaker or write to him, she refused. "I'm sick of always having to fight these racial battles," she said. "I'm sick and tired of always having to educate other people." No amount of convincing on my part could persuade her to become proactive, but this one incident changed her opinion of the speaker. She no longer respected him or his scholarship, and she believed he was a racist who hid his racism behind a social justice research agenda.

The second example was relayed to me by an African American middle school vice principal, whom I consider to be a positive role model for myself and other professional women of color. This woman is intelligent and articulate; dresses immaculately; and treats parents, students, and her colleagues respectfully. On numerous occasions, I have had discussions with her that provided me with important insights about handling adversity in the workplace and dealing with difficult people. One day, she told me about a negative experience that she had had with an African American parent. The parent was upset, because her son, a middle school student, was suspended by the vice principal after he dropped the baggy pants that he was wearing in class. Although his teacher, an eyewitness, insisted he had done it deliberately, his mother said he should not have been suspended, because it was an accident, caused by his failure to wear a belt that day. When the mother realized that the vice principal was not going to rescind the suspension, out of frustration she called the vice principal a "bougie [Ebonics for bourgeoisie] [N word]." Refusing to get visibly angry, the vice principal told the parent the suspension would stand and then politely asked her to leave her office. "Just because she chose to act ugly," she told me, "it didn't mean that I had to stoop to her level." Several months later, the vice principal received a call from the grandmother of the child who had been suspended. The grandmother was calling to apologize on behalf of her adult daughter, the mother who had referred to the vice principal by the N word; she told the vice principal, "My daughter has wanted to telephone you to apologize many times, but she felt too embarrassed and too guilty to do so. Would you please forgive her?"

In my opinion, these examples illustrate why the use of the N word remains controversial and why teachers must exercise wisdom when the word surfaces in their classrooms, through literature or in the speech of African American and other students. Table 6.1 lists guidelines that might be useful to teachers regarding the use of the N word in class.

TABLE 6.1 How to Deal with Students Who Use the N Word in Class.

Strategy	Comments
1. Explain the rules.	On the first day of school, explain your stance and class rules regarding the use of offensive language, such as the N word. You can emphasize the fact that profanity as well as racist, sexist, and other offensive language will not be tolerated in your class, by including a related statement in your course contract or course description and by stating it verbally.
2. Deal with offensive language and behavior swiftly.	If a student violates this rule, it is wise to deal with the situation immediately. Ignoring it may cause hostility to grow toward the student and the teacher, because other students might assume the teacher's silence means he or she condones this behavior.

TABLE 6.1 How to Deal with Students
Who Use the *N* Word in Class, Cont'd.

Strategy	Comments
3. Confer with the "offender" privately as soon as possible.	After the offensive word has been used in class, and you have reprimanded the offender, ask the student to remain after class. This gives you an opportunity to explain that you want every student to feel comfortable in your class, and that no one will be verbally abused by anyone. Then you might ask the student how he or she would feel if a nonblack student used the word to refer to him or her.
4. For repeat offenders, resort to more drastic action.	Have students write standards (after writing "I will not use the *N* word in class" two hundred and fifty times, a student will probably think twice about doing so). Contact a parent. Contact a counselor.
5. Be fair and consistent.	Students are always watching for any sign of favoritism, especially along racial lines. If a teacher lets one student get away with using offensive language, the rest of the class may lose respect for the teacher.

7

What Should I Do When African American Students Accuse Me of Being Racist?

Racism has had a long history, and it continues to exist. According to Giovanni, "the biggest stumbling block to progress in America is still racism."[1] In *Racism: A Short History*, Fredrickson traced the origins of racism to religious practices and concluded that "religious racism" eventually paved the way for the "scientific racism" that has long been used to promote white supremacy and anti-Semitism in modern times. Although racist practices have been common for centuries, Fredrickson reported that "the word 'racism' first came into common usage in the 1930s when a new word was required to describe the theories on which the Nazis based their persecution of the Jews."[2] Nonetheless, Fredrickson asserted that numerous definitions of racism exist and that "our understanding of what beliefs and behaviors are to be considered 'racist' has been unstable."[3] Conversely, Murrell defined racism as "an ideology that positions White people as superior and non-White people as inferior."[4]

In spite of differing definitions of racism, today in the United States the term *racism* and depictions of "racist" acts surface regularly on television, in newspapers, on radio talk shows, and even in schools. According to Nieto, although it is common to blame students' academic problems on their race, class, gender, and the like, racism also plays a role in their educational failure.[5]

One way in which the term *racism* can surface in the classroom is as part of the formal curriculum. For example, a teacher might teach a lesson on racism, a textbook might allude to it, or students might watch a movie in which racist acts are depicted. But according to Loewen, most history textbooks lack detailed information about racism. He wrote, "To function adequately in civic life in our troubled times, students must learn what causes racism, but the textbooks that are used in most schools fail to do this."[6] In fact, only five of the twelve standard textbooks that Loewen analyzed listed "racism, racial prejudice, or any term beginning with race in their indexes,"[7] and he found that "not one textbook connects history and racism."[8]

Racism can also surface in schools in other ways: through the hidden curriculum, institutional racism, and individualized racism.[9] Individualized racism results when an individual is subjected to negative behavior or verbal abuse as a result of his or her race or ethnicity.[10] In *African American Teens Discuss Their Schooling Experiences*, 43 percent of the participants said they experienced racism at their high school. Whereas most of it was perpetrated by other students, nearly one-third of the high school students said the culprit was one or more adults on campus.[11] In *What African American Parents Want Educators to Know*, nearly 30 percent of the parents and guardians said their children had experienced racism at school, but 52 percent said it existed in their children's school district. In addition to providing other examples, several of the parents and guardians said their children, particularly their sons, had been the victims of racial profiling by teachers who had negative beliefs about them and placed detrimental labels on them.[12]

In these studies, the African American parents and guardians were more likely than the high school seniors to describe examples of institutional racism—another form of racism in schools—but some of the high school students also described similar examples. Institutional racism has repeatedly been identified as one of the main causes of the inequality of educational opportunity that plagues the U.S. public school system.[13] It is a well-known fact that public schools do not give all students the same quality of instruction or educational opportunities. Some students receive more benefits than others. In most cases, those who receive less are students of color and poor students. As I have noted previously, students of color are more likely to attend schools where overcrowded classrooms, a lack of textbooks, a lack of instructional materials and supplies, and a disproportionately high percentage of underqualified teachers are common. These problems have a negative impact on the standardized test scores of students of color.[14] Additional examples of inequality of educational opportunity are tracking, low teacher expectations, grade inflation, and unfair discipline practices.[15] Nevertheless, according to Murrell adults at school usually do not examine the reasons inequality exists.[16] Regarding institutional racism and inequality of educational opportunity, in *Learning While Black* Hale wrote, "By confining African Americans to inferior schools and thus inferior skills and credentials, White America maintains the oppression of African Americans, while the myth of freedom and opportunity for all enables them to blame us, the victims, for our status."[17]

Another way racism can manifest itself in schools is through the hidden curriculum. The hidden curriculum, as opposed to the formal curriculum, contains messages that students infer from classroom practices and teachers' actions. For example, as noted previously, in *Aptitude Revisited* Drew illustrated how females and students of color can infer that they do not have the capability to excel at mathematics, particularly higher level math courses, because of negative messages they receive from teachers.[18]

Racism can also surface in classrooms in other ways. For example, during the trainings that I conducted at the middle school and three high schools (discussed in Appendix I) the question "What should I do when African American students accuse me of being racist?" arose. I addressed this issue through the multifaceted approach presented in this chapter:

- I shared a personal example from my freshmen year in college, when I accused a university instructor of being racist, and the reason why I did so.

- I shared examples from my own experience as a first-year high school teacher, when several African American students accused me of discrimination.

- I summarized reasons why African American students or parents might accuse teachers of being racist.

- I described strategies that teachers can use in the event they are accused of being racist or discriminatory.

Why a Teacher Might Be Accused of Being Racist

When allegations of racism surface, some whites (including teachers) conveniently accuse people of color of "playing the race card." Racism is not a game, though, and it is no laughing matter; as I said previously, it is a reality that exists in the United States for many people of color (and for some whites, such as white students in urban schools).

There are at least three reasons why a teacher might be accused of being racist. The most obvious reason African American students, other students, parents, or even other teachers might accuse a teacher of racism is that the teacher actually is racist or has engaged in behavior that gave this impression. For example, a teacher who makes ethnocentric or blatantly racist comments in class gives students the impression that the teacher believes that he or she is superior. A teacher who singles out African American students for misbehavior while permitting nonblack students to engage in the same behavior with impunity can also convey the message that the teacher is racist. In *African American Teens Discuss Their Schooling Experiences* and *What African American Parents Want Educators to Know,* this is a recurring theme. According to Comer and Poussaint, white teachers who are racist tend to have low expectations for African American students and teach less.[19] However, teachers can also be racist without showing blatant signs of racism. In *Learning While Black,* Hale described two components of the "hidden racism" that is common in schools: "unconscious discrimination" by teachers and "the expectation of privilege among upper-class White Americans." The end result, according to Hale, is that "inferior educational outcomes are tolerated for African American children."[20] In both cases—those involving teachers who are blatantly racist and those involving teachers who engage in covert discrimination—such individuals should not be allowed to work with African American children. It is the responsibility of administrators to help these teachers adjust their attitudes and behavior, or to transfer them to another setting.[21]

As I was writing this book, my husband, Rufus, a former middle school social studies and physical education teacher, shared two examples with me of why educators who may not actually be racist or who might not even realize their behavior appears to be racist can be accused of being racist. He said:

> I've actually had an elementary school teacher and one middle school counselor come up to me in tears, saying that African American parents called them racist. The reason they came to me was because there were only two African American employees in the district. For six years, I was the only African American employee. The counselor had told an African American boy that if he kept dressing the way he was dressing, he was going to die. The boy had been dressing in the hip hop style. So, he went home and told his parent. According to the counselor, the father was very respectful, but said that the woman was racist, based on what she told the boy. In my opinion, the counselor was not racist, but she was ignorant. The father also said the reason why she was racist is because kids dress like skinheads everyday at that school, in what they call "Nazi storm trooper boots," plaid shirts, and shaven heads, but nobody said anything to those kids. Whereas with his son, the only trouble he had been in was dress code violations and the implication was that he was in a gang and that's why he was going to die.

The second example involved a new elementary school teacher. According to Rufus:

> The other incident was a lot less subtle. It was based on what an African American parent deemed to be "extreme discipline" by a teacher who appeared to be picking on her son because he was black. The teacher's situation was that she did not know African American culture. This teacher really cared and had children of her own, but she did not know the culture or the way that black parents in that community feel as a result of experiences, like the one I mentioned with the counselor. When you walk into the school and there's only one black man—myself—in the district, there's a perception that there's some racism involved. The teacher gave her students consequences, which led to her having to call the parent. The parent had come from a school district where they let things like talking out of turn, not completing homework assignments, and horseplay slide. The parent came to a parent-teacher conference and accused the teacher of being racist. I walked in shortly after the parent left. The teacher lost it. She was crying, because she was deeply offended and hurt that she had been called a racist. At that time, she was a new teacher, but a very good teacher, I think. She was a victim of the perceived climate of bigotry in the community that the school district served. This is important, because a lot of the parents' experiences outside of the school dictated how they perceived the school. I advised the teacher to stay in contact with the parent and that over time the parent would see that she was fair. That did happen, and the reason for that parent being won over is that her child showed significant academic and social progress in that class. The fact that the parent even came to a parent conference, in the school's eyes, showed that that parent cared, even though parents who do not come to conferences care. But when parents show up at the school, it changes the way the school deals with the child.

Rufus concluded this story with advice to educators:

> Just as African Americans have to be prepared to be called the N word in this society, teachers have to be prepared to be called racist. And any white teacher who thinks that the N word is just a harmless word should think about how she feels when she's called racist. The two aren't equivalent, but multiply how they feel by a thousand, and that's how we feel when we're called the N word by nonblacks.

A second reason why a teacher might be accused of being racist is based on preconceived notions that African American students might have about white teachers. Because of America's racist history and ongoing racist practices that surface on a regular basis, some African American students may believe that all whites are racist. During the teacher trainings I conducted, several white teachers stated that, starting on the first day of school, they felt they had to prove themselves to their African American students.

One high school teacher spoke for many when she remarked: "I have a problem when my students come into my class assuming that I won't treat them fairly because of their race. It seems that they shut down when they see that I'm a red-haired white lady. I don't feel like I get a fair chance." Another teacher asked: "How can I get my African American students to see me first as a teacher, not a 'white' teacher? They have preconceived and predetermined attitudes against me. I want to be able to eliminate that from the start."

A third reason is that the teacher might not be racist, but he or she might be accused of being racist because of ignorance or confusion on the students' part. Nieto stated that "it is sometimes difficult to separate what is racist or discriminatory from what appear to be neutral school policies and practices or behaviors of individual teachers."[22] During the teacher trainings, numerous teachers gave examples of instances when this happened in their classrooms. Hence I used a personal story to illustrate why ignorance and a limited frame of reference can lead to an accusation of racism.

Why I Accused an Instructor of Being Racist

In the late 1970s, I arrived at USC as a result of scholarships and grants. Since I had graduated as the third top-ranked student in my high school class with a 3.7 cumulative grade point average; was a member of the National Honor Society and the California Scholarship Federation; and was associated student body president, editor of the school newspaper (*The Buzz*), and a member of several extracurricular organizations, I was not worried about my academic skills. In fact, I was confident that I would succeed at USC. To my chagrin, however, the academic standards at USC were quite different from my expectations.

Although I was somewhat apprehensive about taking general math, I was excited about freshman composition. In high school, several of my teachers had convinced me that I was a good writer. My writing assignments earned A's and my articles were often published in the school newspaper, so naturally I was shocked when my freshman composition teacher wrote a D on my first essay. My shock turned into outrage when she assigned a D to my second paper. When my third paper earned a low grade, I was convinced that the teacher was racist.

I scheduled a meeting with the instructor during her office hours to share my concerns that she might be grading me unfairly. The meeting was awkward, and I was nervous. When I told her I believed she was assigning low grades to my papers because of my race, she tried to convince me that I was wrong. She attributed the low grades to my weak writing skills. But my mind was made up, and her explanation fell on deaf ears. How could I have believed that it was I and not she who had the problem, when my high school teachers had inflated my ego for years about my writing ability?

In retrospect, I feel sorry for that poor woman. She was attempting to tell me what someone should have told me long before I ever arrived at USC: I did not know the difference between a run-on, fragment, and a complete sentence! Instead of accepting this stark fact, I continued to believe she was biased against me, and therefore I lost interest in her class.

In the meantime, my grade point average plummeted, and as a result I lost one of my scholarships and had to get a part-time job to remain at USC. It took me another semester to realize that I was indeed a poor writer. I only realized this after I had a similar experience in another writing class. After two writing instructors had written the same grades and comments, the magnitude of my problem finally dawned on me. Thereafter, I had to struggle to learn skills that I should have learned in junior high and high school. Night after night, I studied a grammar and composition book by reading each chapter and doing the practice exercises and tests. I had to learn rules about grammar, syntax, and essay organization that my freshmen and sophomore classmates had obviously learned during their precollege schooling.

My writing skills and grade point average did improve eventually. In fact, I graduated on time and on the Dean's Honor Roll. Many years later, when I became a secondary school teacher, I vowed that my own students would never have to experience the humiliation and sense of inferiority that I experienced at USC, as a result of inadequate academic preparation. Thus I began each school year with this story, telling my students why I placed such a strong emphasis on good writing skills. They were also forewarned that they would probably end up doing more writing assignments than their peers in other classes.

The story about my freshman year at USC illustrates a point that a Nigerian doctoral student recently stressed to me. He said: "A lot of African Americans have been conditioned to believe that racism is the source of all of their misfortunes. Sometimes racism is the cause, but sometimes it is not." This student was right. Because of the prevalence of racism in the United States today and because of America's racist history, many African Americans truly do not know when a negative experience stems from racism and when it is from another source. For example, if I am treated rudely by a non-black salesperson in a store, a nonblack waitress in a restaurant, or a nonblack bank teller, I never know if the rudeness is race-related or if it stems from poor manners or simply because the individual is having a bad day.

In the example about my writing course at USC, racism was the culprit—but the instructor was actually innocent. Racism was the culprit because I unknowingly had been subjected to inequality of educational opportunity throughout my K–12 education. I had earned scholarships and high grades and was the third-ranked student in my high school class, the school newspaper editor and author of many articles, but I could not write a decent sentence. My college instructor was the first person to point this out. But since none of my previous teachers had done so, I mistakenly assumed that the instructor was picking on me. This woman was not just innocent; she was caring enough to try to help me improve my writing skills. At the time, however, I did not know this. Hence my naïveté and limited frame of reference caused me to conclude that she was racist.

This story shows how the perpetuation of inequality of educational opportunity through low teaching standards, grade inflation, and a weak curriculum hurts not only the victims—the students—but also teachers who have high standards and who refuse to indulge in these practices. The consequences are played out in classrooms all the time. Three stories from my first year as a high school teacher relate to this point.

Why My Own African American Students Accused Me of Discrimination

As a result of my own experiences as a victim of inequality of educational opportunity, I always had extremely high standards for my junior high school students, and later for my high school students, about their academic performance and classroom behavior. I wanted them to be well prepared for college so that they could avoid the humiliation and rude awakening I experienced. Moreover, I never assumed that they were not college material. Instead I believed that I had a moral and professional obligation to prepare all students for college. Then, if they decided not to go, it would be their decision and not mine. Unfortunately, many of my own students—who were primarily children of color in urban schools—

had already been subjected to numerous forms of inequality of educational opportunity prior to taking my classes. They were conditioned by low standards, low expectations, a nonchallenging curriculum, and sometimes even weak classroom management skills. Just as I in ignorance once lashed out and accused a USC instructor of racism, some of my own African American high school students accused me—an African American educator—of discriminatory behavior.

One example involved a football player, an only child. This student took one of the first high school courses that I taught, tenth grade English and language arts. Evidently, from the start he was appalled at all of the requirements for the course and believed that the workload, particularly the number of writing assignments, was excessive and punitive. Soon he began to relay negative messages to me from his mother. By way of her son, she constantly complained about the homework I assigned. "My mother wants to know why I have to write so many essays," he would inquire. Ignoring my explanations, his mother constantly sent notes or verbal messages through her son. "My mom wants to know why you keep giving me so much writing," he would whine; "my last English teacher didn't do that." On and on it went. Neither son nor mother was satisfied with the writing requirements for my class, or with my explanation that I was trying to prepare her son for college and for the workforce. Instead, they believed I was picking on the student out of vindictiveness. Finally, in exasperation, at the end of the first semester, the mother had her son transferred to another English class.

Three years later, on an extremely stressful day at work, I had just turned off the lights in my classroom, kicked off my shoes and elevated my feet, hoping to get a nap before lunchtime ended. All of a sudden, there was a knock on the door. I was tired and decided to ignore it. The knocking, however, became more insistent, so I put on my shoes, flipped on the lights, and flung the door open. To my surprise, there stood the former student. "I just came to tell you thanks," he said. "Because of you, I'm getting A's in my English class at [a] community college." His news surprised me even more than his presence.

I invited him inside the classroom, and we spent the rest of the lunch hour conversing. He told me that when he enrolled in the community college, his English instructor was surprised that he already knew how to use the six-step writing process I required. Before he left, however, I could not resist asking one question. "Did you tell your mother all of this?" He hung his head a little and smiled sheepishly before replying, "Yes, I told her." Recently, I was thrilled to finally meet his mother in person. When I told her that I was the former teacher whom she had routinely complained about, she thanked me for all that I had done for her son (who is now a married father of four children).

Another example involved three African American students who were enrolled in a ninth grade English and language arts summer school class I taught. One day, they asked to speak with me after class. I was surprised to hear they felt I was picking on them. "You're harder on us than other students," they complained. When I asked for examples, they described instances where I reprimanded one or more of them for talking in class when the class was asked to work quietly, and times when I reprimanded one or more of them for not handing in homework. They were angry at me and wanted me to admit that I had been treating them unfairly.

I tried to explain to them that my policies applied to all students and that my high standards regarding course work, homework, and class behavior stemmed from my desire to prepare them for college and the workforce. But in the same way the USC instructor's explanation to me had fallen on deaf ears, these students seemed unconvinced by my explanation. Their accusations troubled me long after the class ended and I arrived home. After pondering my dilemma for several hours, I decided I had to make a choice. I could choose to lower my standards and become more popular with certain students, or I could stick to my high standards and remain very unpopular with some, among them the three African American students who were under the impression I was picking on them. In the end, I decided that I would much rather have young, impressionable, and often fickle teenage students dislike me in the short run, because I believed that as they matured they would eventually realize why I maintained such high standards and how my standards benefited them. In short, I decided their current dislike was not nearly as important as their eventual respect for a teacher who cared enough about them to try to equip them with skills that would enable them to improve the quality of their lives. Recently, I had similar experiences with a few African American doctoral students, an indication of how little things have changed.

The third example pertains to classroom management. During the teacher trainings, I discovered that most of the teachers who said they had been accused of being racist were blamed for engaging in unfair discipline practices toward African American students. On several occasions, particularly during my first year of teaching junior high school and later during my first year as a high school teacher, I had similar experiences. One case involved an African American tenth grade male.

For some reason this student seemed to believe that my class rules did not apply to him. He talked out of turn, chatted with his classmates whenever he felt like it—thereby distracting them from their work—and spent more time off-task than doing his class work. When I asked him to be quiet or to get to work, he would either ignore me or comply for a short time before resuming his misbehavior.

The last straw was his behavior during an actual earthquake. When the classroom—a rickety old portable—started to shake, I ordered students to get under their desks. Then, I maneuvered my huge, seven-months-pregnant body under my own desk. To my dismay, this male student crawled from under his desk and ran to the classroom door. He stood in the doorway, laughing. Pointing at me, he jeered, "She's just scared that her baby is going to die." I ordered him to get back under his desk, but he refused. At that moment, I felt helpless. As the adult in charge, I was responsible for my own safety and that of my students, including the one who refused to cooperate. If he were injured, I would be liable.

After a few moments, but what seemed an eternity, the earthquake ended. Classrooms were evacuated and school administrators took charge. I was relieved that it was over, but I was thoroughly fed up with the uncooperative student's behavior. During my preparation period, I left a telephone message with his aunt, requesting a meeting with his mother, who was not home at the time. The aunt, who also had a child in my class, was very sympathetic. She promised to relay the message to the boy's mother.

The next day, the boy's mother came to the school. I was totally unprepared for her behavior. She was rude and repeatedly accused me of picking on her son. At one point, she stated, "I can see why my son doesn't like you. I don't like you either!" I spent my entire preparation hour trying to explain my goals, class rules, and classroom practices to this mother, but every comment or explanation was met with resistance and disbelief. She had arrived at the meeting with the belief that a mean black teacher was picking on her precious son, and she left unchanged—or so it seemed.

By the end of the meeting, I was fighting back tears, but I willed myself not to let her see me cry. Not only was I wrongly accused, but I had failed to convince this parent I was a dedicated and caring teacher who had my students' best interests at heart. As a last resort, I asked her to have her son transferred to another class. "Since you and your son are convinced that I'm picking on him," I stated, "there's nothing that I can do. Your son knows that you will take his side against me, so his behavior is going to get worse in my class." The mother bristled at my suggestion. For some reason, she was not in a hurry to have her son moved to another class. When I repeated that I wanted her to see her son's counselor to request the transfer that very day, she unconvincingly replied that she would think about it.

When I returned to my classroom a few minutes before my next class was scheduled to begin, I felt battered. The flood of tears I had successfully suppressed during the parent meeting erupted with a vengeance. When my students arrived for class, they found their pregnant teacher crying uncontrollably at her desk.

They tiptoed to their seats and tried not to look at me. When the bell rang, the students read the lesson plan I had written on the chalkboard and began to read their literature books silently, without any instruction from me. (Later, I learned they thought I was crying from labor pains and feared that I was in the process of giving birth.) I tried to regain my composure, but every time I attempted to speak, my sobbing prevented me from sounding coherent. Finally, an African American boy left the classroom quietly. Soon, he returned with an assistant principal, another African American male. The assistant principal asked me to step outside, and proceeded to question me about the source of my distress.

As soon as I mentioned the parent's name, he exclaimed, "I know her very well. She's cursed me out on numerous occasions!" The assistant principal told me that this parent had a reputation for being difficult and confrontational. She was used to bullying people and upholding her son's misbehavior, which was one of the main reasons he behaved as he did in class. Therefore I should not take her rudeness personally. Although his comments were reassuring, I was still adamant about having the student transferred out of my class, because I strongly believe that no child should be able to prevent other students from learning or the teacher from teaching. I told the assistant principal I felt my hands were tied with this student. Moreover, his presence in the class would limit my effectiveness with other students. If they saw him misbehave with impunity—merely because his mother had intimidated the teacher—they would conclude that I was engaging in unfair disciplinary practices. The assistant principal agreed that the student should be transferred to another class, and he made the necessary arrangements. I was relieved, but my relief was short-lived.

The next morning, when I arrived at school, I was summoned to the assistant principal's office. It turned out he had already been berated—first thing in the morning—by the same parent. The assistant principal told me, "She's very upset that her son was transferred out of your class without her permission. She said that you're a good black teacher and her son needs to remain in your class!" I was shocked and confused by this turn of events. Nevertheless, I continued to insist that it would be counterproductive for myself and my other students to permit the boy to return. The assistant principal supported me, and the transfer remained in effect.

A few years later, I learned that the student had offended another teenager, and his throat was slashed. He survived the attack, but from all accounts he became kinder and more respectful toward others.

What Teachers Can Do When They Are Accused of Being Racist

There are specific steps that teachers should take when they are accused of racism or discrimination. First, they should not ignore the accusation. Doing so might give students—even those who do not believe it—the impression that the allegation is true. It might also cause ill will toward the teacher.

Second, once the allegation has been made, the teacher should examine his or her beliefs, attitudes, and actions to see how they might have led to the accusation. The three-part long-term professional growth plan that is included at the end of this book can be used as a guide. As noted there, throughout this book, and by numerous researchers, teachers' beliefs have a powerful impact—either negative or positive—on the way that students are perceived and treated, and on the quality of education they receive. Therefore, whenever the allegation of racism arises against a teacher, the first place to start is with self-examination.

Third, the teacher should use the incident as a teachable moment opportunity. This requires careful planning on the teacher's part. Hence, designing a related lesson plan or unit in advance can be beneficial. Moreover, since racism and related issues should always be incorporated into school curricula anyway, teachers should not wait until they are accused of racism to teach a lesson on it. The lesson plan can take several days or weeks, or even an entire school quarter, to cover. Teaching a lesson or a unit on racism can have far-reaching positive consequences for the entire class. The unit should include at least four components: (1) defining racism, (2) examples of racism, (3) related class work and homework, and (4) empowering students to deal with racism.

The first component of the unit, defining racism, is important because many students, including whites, African Americans, and other students of color, do not know the definition of *racism* or understand what it is. Therefore, an allegation of racism can give the teacher an opportunity to teach students how to identify racism and how to differentiate it from such similar words as "oppression," "prejudice," "discrimination," and "stereotyping." These words might be assigned as vocabulary. Students should have repeated exposure to the words through class discussion, reading assignments, writing assignments, games, and projects that are related to the unit.

The second component, examples of racism, requires the teacher to share specific examples of racism, prejudice, and discrimination with the class. Students could read examples of racism from current events and literature, such as *Black Boy*[23] by Richard Wright, *The Friends*[24] by Rosa Guy, poems by Maya Angelou and Langston Hughes, or other multicultural works that have been recommended by the local school district or state department of education. Providing students with examples from current events in newspaper and magazine articles is also a good way to help them better understand racism. Examples of individualized and institutional racism, including the inequality of educational opportunity that prevails in schools for children of color, should also be included.

The third component of a good unit on racism consists of extension activities to be assigned as class work and homework. Once students understand the definition of racism and can identify and describe examples in literature and current events, this knowledge can be reinforced through additional writing assignments, individualized projects, and group projects. For example, writing assignments might require students to write about instances when they have experienced racism, someone they know who experienced it, or when they witnessed racist behavior. Students might also interview their parents, guardians, or other adult relatives about their own personal experiences with racism. Another extension exercise might require students to write a research paper on the history of racism in the United States.

The fourth component of the lesson plan, empowering students, requires that the teacher help students develop strategies to deal with racism. In other words, after students are clear about what racism actually is, they need to be equipped with the tools to address the racism that they are already facing or might eventually face in American society. The teacher could begin by having students review examples from literature and current events regarding how other individuals dealt with specific racist acts. Then the class can discuss (with a partner, in small groups, or as a whole class) whether or not the individual chose the best option. For each specific example, the class can develop other options. Students can also share strategies that their parents and guardians have encouraged them to use in case they are followed in a store, harassed by police, called a racially derogatory name, or experience other forms of racism.

Summary

Racism continues to exist in American society. The fact is indisputable, and its manifestations can be seen at every level of our society, from individual acts to policies and practices that are deeply embedded in institutions such as K–12 schools, universities, political machines, corporations, and even churches and other places of worship. Teachers who deny that racism exists or who use the offensive statement that "they're playing the 'race card'" merely demonstrate their ignorance, cultural insensitivity, and denial of painful realities that many people of color and some whites regularly face.

When a teacher is accused of racism or discrimination, the allegation can result in a bittersweet experience. A teacher who actually is a racist but in denial has the opportunity to change damaging beliefs, attitudes, and actions toward students. A teacher who is racist and chooses to remain in denial, however, will have limited efficacy with students of color and will do them much harm.

In April 2003, I had already finished this chapter when I had a conversation with a retired white teacher from a rural area of Minnesota. I decided to add this conversation (with her enthusiastic permission) to this chapter because she spoke candidly about many of the culturally sensitive topics—particularly racism—that I have attempted to deal with in this book. At the time, I was on my way to Chicago for the American Educational Research Association annual conference, and we ended up sitting next to each other on an airplane that was headed for Denver.

This sixty-three-year-old woman, whom I'll refer to as Mrs. G., was the mother of five adult biological children and had been a foster mother to numerous children, including three teens who were currently living in her home. She had grown up in a predominantly Norwegian and German town sixty miles from Minneapolis, in a poor farming family. "During elementary school, we were so poor that I only had one dress to wear to school," she said. "I was much poorer than any of my students." Although her father was abusive, he stressed the value of education and told his children that the best thing about America was that it educated its poor. When she was six years old, she traveled to Iowa with her family to attend her great-grandmother's funeral. "The only thing that I remember about that trip," she told me, "was that my maternal grandmother pointed at a group of black people and told me 'You want to stay away from *those* people, because they're dirty and dangerous.' She showed me segregated drinking fountains, and I thought it was stupid."

After graduating from high school, Mrs. G. married and became a full-time housewife. Once her children became adults, she returned to school and earned a teaching credential. She had planned to teach special education classes, but in the K–12 rural school at which she was hired she ending up heading the program for emotionally and behaviorally disturbed (EBD) students. "We only had three black students in the whole school," she said. "Of course, they all ended up in special ed—EBD on top of that. In a small town, kids of color stick out, and any other difference makes it worse for them. Not every kid can handle it."

Two of the students of color that Mrs. G. talked extensively about were Kim (not her real name), a dark Filipina, and JoBari (not his real name), an African American. Both students believed that teachers were biased against them and treated them unfairly. According to Mrs. G., "Teachers like to think that they're colorblind. I don't believe it, but teachers like to believe that they are because they don't like to think that they're biased. But they're very biased, because they're human."

They both believed that teachers were biased against them, but JoBari and Kim had different experiences at the school. Mrs. G. said Kim was obsessed with her dark skin and constantly accused people of staring at her because her skin was "black." She eventually had to be hospitalized for psychological problems.

Like Kim, JoBari also believed that teachers were biased against him because he was black. This included Mrs. G. When he was assigned to her class as a seventh grader, she attempted to administer the reading assessment she gave to all incoming students. This assessment required the student to read a series of books starting at the lowest level, kindergarten, and then progressing to books at a higher readability level. However, when JoBari learned that Mrs. G. expected him to demonstrate his reading skills by reading a "baby book," he told her she was racist. Mrs. G. gave him an ultimatum: He would either read the book or go to the principal's office. JoBari replied with an expletive. Instead of sending him to the principal's office, Mrs. G. told him she had family members of color (two Latina daughters-in-law and biracial grandchildren) and that JoBari was not to ever accuse her of being racist. "I just jumped him from the git-go," she explained, "because he was going to be in my class for six years. I never had another problem with him." Concerning what she learned about JoBari during those six years, Mrs. G. stated:

JoBari was more of a conduct-disordered kid. He had a reputation for not doing his work and for swearing at teachers, plus his mother wanted him to get some help, because she valued his education. Obviously, JoBari was one of my favorites, but the other teachers hated him. I was a teacher who stayed out of the teachers' lounge because if you went in there, you heard negative stuff and it wouldn't take me very long before I was giving them negative information to use against the kids. I'll bet in my thirty years of teaching, I barely spent twenty hours in the lounge. It's a good place to stay out of unless you want to get negative. I noticed that my own biological kids could get away with stuff all of the time, just because they came from a "good" family. But my special ed kids couldn't get away with anything. Teachers were always on them. That always made me mad. I always said: "JoBari, they don't dislike you because you're black; they dislike you because you're a brat! They both start with *b*." And he was a brat. It doesn't hurt to lie some-times, and I think that some of that was true. I think that he stopped saying that teachers were picking on him by the end of his sophomore year.

Near the end of our conversation, Mrs. G. told me there is a great need for the work I am attempting to do with teachers. However, she also warned me to expect hostility from some. When I told her that the questionnaire results (see Appendix I) indicated 15 per-cent of the teachers were resentful about attending the trainings that I conducted at the middle school and the three high schools, she was skeptical. "I'll bet it's really closer to 55 percent," she de-clared. She also said, "People are very different and yet they're all the same. If you dig deep you find some basic similarities. Some white teachers are going to have trouble with you as a black woman because they think you have your own axe to grind. They may think, 'Well, she's got her own baggage, her own agenda'—and bag-gage does count."

This story indicates that a teacher who has been wrongfully ac-cused of racism can use the experience as a powerful teachable mo-ment opportunity that can be mutually beneficial. It can benefit the teacher in that it requires him or her to take charge of a po-tentially volatile situation in a way that can actually bring the class closer together as a community of learners, instead of racially po-larized groups. It can benefit students because it brings an important topic that needs to be addressed out in the open. Furthermore, it broadens students' and the teacher's knowledge about the topic and empowers students by arming them with a repertoire of strategies to use when they are subjected to racism.

Hence, although racism continues to be an ongoing problem in schools and in the larger society, teachers can use their time and ac-cess to students in ways that can (1) improve interethnic and in-terracial group relations, (2) give all students an opportunity to better understand racism, and (3) help students develop crucial skills.

More important, teachers can convey this message to students: "Yes, racism does exist in American society, but knowledge is power and you, as students, can use education and the information that is available to you to change the status quo, for although racism con-tinues to remain prevalent in this country, the United States is one of the few countries in the world in which racism does not have to be the ultimate determiner of your fate."

Given the school system's unique position of having access to students from diverse backgrounds for a sustained amount of time, elementary teachers should begin this work, and middle school teachers and high school teachers should continue it. This would ensure that all students are provided with this important informa-tion throughout their K–12 schooling.

8

Why Do African American Students Need a Culturally Relevant Education?

In one of my graduate courses, an African American high school principal described an experience she had at a conference for high school student leaders. During one of the activities, the students were required to become a race or ethnicity that was different from their own. The only race or ethnicity that the nonblack students refused to select was "African American," the principal pointed out. When she asked them why, the students explained they did not want to be African American because they believed it would be too difficult to survive in American society as an African American.

In forming opinions about African Americans, these students, like all Americans, have been influenced by many sources, including the media, and particularly the news media. It is no secret that there are great disparities in how the news media cover African American issues versus those pertaining to whites. More than a decade ago, Harvard professor Andrew Hacker's *Two Nations: Black, and White, Separate, Hostile, Unequal*[1] and Jonathan Kozol's *Savage Inequalities*[2] addressed this problem. More recently, in *Don't Believe the Hype*,[3] Farai Chideya, a former news reporter, and Michael Moore, author of the best-selling *Stupid White Men and Other Sorry Excuses for the State of the Nation*,[4] also mentioned this antiblack media bias. According to Chideya, the result is that as much as 61 percent of the news that is reported about African Americans is negative. Moreover, Chideya said the media manipulate numbers to sensationalize news regarding African Americans. Instead of focusing on the positive, they deliberately focus on the negative.

The media have been responsible for disseminating much negativity about African Americans, but K–12 educators, university professors, and textbook authors have also done their part—by omission or commission. Today, the classroom is one arena in which the traditional Eurocentric perspective is most obvious. Because negativity and hopelessness predominate in news reports and research regarding African Americans[5] and because most textbooks reflect a Eurocentric bias, in most high school history classes the students are likely to hear about slavery, Martin Luther King, Jr., and possibly Rosa Parks. They are unlikely to learn much else about African Americans, even though there are plenty of positive facts about African Americans that could broaden their education. For example, they do not learn that in spite of many obstacles, racism and much oppression, nearly four hundred African American men and women earned doctorates from the period spanning the late 1800s to World War II; that one of the founders of Georgetown University was a half-black man who had earned a Ph.D. in Belgium before the Civil War[6]; or that Matthew Henson, a black man, "discovered" the North Pole along with Admiral Peary. In fact, the list of positive information and contributions about African Americans and other nonwhite groups that has been omitted from school curricula is endless.

Unfortunately, not only are K–12 students kept ignorant about the histories and contributions that most ethnic-minority groups have made to American society, but a substantial number are also being miseducated. Back in 1933, Woodson described the methods by which African Americans have been shortchanged, misled, and miseducated by their schooling.[7] He criticized school curricula for excluding the contributions of African Americans, and he concluded that the public school system sought to convince African American children that they were grossly inferior to whites in every way. Today, it can also be said that the majority of American students of all races and ethnicities continue to be miseducated, because huge periods of history are not included in most curricula, and students of color rarely see their culture reflected in a positive way. In *Lies My Teacher Told Me*, Loewen wrote that although most high school students hate history, this hatred is more common among students of color.[8] The most obvious reason is that in many classrooms, history is presented in a way that gives students of color very little to be proud of.

One way educators have attempted to reduce interracial conflicts and to make curricula more representative of nonmainstream cultures is through multicultural education. Although multicultural education and culturally relevant teaching have been discussed in academic circles for decades, they are still topics of debate, confusion, and resistance among educators. There are several reasons why. Among them are cultural insensitivity, cultural ignorance, and teachers' resistance. These issues are discussed in the remainder of this chapter, along with the reasons African American students need a culturally relevant education.

Attempts to Diversify the Curriculum

According to Nieto, "Both multicultural and bilingual education were direct outgrowths of the Civil Rights movement and they developed in response to racism, ethnocentrism, and language discrimination in education."[9] Bennett defined multicultural education as an approach to teaching and learning that is based upon democratic values and beliefs and that affirms cultural pluralism. Bennett's conceptualization of multicultural education encompasses four components: (1) the movement toward equity, (2) curriculum reform, (3) the process of becoming interculturally competent, and (4) the commitment to combat prejudice and discrimination, especially racism.[10] Diamond and Moore used the term *multicultural literacy* to describe curricular and instructional practices that build on students' cultures, histories, and languages. Their model is based on a number of principles, including the belief that all students can learn and benefit from multicultural educational practices, and the fact that teachers' attitudes and expectations have an impact on student achievement. Diamond and Moore encouraged educators to help students overcome ignorance and fear by teaching them to value and understand other cultures. One direct consequence, they noted, is that once they are employed in the workforce, students are better prepared to interact with coworkers from different backgrounds.[11]

Teachers' Fear and Resistance as Barriers to Diversifying the Curriculum

One reason some teachers oppose a culturally diverse curriculum is that they fail to see its value.[12] For example, there are educators who believe that only the "Western canon," which includes the information that has traditionally been taught, has value. A second reason is that some educators oppose diversifying the curriculum because it requires them to address issues and beliefs that make them feel uncomfortable. Nieto attributed teachers' resistance to the fact that multicultural education challenges the status quo and that some teachers are reluctant to face racism.[13] I witnessed this firsthand in two graduate courses for teachers that I taught at two different universities. The two stories follow.

Several years ago, I taught at a large comprehensive university located in a region in which children from nonmainstream backgrounds made up more than 60 percent of the public school enrollment. Given that this region had one of the lowest college-attendance rates nationwide, it was apparent to me that there was much work to be done, particularly to improve the schooling experiences of struggling students. These were some of the reasons I was eager to teach a graduate reading course called Issues in Multicultural Literacy during one quarter. All but three of the twenty-four students in the class were public elementary school teachers who were working on their reading specialist certificate. The other three were secondary school teachers. There were four major assignments in this class. First, students had to create a cultural awareness project (see

Appendix C). Second, they had to write a reflective paper on Kathryn Au's *Literacy Instruction in Multicultural Settings*.[14] Third, they had to write a reflective paper on Lisa Delpit's *Other People's Children*.[15] Fourth, they had to create a directed reading lesson. What I learned from how the class reacted to some of the assignments gave me some important insights regarding teachers' attitudes and race relations.

On the first night of class, although it started well, before the class ended there was palpable tension in the air. A number of students in this mostly white class (in which there were no Asians or African Americans and only two Latinos, one biracial woman, and only one male) were upset that they would have to do a cultural awareness presentation about their own culture. The guidelines were explicitly stated in the syllabus. We spent a considerable amount of time discussing the assignment, yet there were many questions and much anger and frustration. One woman said, "I grew up with the typical American culture, so I don't know what you expect me to do. I can't put on a show." When I asked her if she grew up eating collard greens, pigs' feet, black-eyed peas and cornbread, and listening to Motown, she said no and was clearly taken aback by the question. Then I explained that even though I grew up as an "American"—an African American that is—this is what I grew up eating and listening to. I wanted the class to see that there is no such thing as one single "American culture," and that as educators we cannot assume that everyone grew up observing the same customs, values, and practices that we observed and practiced. I answered all questions and challenging comments as well as I could, but by the looks on some of the students' faces, I knew it was going to be a long quarter.

Three weeks later, the first group of students presented their projects to the class. Several women had e-mailed me or visited during office hours for further clarification about the project guidelines. During the first night of presentations, I was pleased at the quality of work and effort that the students had devoted to their projects. As I praised each student after her presentation, the classroom climate appeared to change. The anger, fear, and frustration I had noticed earlier seemed to dissipate. That night a community of learners was formed. As students shared photos, memorabilia, books, demographics, historical facts, and other information about their culture and childhood experiences, it seemed that the assignment was successful. Two weeks later, when the last group of students presented their projects, I had the same feeling. Every student earned the full thirty points, one-third of the entire grade, on this assignment. We had heard wonderful presentations about Irish Americans, Italian Americans, Swedish Americans, Mormon Americans, Basque Americans, Norwegian Americans, white Anglo Saxon Protestants, French Americans, and many other groups.

The following week, we discussed what we had learned about our own culture and that of others from the presentations. There were three recurring themes:

1. Many of the students feared doing the project because they had never thought about culture before and assumed that everyone had grown up as they had.

2. Many students discovered a lost heritage and needed to contact older relatives to find out information about their culture.

3. Some students had already shared their projects with their own students, and many planned to start the next academic year by presenting their project to their students and assigning a modified version of the project to establish a community of learners.

During the time when students were presenting their projects to the class, they were reading Au's *Literacy Instruction in Multicultural Settings*[16] for homework. Class discussion and related reflective papers they wrote indicated that the students were learning a lot from the book. Moreover, most students liked the book and had actually begun to incorporate some of the information into their own instructional practices. One theme that surfaced repeatedly was that the students were unaware of different interactional patterns along cultural lines, until they read this book. They constantly mentioned learning, for example, that many African American children use a topic-associating versus a topic-centered style of discourse; this helped them work more effectively with some of the African American children in their classes. One student said she learned that an African American child labeled as a "poor comprehender" really could comprehend text when her topic-associating style was understood. Only one student in the class wrote that she had not learned anything at all from Au's book and that it was totally unrealistic.

During the next few weeks we discussed Delpit's *Other People's Children*.[17] Subsequently, the community of learners divided into two camps. About half of the class seemed to feel that Delpit had something of value to say. The other half felt Delpit was racist and attacking all white teachers. One student said, "I'm offended because I'm not the type of teacher that she is describing." Another student said, "I could not get anything out of this book because this woman is angry and bitter." When I mentioned that Delpit had clearly stated in the conclusion that she knew many excellent white teachers, as well as some bad black teachers, the student said, "It was too little too late. She should have put that in her introduction, instead of at the end."

I have drawn upon Delpit's book repeatedly in my own research because it contains many powerful lessons for educators and researchers, so I was totally unprepared for the strong negative reaction from some students. I was also concerned that the community of learners that had been established would disappear. I wanted, however, to really understand the views of students who were offended by the book. I made it clear to them I wanted to hear their honest opinions during class discussions, as well as when they wrote their reflective papers. Although I think I was successful in not silencing the voices of the dissenters, what became painfully and increasingly clear to me was that they were not offended by what Delpit said. They were offended by who she was: an African American woman who was addressing some racially sensitive issues that struck a nerve they did not want struck.

At this point, information that had been buried in my subconscious surfaced. A comment I heard from a woman in the class came to mind. She prefaced her cultural awareness presentation by saying, "I'm from the bad race, the white race." At the time, I had wondered why she made the comment, because at no point whatsoever did anyone in the class, myself included, say that the "white race" was bad. Another troubling incident came to mind. A white colleague informed me that at the beginning of the quarter two of the women in the class had told him that I was a racist. When I mentioned this to the class, there were audible gasps of disbelief, and one woman blurted out "I didn't tell him that!" Others offered to speak to my department chair on my behalf. One woman gave me a beautiful and encouraging note. She said I was a great teacher, yet on the first night of class some of the women who were "negative and jealous" (according to the student who gave me the encouraging note) were put off by my direct style, especially when I asked a white student if she had grown up eating collard greens, pigs' feet, black-eyed peas and cornbread, and listening to Motown. Another student in the class sent me a touching and positive e-mail. One woman approached me during break time and said she would do anything I needed to clear things up with my department chair. This entire incident disturbed me and made me guarded for the rest of the quarter. I remained uneasy even after the colleague told me that three students in the class had gone to him and told him I was an excellent teacher. More than anything, this incident made me decide not to teach the course the following quarter. I felt this was in my best interest because junior faculty cannot risk getting negative teaching evaluations before they are tenured.

When I thought about this incident and some of the comments and facial expressions I had noticed from a few students since the first night of class, a light bulb went on in my head. Those who rejected Delpit's book did so because she was an African American woman who was addressing some racially sensitive issues. Couldn't some of the negative reactions I had experienced from a few students in the class have the same origins? Could it be that some of the students put up a wall of resistance between themselves and me from the moment I walked into the classroom and they learned I was the professor, instead of another student, as they assumed? My suspicions were confirmed by two students in the class. One pleaded with me privately to teach the same course the following quarter. She told me that the resistance stemmed from jealousy and resentment, but the resisters and others like them needed to hear the messages that were conveyed through the assigned readings, lectures, and class discussions. Another student made similar comments. In the end, I did decide to teach the class the following quarter.

More recently, my suspicions were confirmed again. I told the students in one of my doctoral classes about how students at another university had reacted to Delpit's *Other People's Children*. A middle-aged white woman declared, "I was assigned to read that book in an all-white class by a white professor and nobody got mad. I'll bet those students resented the fact that you were a black woman making them read that book."

The second blatant example of teachers' resistance to diversifying the curriculum that I witnessed took place at another university at which I taught a graduate course called Using Multicultural Literature to Foster Seeds of Resiliency in Secondary School Students. Although the students knew ahead of time that they would be reading multicultural literature and that the professor was African American, one student, a first-year, progressive, young white teacher who claimed to be colorblind to racial and ethnic differences, grew increasingly upset about the issues that surfaced in some of the required texts. Two of the books that were most upsetting to her were Wright's *Black Boy*[18] and *The Circuit: Stories from the Life of a Migrant Child*,[19] Francisco Jimenez's autobiography.

During one class session, she burst into tears and exclaimed, "Why do we have to talk about all of this stuff? It's starting to make me racist!" I was shocked. We were reading and discussing incidents from the lives of real individuals. Moreover, the issues that surfaced were issues that children in classrooms throughout the nation wrestle with daily. Nonetheless, this teacher was offended by a discussion of these realities. Before I could respond to her outburst, an African American student in the class told her that she was offended by the number of times she had sat in undergraduate and graduate classrooms and heard white students voice similar complaints. She angrily rebuffed the white student with, "I get followed in stores, have difficulty finding jobs—even though I have a master's degree—and you sit there and say that you don't want to discuss these topics!"

At this point, I recovered from my initial shock. I asked the other white students in the class if they were also feeling offended by the readings and the class discussions. They all said they were not. This could be attributed to fear of admitting they were offended, as a result of the African American student's response, or it could be that they actually were not. Then I asked the teacher who had initially expressed her displeasure if her reaction to the readings and the class discussions might really be based on her refusal to face some unexamined personal issues. She said she did not know. I encouraged her to spend some time engaged in self-reflection, and the class discussion moved in another direction. However, for the duration of the class session, the student clearly continued to be upset, and she even sulked.

A few days later, in one of the most blatant examples of "white privilege" I have ever seen (another was when a group of white teachers told me they did not feel like taking notes in my class, so could I photocopy my lecture notes each week and give them to them? And the most recent was when a young white woman threatened to call security on me at work because I had refused to move my doctoral students to another classroom; I am positive that she would never have threatened a tenured white professor—male or female— in this manner), I received a strongly worded e-mail from her. The student urged me to stop having discussions about racial issues in the class. She also indicated she was seriously considering dropping the class. I wondered if she would have had the nerve to tell a white professor how to teach his or her class.

Because I was still an untenured junior professor at the time, I discussed the issue with two colleagues. Both of them, a white male and a white female, supported the work I was doing in my class. In fact, the male professor reassuringly told me, "The fact that a white student cried in your class should be the least of your worries at this time." Then I wrote a reply to the student. In the reply, I stated that I would continue to talk about the racial issues that surfaced in the class readings, and that dropping the class was an option that remained open to her. For some reason, the student decided to remain in the class, but her comments and behavior continued to indicate that she was extremely unhappy about the race-related subject matter.

These two incidents taught me several lessons. The main lesson I learned is that whereas many teachers are receptive to topics pertaining to diversity, those who are resistant can go to great lengths to prevent related discussion. Instead of doing the personal growth work they are in dire need of, they would much rather project their resistance onto others. This often results in peer pressure, in which other teachers are pressured to align with the resister. This occurs not just in graduate education classrooms but at school sites as well. For example, several first-year white teachers recently told me that when it comes to diversity issues, white teachers receive pressure from two groups. On the one hand, they may be dissuaded by white teachers from selling out. On the other hand, they may be criticized by people of color who accuse them of not having legitimacy or the right to teach about other cultures. These problems can make it difficult for receptive teachers to reach a level of comfort in discussing cultural issues.

Cultural Insensitivity and Cultural Ignorance

Another controversy associated with diversifying the curriculum is that some teachers are uncertain about which topics and materials are acceptable and which are unacceptable for classroom use. Three stories illustrate this point. The first relates to my own childhood. The second pertains to one of my daughter's experiences at school, and the third story describes a case that made the national news several years ago.

When I was an elementary school student, my teachers occasionally showed movies to reward us for good behavior. Although I am certain that I saw numerous movies during those years, only one remains vivid in my mind. The classic *Birth of a Nation*, which depicted the Ku Klux Klan attacking terrified African Americans, frightened and depressed me. Today, in retrospect, I do not know if the teacher showed this film to a classroom full of African American children as a reward or to send a message to us about our place in society—maybe even our place in her classroom. I do know, though, that whatever her motive, showing the film to young, impressionable children who happened to be of the same race as the victims on the screen was inappropriate, to say the least.

In the twenty-first century—the age of rapid change, ongoing technological advancement, and political correctness—most teachers would know that it is totally unwise and inappropriate to show this film not only to African American children but to any elementary school age children. Or would they? This question is pertinent to a discussion about attempts to diversify the curriculum because many well-meaning teachers make mistakes in their efforts to include multicultural films and books in the curriculum. So although a culturally relevant curriculum is extremely important, informing teachers of related controversies and issues is also necessary. My daughter's experience underscores this point.

Two years ago, my daughter NaChé, an eighth grader at the time, returned from school in a huff. She had been watching *Roots* in her history class and found it to be an extremely upsetting experience, for two reasons. First, as the descendant of African slaves, it was painful for her to watch people who looked like her and her ancestors being dehumanized. The violence to which they were subjected overwhelmed her, angered her, and made her weep quietly in class. However, the reaction of some of her non-African American classmates enraged her. (Today, when she discusses her *Roots* experience, it is the classmates' behavior versus the actual movie that continues to infuriate her.) "They were laughing," she said. "Kids were laughing when people got raped and beaten." As a result, NaChé refused to speak to the offenders for the remainder of the school year. Instead of confronting them directly, she resorted to passive-aggressive defense mechanisms. Her experience reminded me of my own reaction to *Roots*, and I saw similarities and differences.

At the time when *Roots* first aired on television, I was a college freshman at USC. A small group of my African American friends and acquaintances and I watched the miniseries in the privacy of a dorm room. There, we could cry, complain, and express anger in a safe environment. Although I was several years older than NaChé was when she viewed the movie, the movie also made me both sad and angry. The difference, however, was that my anger was directed solely at the injustices depicted on television and the historical ramifications stemming from the slavery era. There were no insensitive viewers in my immediate vicinity. In my daughter's case, although the teacher, an African American, undoubtedly had good intentions in showing the movie, his failure to prepare the class for the scenes made the viewing of the movie somewhat counterproductive. Moreover, his failure to stop the movie when students began to exhibit signs of insensitivity and use their behavior as a teachable moment opportunity was unwise.

The topic of what is appropriate material for classroom use also received national attention several years ago as the result of an incident in New York. In the end, Ruth Ann Sherman, a white third grade teacher, learned that having good intentions is not enough. When it comes to diversifying the curriculum, cultural ignorance can be dangerous.

In September 1998, Sherman read *Nappy Hair*,[20] a beautifully illustrated multicultural book, to her mainly black and Latino class. Her goal was to teach the students "about self-acceptance and acceptance of racial differences."[21] The book, which was written by Carolivia Herron, a black professor, promotes a positive message of self-acceptance. Moreover, it gives readers an excellent example of the call-and-recall style of discourse that is common in African American culture.

After reading the book aloud to the class, Sherman gave the students photocopied pages to take home. Two months later, a parent found the pages in her child's folder and became outraged. She made copies of the excerpts, attached an unflattering note to them about the teacher, and distributed them throughout her neighborhood.

Soon, other parents—most of whom did not have children in Sherman's class—were so angry that they started demanding that Sherman resign from teaching. At a heated school board meeting, a group of irate parents allegedly "hurled racial epithets and profanities at Ms. Sherman as well as verbally and physically threatened her."[22]

After an investigation, the school board completely exonerated Sherman. They also urged her to continue to teach the same class and promised to provide her with security. Although her students and their parents asked Sherman to stay, she decided to transfer to another school. In numerous related news reports and editorials, the parents who criticized and threatened Sherman were vilified. They were referred to as racist, bad people, and individuals who were too backward to have even read the entire book before jumping to conclusions.

During the time when the controversy first became a national news item, as a parent and as an educator I wanted to know what my own son and two daughters thought of the book and the controversy. At that time, they were in the fourth, sixth, and eleventh grades and enrolled in mostly white private schools.

After we read the book, I asked each child to share his or her thoughts. All three loved the story and the colorful illustrations. The main character had dark skin and a hair texture that was similar to their own, and the story contained a positive message. Then I asked how they would feel if a white teacher read the book to them in class. My oldest child said she would not want any white teacher reading the book to her in class under any circumstance whatsoever, especially if white students were present in the classroom. "I like the book, but I would rather read it privately, because the white kids would make fun of it," she explained. She feared that the book's positive message would be lost on her white classmates. Her response undoubtedly stemmed from the many years in which her white classmates had made fun of her speech (by telling her she did not "sound black" enough), her skin color, and her physical features. My second child, the sixth grader, said it would depend on the teacher. She explained that if a white teacher whom she respected for being fair to all students read the book in class, it would be OK. However, if certain teachers (and she named some of her former teachers) whom she suspected of being racist read the book in class, she would "think that they were making fun of black people," she said. My son, who was in fourth grade at that time, said, "I wouldn't care if a teacher read the book in class or not, and I wouldn't care if white kids laughed!"

Recently, I asked them if they still felt the same way. Although the oldest is now a junior in college, the second child is now a tenth grader, and my son is now an eighth grader, they still feel the same way they did when I initially asked them the question.

My children's responses are indicative of the diversity that exists among African Americans and within all groups. Although they were reared in the same household by the same parents, they responded to the question differently. Personality differences, age differences, schooling experiences, and their previous interethnic and interracial experiences affected their responses. The New York case and my children's responses illustrate an important point: in dealing with racial issues, one can never be certain of the outcome. Given historical interracial and interethnic animosity, polarization, and ongoing tension, there is always the risk of being maligned, disparaged, misunderstood, or attacked when it comes to racial issues. However, the case also underscores the danger of assuming that all persons of color are of the same mind-set about what is and what is not acceptable for classroom use.

Today, many African Americans are proud of their natural hair texture, as evidenced by numerous hairstyles, such as braids, twists, Afros, dreadlocks, sisterlocks, and so on. Hence "nappy hair" has become a source of great pride, just as it was during the "Say it loud;

I'm black and I'm proud" era of the sixties. In fact, many whites and other nonblacks, including some entertainers, have copied these styles. Still, old wounds passed on generationally for centuries have not healed completely. Countless African Americans have been told by the media, family members, and others that they are unattractive and even downright ugly because of their nappy hair and African features. In fact, throughout history, nappy hair was often contrasted with "good hair," or hair that was more similar to white people's hair than to "African hair." Perhaps these wounds surfaced when the irate parent and her neighbors read the excerpts from the book.

One way in which the controversy might have been avoided is if Sherman had shared her plan to use the book in her classroom with parents and teachers of color prior to doing so. This would have given parents and teachers an opportunity to share their concerns with her ahead of time and to understand her motives. Someone would have undoubtedly warned her that just as the N word is commonly used by many African Americans (see Chapter Six), so is the word *nappy* in reference to hair. However, just as it continues to be dangerous for whites and other nonblacks to use the N word in reference to African Americans, there are other words, "nappy hair" included, that many African Americans continue to find offensive when used by non-blacks. For numerous African Americans, both terms ("nappy hair" and the N word) remain pejorative terms, not terms of endearment. This issue of "offensive terms" is revisited in Chapter Nine, "Other Controversial Issues."

Tokenism: The Wrong Approach to Diversifying the Curriculum

"Tokenism" is another problem that has been associated with diversifying the curriculum. Ideally the contributions of people of color, and issues and topics pertaining to groups that have traditionally been excluded from curricula, should be integrated into every student's K–college education continuously and comprehensively. Too often, though, attempts to diversify the curriculum have been reduced to Black History Month, Cinco de Mayo activities, and potlucks. In other words, either out of ignorance or a desire to be able to say that they have offered a multicultural curriculum, some teachers have reduced diversifying the curriculum to tokenism. Recently, a high school teacher told me that as a result of this reduction of multicultural education into token events, "the black kids tune out when it's the Mexican kids' turn, and the Mexican kids tune out during Black History Month." In *What African American Parents Want Educators to Know*, one parent told me: "I feel they should do more things that pertain to our culture. . . . Teaching about George Washington and Abraham Lincoln is great. But teach me about some black people. Not only in February, the shortest month of the year, but teach me that all year long, because I want to know. . . . Just like you do George and Lincoln, teach me about them all year long. African American children need to know about what their people have accomplished."[23]

From Multicultural Education to a Culturally Relevant Curriculum

Proponents of multicultural education clearly have good intentions, and multicultural education has been used to expose students to information about groups from nonmainstream backgrounds. As a result, students are required to read a more culturally diverse body of literature, instead of just literature from the Western canon. Furthermore, many teachers have incorporated exercises and assignments into their curricula that encourage students to showcase aspects of their heritage, such as ethnic foods, clothing, artifacts, and so forth. However, some educators and researchers found that multicultural education fell short in actually improving the academic performance of African American students. Moreover, some educators, such as Murrell,[24] have stated that multicultural education can actually be counterproductive. For example, Murrell found it to be more beneficial for white students than for African American students.

Therefore, new solutions have been sought. One of the results is the emergence of a new theory pertaining to a culturally relevant curriculum. Proponents of this theory maintain that African Americans and other students of color must have a culturally relevant curriculum in order to achieve academically. However, unlike multicultural education, which promotes tolerance and exposes students to the diversity that exists among culturally different groups, a culturally relevant curriculum is designed to empower students on the personal and societal levels. Gay wrote, "Just as the evocation of their European American, middle-class heritage contributes to the achievement of White students, using the cultures and experiences of Native Americans, Asian and Pacific Islander Americans, Latino Americans, and African Americans facilitates their school success."[25]

Defining a Culturally Relevant Pedagogy

According to Ladson-Billings, a culturally relevant pedagogy "is a theoretical construct that rests on three propositions: Successful teaching focuses on students' achievement; successful teaching supports students' cultural competence, and successful teaching promotes students' socio-political consciousness."[26] In other words, a culturally relevant pedagogy involves educating and empowering students holistically. Students must be excelling academically. However, instead of feeling that they have to act white or eradicate their own culture in order to do well in school, they must also be taught in ways that value and build on their culture. Ladson-Billings said: "Cultural competence refers to the ability of students to grow in understanding and respect for their culture of origin. Rather than experiencing the alienating effects of education where school-based learning detaches students from their home culture, cultural competence is a way for students to be bicultural and facile in the ability to move between school and home cultures."[27]

As an example, Ladson-Billings described a teacher who used music that students brought to class in order to teach them how to identify the poetic devices within the songs.[28] In Chapter Five of this book, the strategies that Baker, a Boston public school teacher, used to expand her students' oral and written communication skills by building on their home language illustrate this important component of a culturally relevant pedagogy. According to Ladson-Billings, the third component of a culturally relevant pedagogy is a "socio-political consciousness," designed to help students "ask larger socio-political questions about how schools and the society work to expose ongoing inequity and social injustice."[29] As an example, she described a teacher whose class was given a set of out-of-date textbooks to use. The teacher raised the students' sociopolitical consciousness by supplementing the old texts with more recent information about the topics they were required to learn. She empowered the students to become proactive and "political" by having them write letters to newspaper editors. In addition to educating students holistically, as with critical pedagogy "culturally relevant teaching is designed to help students move past a blaming the victim mentality in search for the structural and symbolic foundations of inequity and injustice," Ladson-Billings said.[30] Gay's five-point summary of the components of a culturally relevant pedagogy can be useful to teachers:

1. It acknowledges the legitimacy of the cultural heritages of different ethnic groups.
2. It connects school and home experiences.
3. It uses different instructional strategies to address all learning styles.
4. It teaches students to value their own cultural heritage and that of others.
5. It incorporates multicultural materials into the curriculum.[31]

Summary

If African American students are going to thrive in classrooms and excel academically, they need a culturally relevant and culturally responsive education. A culturally responsive education can increase the likelihood of students receiving an education that empowers them to improve society. Instead of merely teaching students to memorize facts and figures in order to pass tests, a culturally relevant education can give them knowledge that permits them to think critically and become aware of options that are available to them.

As Boykin stated, "Schools for Black children should be sites for talent development. They should accomplish a range of objectives. They should prepare these children to acquire a broad range of marketable skills, but they should also prepare them to appreciate their cultural legacy and to use it to be proactive contributors to changing their own life circumstances and to enhancing the life quality of others in their community if not in society at large."[32] However, before teachers can become successful teachers of African American students, they must be willing to address their own issues and biases pertaining to African American children and African American culture and language.

These themes, particularly that teachers' beliefs affect students' learning, have surfaced repeatedly throughout this book. If teachers are fearful of facing their own issues and biases, these problems will manifest themselves in the classroom and impede their progress with African American students. African American students need a culturally relevant curriculum, but they cannot receive it from fearful teachers, teachers who refuse to acknowledge and face the realities and inequities that continue to exist in society, or from teachers who will not take the time to use the African American community as a resource to improve their pedagogy. The conclusion of this book, which contains a long-term professional growth plan for teachers, can be a starting point for teachers who want to begin to examine some of these issues in private.

9

Other Controversial Issues

During the teacher trainings for the middle school and three high schools, some teachers raised additional questions. Four of them are addressed in this chapter:

1. "Black" or "African American": Which term should we use?
2. Why are African Americans so loud?
3. Why do some African Americans have such a bad attitude?
4. Are African American teachers more effective with African American students than nonblack teachers?

I have also included a story ("Why Can't We Call Them Monkeys? To Offend or Not to Offend; That Is the Question") about cultural insensitivity that I shared during the trainings, and the responses of two teachers to this story.

Black or African American: Which Term Should We Use?

There is some confusion about the actual definition of the term *African American*. Some older African Americans prefer the term *black* to *African American*. One professor recently said, "I'm black, not Afro American." His comment illustrated the frustration that some individuals feel over the number of terms—colored, Negro, Afro-American, black, and African American—used to describe black people in the United States during the twentieth century alone. This same professor also raised an important point: he mentioned that many indigenous Africans who come to the United States to attend college have children while they are here. Their children are entitled to dual citizenship, in America and in their parents' native countries. The professor said that even though these children are reared in homes in which their parents may adhere to their native African customs, they can also be labeled African Americans.

In my opinion, *African American* generally has a limited meaning but *black* has a more encompassing meaning. The former usually refers to individuals of African descent whose ancestors lived in the United States before the slavery era or arrived here during that time, and who consider themselves to be black Americans, African Americans, or Afro-Americans (a term that has become obsolete). All three have traditionally been used to describe the same cultural group, the overwhelming majority of whom had ancestors who were slaves in the United States.

The distinction between African American or black American and other groups of blacks must be made for several reasons. First, many Africans (blacks who were born in Africa or whose parents were born in Africa) and West Indian or Caribbean blacks (those who were born in the Caribbean or whose parents were born in the Caribbean) do not consider themselves to be African Americans or black Americans. For example, a black person from one of these groups might identify himself or herself as a Nigerian, Ghanaian, Jamaican, or Haitian, but rarely as an African American. Moreover, although there are many similarities there are also strong cultural differences among Africans, West Indians, and African Americans.

In many regions of the United States, there are significant populations of Nigerian, West Indian, and African American students. Therefore, it would be unwise for teachers to assume that all of the black students in class share a common recent heritage. In other words, some groups of black students are a lot closer to their African roots than others. This makes a huge difference, in my opinion, when it comes to self-esteem, self-concept, and self-image. Two decades ago, when I lived in Africa (in Cameroun and Zaire), one of the first things I noticed was the difference in how I felt while living in countries in which people who looked like me had majority rather than minority status. Seeing portraits of black people on the currency being used and in all positions of power (including the presidency), at all levels of government, and as most of the business owners I encountered was empowering. Unless I opened my mouth and thus indicated by my accent that I was an American, most people assumed that I was an African; I blended in, and it felt great. Conversely, most African Americans have never had the opportunity to experience this majority status and the sense of pride and empowerment that comes with it.

To avoid confusing and offending students, teachers can simply ask them which term best describes them. This simple strategy is especially useful in urban schools in which there may be numerous heterogeneous groups of black children. The cultural awareness project in Appendix C can be useful in this regard. Autobiographical writing assignments, the "All About Me" assignment in Appendix B, and class discussions at the beginning of the school year can also be useful.

Why Can't We Call Them Monkeys? To Offend or Not to Offend; That Is the Question

One of my former graduate students, a white middle school teacher, said that one of her African American students developed a bad attitude after the teacher told her "to stop dressing like a hoochie." The teacher could not understand why the student hated her. She believed she was acting in the child's best interest, but I could see the problem clearly. Although *hoochie* is a word commonly used by some African American and other youths, a white teacher who uses this word in reference to an African American student is asking for trouble. To refer to an individual as a hoochie is to say basically that the person is behaving or dressing like a prostitute. If the student had gone home and told her mother about the teacher's comment, the teacher would have undoubtedly gotten a worse reaction than a mere bad attitude (a topic that will be addressed later in this chapter).

This incident illustrates that when it comes to race relations and cultural sensitivity, there are clearly defined taboos. As noted in previous chapters, the N word and "nappy hair" are not options that nonblacks can use with impunity in reference to African Americans. However, there are also gray areas—lesser-known topics, words, and actions that may or may not be considered racist, culturally insensitive, or culturally offensive. It is often the gray areas that cause a problem in the classroom. One gray area became a source of controversy during the inservice that I conducted at the middle school. The incident, the story that led to it, and my advice to teachers are recounted here.

At one point near the beginning of the inservice at the middle school, I shared a story that had recently been told to me by a teacher who was attending a three-day Improving Students' Writing Skills workshop I was conducting at a large Los Angeles County high school. At the end of the second day, the teacher, a Latina who taught special education classes, told me, "I made a big mistake with one of my classes. One day, my students were very noisy and uncooperative. So, I told them, 'You guys are acting just like monkeys!'" According to the teacher, one of her African American students became extremely upset and told her that the comment had offended him. At this point, the teacher had several choices regarding how to respond. One option was to ignore the student's remark. Another option was to tell him that the class was to blame for her comment. After all, if they had not been so noisy, she would never have made the comment in the first place. A third option was to accept responsibility for the comment, which is the option the teacher chose.

She told the student she did not know the comment would offend him, and she immediately apologized, to this student and to the entire class. Although the teacher handled this sensitive situation sensibly, the matter did not end with her apology. The student went home and told his grandmother about the teacher's comment. The grandmother immediately telephoned the teacher and voiced her outrage. Again, the teacher had several options regarding how to respond. Nevertheless, for the second time in the same day, she chose the third option. She apologized to the grandmother and explained that she had been unaware that her comment would offend the woman's grandson. At this point, a situation that could have become more volatile was defused. The grandmother accepted the teacher's apology and explained why comparing her grandson's behavior to a monkey was so upsetting to both the student and her.

Like many older African Americans, the grandmother was aware that for decades African Americans were compared to monkeys, apes, and gorillas. Historically, comparisons were made between the physical features of African Americans and apes, and conclusions were drawn that African Americans were actually subhuman. Thus comparing an African American child to a monkey or an ape conjures up the long and painful period throughout history when the proponents of eugenics, biological determinism, polygenism, and hereditarianism sought to convince the world that since African Americans were less human than whites, they were incapable of excelling academically to the same extent as whites, and they deserved their socioeconomic plight in society.[1]

In Isaac's book on the history of the N word and the origins of antiblack racism, the author (a veteran African American teacher) cited numerous instances when whites used the Bible to attempt to prove that African Americans were actually apes. Throughout her book, Isaac quoted directly from a racist document she inherited from a family member. For example, one passage states:

> The Bible is simply a history of the long conflict which has raged between God and man, as the result of man's criminal relations with the Negro. Hence, when we recognize the Negro as a man, we can make no more sense out of the Bible . . . but when we accept the teachings of scripture that man is a

distinct creation "in the image of God" and that the Negro is an ape . . . the mystery with which atheism has enveloped the Bible disappears. . . .[2]

During the inservices that I conducted for the middle school and three high schools, I shared the aforementioned story about the special education teacher, how the teacher handled both situations, and related research with the participants. Whereas most of the high school teachers and middle school teachers appeared to understand why the teacher's apology was warranted, one middle school teacher not only disagreed but became quite agitated. In fact, when I tried to explain why the circumstances warranted an apology and why it was unwise for teachers—once they knew better—to continue to use culturally offensive terms in reference to their students, the teacher's irritation became more apparent. At one point, in exasperation, she said she was sick of hearing about the sensitivity of blacks. "I constantly tell my students that they act like little monkeys," she remarked, "and I will continue to do so. I even call my own daughter 'monkey,' and 'monkey' is a term of endearment for me." The teacher added, "Instead of apologizing to my African American students when they get offended, I'm going to teach them to toughen up. They need to stop getting their feelings hurt so easily and realize that the rest of the world can't cater to them."

When I relayed these incidents to another group of educators at another training, a veteran teacher (a white woman) said she did not like the way that either teacher—the Latina or the white middle school teacher—responded. "Both were knee-jerk reactions," she explained. Instead, she believed that the Latina teacher should have used the incident as a teachable moment opportunity. Although an apology may have been warranted, the veteran teacher thought a better solution would have been for the teacher to ask the African American student why he was offended. The related discussion could have benefited the entire class. First, it could have helped the African American student to understand his anger and verbalize the causes. Second, it could have helped the teacher and the entire class understand what the boy's grandmother would later explain. Third, it could have resulted in a minihistory lesson for the entire class.

These three responses indicate that although there is no blueprint for handling the gray areas of race relations, teachers can use similar situations in a way that exacerbates or silences—or serves as an opportunity for growth.

Why Are African Americans so Loud?

At the end of March 2003, my husband, kids, and I were sitting in an Italian restaurant celebrating my husband's birthday. I was in the process of remarking to my family that an African American waiter had nice braids, when almost simultaneously both of my daughters said, "Shh. Mom, you're talking loud." I totally disagreed, and a debate ensued. The end result was that I failed to convince my daughters I had not been talking loudly, and they failed to convince me that I had. I concluded that my children's perception stemmed from messages they internalized while attending predominantly white private schools for many years.

This scenario is an example of a pervasive problem in schools. When African American students speak in class or other places on campus, there is often a perception that they speak too loudly, and loud talk is equated with trouble. For example, a white elementary school principal told me that at his school he kept noticing that every day the playground aides were placing several African American and Latino boys on "time out," which meant they had to sit on a bench or stand against a wall, instead of playing. Finally, he asked the aides what the boys kept doing wrong to warrant the time outs. The principal was surprised to hear that the boys were merely "talking loudly." Additional questioning revealed that the boys were not even arguing. However, because of their raised voices, the aides feared the students would eventually end up in a fight, if they did not place them on a time out. Thereafter, the principal began to go to the playground to listen to the boys talk. He soon learned that their loud talking took place as they were joking with each other. In fact, he detected no animosity at all, he told me. Subsequently, he forced the playground aides to stop punishing the boys for merely talking in a way that the aides assumed would eventually lead to trouble.

Several years ago, I heard a related story while I was attending an educational conference in Minnesota. A Nigerian professor described problems that her son, an elementary school student, was having in school. At the beginning of the school year, he was excited and eager about attending. Before long, however, he was feigning sickness to get out of going to school. Some mornings he complained that his stomach hurt too badly for him to get out of bed. It seemed that he had gone from enjoying school to looking for excuses to be absent. After conducting an informal investigation, his mother learned the reason. The boy dreaded going to school because almost every time he opened his mouth his teacher told him he was speaking too loudly. "Use your classroom voice," she repeatedly chided. The child became confused. At home, his parents told him to speak clearly and assertively. According to his mother, this was an important part of his culture that was instilled in all of the males. At school, however, the boy was told that how he had been socialized to speak from as far back as he could remember was unacceptable. As a result, he decided to avoid going to school whenever possible. The conflicting messages from school and home were too stressful for him to handle.

I have never conducted a study regarding why some African Americans speak loudly, but my own experience and observations have led me to several conclusions. The first is that people who assume all African Americans are loud are ignorant; they fail to realize that African Americans are a diverse group. Just as there are some loud, some quiet, and some in-between whites, Latinos, and Asians, the same is true of African Americans. In every classroom in which there are numerous African American students, there are talkative ones and shy and soft-spoken ones. Individuals who believe that "all" African Americans are loud have either had limited exposure to African Americans, lump them all together, or choose not to see

African Americans as individuals who have different behaviors and personalities.

The problem of lumping them all together and assuming that African American students speak louder than other students is pervasive in classrooms. As I noted previously, my husband is an educator. After twenty years of working in a predominantly white school district, Rufus has developed a theory about why African American students are disproportionately punished for talking in class. He stated:

> My theory is that when students are in a class and the class is told to be quiet, the rest of the class is still talking, but it's just that the African American students are often talking louder or they appear to be doing so, because they stand out more than the other kids. It's called "figure ground discrimination." What it basically means is you look for contrast. It's a human trait. You look for contrast, or differences in the environment. When teachers look up, they see black kids and they see their mouths moving. So the black kids get in trouble first, because the teacher can hear them over the rest of the class. It's not so much that the black kids are talking; the other kids are talking too, but when the teacher looks up, she automatically sees the black kids first, and that tends to get the black kids in trouble. Then, the black kids say, "Well everyone else is talking," which is true. But the teacher didn't see everybody else. When she first looks up, she sees the black kids. That becomes a pattern over time. The kids go home, tell their parents, and their parents say, "Well, was anybody else talking?" and the black kids say, "Yeah, the people right next to me were talking." But the teacher doesn't actually see those people talking because when she looks up, she only sees the black kids and their lips are moving.

My second and most obvious conclusion is that some African Americans speak loudly in order to be heard or to get attention. In the United States the voices of African Americans have historically been disparaged, ridiculed, and ignored. On countless occasions, I have noticed that some people will not take an African American seriously—particularly if the individual is speaking Ebonics—until the individual speaks forcefully. I have seen individuals who felt strongly about an issue, but who believed their opinions were being ignored, raise their voices in an effort to show they meant business or that they wanted to be taken seriously. I myself have done this on numerous occasions. I have realized that when I feel strongly about a point I am attempting to make, I get emotional. Although the emotion in my voice stems from my desire to make a point that is important to me, some whites equate this with anger. I have seen numerous white men do the same thing, especially in meetings, and it is clear to me that a double standard exists. When an African American speaks passionately about a topic that is important to him or her, it is usually perceived as anger, as in the example of the boys being punished on the school playground. When white men speak forcefully and passionately about a topic, it is viewed as acceptable behavior or their privilege as white males. In fact, a number of white men have gotten jobs as television and radio program hosts for this very reason.

My third conclusion is that some African Americans speak loudly because it is a cultural norm they learned in their family and community of origin. For example, in a large family, such as my family of origin, when my siblings and I were conversing sometimes—like many children—we would speak at the same time. For my voice to be heard above the others, I felt that speaking loudly was what I had to do.

Recently, a Panamanian American friend and I were discussing this very issue and the consequences. This friend, Camille Mayers, a professor of counseling psychology, has studied the relationship between identity development and status characteristics. She is particularly knowledgeable about how factors such as work, gender, socioeconomic status, and beauty (and the perceived absence of beauty) shape experiences, and how experiences affect how individuals interact with the world. Regarding styles of discourse and loudness, she shared some thoughts with me during a telephone conversation:

Black people start to create an energy when we communicate and it draws us in. We talk loud when we're happy; we talk loud when we're sad; we talk loud when we're tender and it's not the volume that assigns the meaning; it's the intended message and the heart that it's coming from.

One of the things that white people make attributions that are usually inaccurate about is emotions. When they hear emotions attached to a message coming out of a black mouth, they shut down and dismiss it, and they usually attach a label of "militance" or "radicalism," when in fact what might be being conveyed is reasoned and accurate thought. Black people gravitate toward emotional expression of any kind. We do not fear it. Emotional expression is our salvation. But white people tend to step back from that, experience guilt, and wonder if they're the cause of whatever the message bearer is expressing.

A fourth conclusion that I have drawn is similar to what Camille stated: because whites and blacks are usually socialized differently, this increases the likelihood of miscommunication between them.[3] The problem is compounded by many white women from middle-class backgrounds having been socialized to speak nonauthoritatively and maybe feeling uncomfortable exerting authority in the classroom.[4] One result can be that African American students may not take them seriously, which can result in behavioral problems.[5] Another result, in my opinion, is that teachers can actually convey the message they are fearful of African American students who speak in a way that the teacher presumes to be loud or too direct. In the case of older students, the teacher may be accused of being racist for singling out African American students, or the students may react passive-aggressively.

Another conclusion I have drawn is that many African Americans and other blacks are socialized to view discourse as interactive and dynamic, not static, passive, and one-dimensional. I have already noted that in many black churches during the sermon the congregation is expected to interact in verbal exchanges with the minister. The same thing happens when the choir or a soloist sings.

Regardless of the reasons why some African Americans speak loudly and why they are presumed to do so even when they believe they are not speaking loudly, each teacher must decide how to handle this widespread problem on an individual basis. Rufus made these suggestions to teachers: "When the class is talking, stop, look, and then listen. Just like walking across the street—you hear the conversations going on, you look up, you stop what you're doing, you look up, you survey the class, and if you see other people's mouths moving besides the black kids' mouths moving, then everybody that's talking gets into trouble, not just the black kids, or the Latino kids, or the kids of color, because it's a contrast thing, initially." I conclude this section with some of author Ralph Wiley's explanations for why some African Americans tend to "shout":

- Black people tend to shout in churches, movie theatres, and anywhere else they feel the need to shout, because . . . the uproar [caused by emotions] is too big to hold inside. The feeling must be aired.

- When you have read that bits [from horses' bridles] were put in some of your ancestors' mouths, you tend to shout.

- Poverty has something to do with the shouting too. Most black people can't afford to be quiet.

- Black people shout because they want the answers to questions that go unanswered, like, "Who knocked the nose and lips off the Sphinx?"

- Black people tend to shout because they dare to have the nerve not to be silent.[6]

Why Do Some African Americans Have Such a Bad Attitude?

Another recurring theme about African Americans is a widespread perception among teachers and others that we have a bad attitude.

When I appeared on Tavis Smiley's National Public Radio program in 2002, I mentioned this point. Smiley replied that he often gave presentations at schools and found that "some black kids are bad!" I agreed with him but countered with the statement that "some white kids, Asian kids, and Latino kids are bad too!" We were both correct. However, rightly or wrongly, African Americans are more likely than the other groups to be perceived as having a bad attitude, or even as being bad people. The media's history of concentrating on negativity rather than the positive accomplishments of African Americans is one reason. (For example, an African American woman recently told me that her nephew had just gotten a full scholarship to Juilliard. She wanted to know why stories such as this are rarely reported by the media; every time she opened a newspaper or turned on the television she'd read or hear about some "black suspect." "They make it seem like none of our kids are doing anything positive," she complained.) The high percentage of African Americans who are incarcerated is another. A third reason is that African Americans are disproportionately represented among the students who are suspended and expelled from school, as has already been noted. Even though there is extensive proof that the American judicial system and school discipline policies and practices are tainted by racism, the perception that African Americans are bad, dangerous, and have a bad attitude is entrenched in the American psyche.

I experienced this firsthand more than a decade ago during the Los Angeles uprising after the police officers who beat Rodney King were acquitted. At that time, my family and I lived in a house bordered on the right by an African American family and on the left by a white family, consisting of a young couple and their two daughters. Although we tend to be loners, my family and I had good relations with both groups of neighbors and had even purchased furniture from our white neighbors' store. Therefore, I was very surprised during the Los Angeles uprising when the white neighbor informed me that he and his wife had purchased guns to protect themselves. We lived fifty-five miles from Los Angeles, and no trouble had erupted in our city at all, yet he was telling me that they were armed. Television news scenes of African American youths attacking an innocent white man and of African Americans and Latinos looting unleashed dormant fears in this couple. In my opinion—and I could be wrong—overnight my family and I went from being quiet neighbors who kept to ourselves to potentially dangerous suspects. Before the conversation ended, I suspected that his goal was to convey a subtle message to me: in case my husband and I were really "big bad Negroes"—the kind that, according to Michael Moore,[7] every white American has been socialized to fear—they were prepared for us. Of course, that was the last long conversation I ever had with these neighbors, and by the time they moved to a less diverse community in another city nearby I could barely open my mouth to speak to them.

The aforementioned experience is an example of why some African Americans do develop a bad attitude. If I reacted this way as an adult, how much more difficult must it be for a young and impressionable African American youth not to develop a negative attitude. The pressure that results from ongoing disparagement, being followed in stores, and constantly having to prove oneself can create a self-fulfilling prophecy. The media role, though, is just one of many reasons for this widespread perception. For youths, in addition to hormonal changes and peer pressure there may be personal problems, the self-protective cool pose discussed earlier, teachers' attitudes, and classroom policies.

In Chapters Three and Four, the way in which personal problems and academic problems can lead to misbehavior was described; in Chapter Four I discussed how my own personal problems during childhood affected my schooling experiences. Students' personal problems can also result in the perception that they have a bad attitude. Two of my former African American male tenth graders were in this category. One of the boys appeared to have a chip on his shoulder. He would scowl at me, suck his teeth, and often appeared to be uncooperative yet not openly defiant. Nevertheless, it was apparent to me that he disliked me. One day, I was shocked to learn that he was living in a foster home. He had been taken from his parents as a result of extreme abuse. During a conversation with him, he told me that my strict authoritative style actually reminded him of his parents! My dilemma became to find a way to show this student that my strictness, authoritativeness, and high expectations stemmed from having his best interests, instead of the worst, at heart. If I were an abusive teacher, I would resort to the "educational malpractice"[8] comprising low expectations, weak classroom management, a substandard curriculum, and inferior quality of instruction that would fail to equip him with the skills and knowledge needed to improve the quality of his future. Over time, our relationship improved. The student learned about the importance of prejudging people as a result of his personal problems, and I learned about the importance of trying to uncover the often hidden causes of unacceptable student behavior. Nevertheless, throughout my years as a secondary school teacher I had to keep learning this same lesson, as illustrated by the next example.

One year, I had an African American football player who was also on the school basketball team in my class. This student angered me. Unlike the student I was just discussing, this young man was never defiant, and he never displayed a hostile attitude. The main problem was that he was working below his potential and often fell asleep in class. Although his working below his potential troubled me, what angered me was that he had the nerve to sleep in my class. Part of my outrage was that I assumed that the student believed his status as a jock on campus meant my no-sleeping-in-class policy did not apply to him. In other words, I assumed he had a cocky attitude.

One day, I got so mad that I tiptoed over to the desk on which was his sleeping head and rapped on the corner of the desk with a ruler. When he bolted upright, obviously startled, his classmates howled with laughter. He looked around in embarrassment and I smugly returned to my desk, certain I had taught him a lesson. For the duration of the class session, he managed to stay awake. Afterward, I asked him privately yet again why he persisted in falling asleep. He said he did not know. In response to specific questions, such as "Are you staying up late at night talking on the telephone?" he replied "No." Again, as I had done before, I told him he needed to stop sleeping in class. As he had promised before, the student said he would try. And try he did. His grade eventually went from a D to a B in my class.

One day, during my preparation period, I was standing outside the building, talking to one of the school proctors (unarmed security personnel), when the student walked by. Speaking loudly enough for the student to hear, I told the proctor, an African American woman who had a good rapport with most of the students at the school, how proud I was that he had drastically improved his grade in my class. When he heard this, the student smiled at us and seemed to walk with more pride. When he was out of earshot, the proctor said to me, "You know he was sleeping in a dumpster earlier in the year, right?"

Once again, I was shocked. No, I did not know this, nor did I know that both of the student's parents were currently incarcerated on drug-related charges. Moreover, I was unaware that his football and basketball coaches had paid his sports fees and purchased his uniforms, or that he sometimes spent the night at the homes of teammates because he did not want to go into the foster care system. Instead, he wanted to be reunited with his parents when they were eventually released.

My shock quickly turned to shame. No wonder the teen had been sleeping in class. On the occasions when he slept in class, perhaps he had not had a bed or even a building to sleep in the previous night. This shame prompted me to search for him. When I found him, I told him I knew a good social worker who could place him in a good foster home until his parents returned. However, he made it clear that he did not want to go into the foster care system and that a schoolmate's family had recently let him move into their home until his parents' release. Thereafter (mostly to assuage my guilt), I gave him a weekly allowance to be used for lunch money. On another occasion, I bought a pair of sneakers he needed. During his senior year, another African American teacher and I paid for his prom ticket and tuxedo. Throughout these years, his coaches continued to pay his sports fees, buy his uniforms, and often took him to dinner.

When the student told me that several universities were expressing interest in recruiting him to play basketball, I was elated. College was going to be his ticket to a stable home environment. In the end, his ACT scores prevented him from going to the four-year university of his choice; he opted to play basketball at a community college in another city that had recruited him. During our last conversation, he convinced me that he was serious about working on improving his ACT scores so that he could eventually play basketball at the university he dreamed of attending. My experiences with this student illustrate how easy it is to make wrong assumptions about students.

Another reason an African American student may appear to have a bad attitude or actually develop one is that the student is sending a message to the teacher, as noted in the chapter on classroom management. When students believe that a teacher is unfair or that the class rules are unfair or unrealistic, a bad attitude or the perception that the student has a bad attitude may result. One of my experiences as a junior high school teacher makes this point.

An African American girl in one of my classes was extremely outspoken and opinionated. When she disagreed with anything, she was quick to verbalize her opinion. At the time, my rule regarding giving students restroom passes was a rule that she clearly disagreed with. My policy was simple: unless it was an emergency, I would not give a pass, because I believed that students had time to go to the restroom during the breaks between classes, during their physical education class, and at lunch. I had adopted this policy because of previous negative experiences, finding that when I gave one student a restroom pass it resulted in a chain reaction. Thereafter, one student after another would all of a sudden need to go to the restroom, which became disruptive to my lesson plans. Consequently, I had adopted a "no restroom pass" policy. It was clearly extreme, demeaning, and subject to abuse, for there was really no way I could determine if a student had a real emergency or not.

Although she had often complained about the policy, the student did not openly defy me until one surprising day when she asked for a restroom pass. I asked if it were an emergency and she said no, but she needed to go to the restroom anyway. When I replied that she would have to wait until the class ended, she exclaimed, "My grandmother said that if you won't let me go to the restroom, I can pee on the floor!" Her statement, and the fact that it was sanctioned by her guardian, placed me in a difficult predicament. If I capitulated, I would appear to be weak; hence other students might take advantage of me. If I did not, the student might act on her threat. Just as I did during my days as a substitute teacher, I resorted to the law of the street and called her bluff. "Go ahead and pee then," I said, "but when you're finished, clean it up."

I was extremely grateful the student did not accept my challenge, but the entire incident troubled me. I realized if a student felt so strongly about the unfairness of this policy that she asked her grandmother for a solution, then my policy clearly needed to be reexamined. I kept the policy for the remainder of the school year, but in ensuing years I adopted a wiser, more realistic, and more humane policy. Thereafter, the rule was that any student could request a restroom pass at anytime, and I would give him or her the pass. However, the student would have to come after school to make up the class time that he or she lost while out of the classroom. This solved the problem. Since most students do not want to stay after school, unless it is for extracurricular activities, the new rule reduced the likelihood that students would take advantage of the policy merely to get out of class. Moreover, it prevented students with a genuine emergency from being humiliated when they needed to go to the restroom. The lesson I learned from the incident that prompted me to examine my policy was that if a student feels strongly enough to risk possible punishment to challenge a class rule or teaching practice, it cannot harm the teacher at the very least to consider other options. (It is important for me to stress that the restroom policy works for secondary students, but it should not be used for younger students, who are prone to "accidents.")

A third reason why a student may have a bad attitude, or appear to have one, might stem from messages the teacher covertly or overtly sends. As repeated throughout this book, a teacher's attitude and expectations about African American students can have far-reaching consequences that affect a student's schooling experiences. The classroom management chapter presented examples of African American boys who were perceived to be discipline problems and assumed to be suffering from ADD early in their schooling. One result can be that the students do actually adopt a bad attitude because they believe their teachers will not give them a fair chance to prove themselves anyway. I was guilty of this with one of my former African American students.

The problem started in the middle of a tenth grade class. I was standing in front of the room leading a class discussion when a stranger burst into the room. She was overweight, scowling, and heading in my direction. A message from my urban upbringing kicked in. My instinct told me that this teen was armed and dangerous. Without thinking, I ducked for cover. The class burst into laughter. When I stood up, the girl gave me a hateful look and handed me a sheet of paper. According to the paper, she was a new student, transferring from a Los Angeles school. I apologized for my behavior and explained that when she opened the door, she looked so angry that I did not know what to expect. Unmoved by my apology, the student took her assigned seat and glared at me for the duration of the class session.

That initial meeting foreshadowed the next few months. Not only did the student refuse to forgive me, as evidenced by her negative body language and silence that spoke volumes, but she barely did any classwork and never completed homework assignments. When I spoke with her mother by telephone, the parent expressed both concern and helplessness. The story she told me convinced me, though, to change my approach with the student. According to the mother, they had moved from Los Angeles because the girl was heavily involved in a notorious black gang. Her older brother, a member of the gang, had been arrested and was incarcerated. Moving her daughter and two younger children out of Los Angeles was the mother's attempt to rescue her from her older brother's fate.

I have always used storytelling throughout my teaching, but I began to share more stories with my students about individuals who have overcome adversity. We discussed literature and current events that contained pertinent examples, I told more stories about people I knew personally, and I shared stories from my own life. On several occasions, although she never actively participated, I noticed that the girl appeared to be captivated by the stories and discussions. Another difference I noticed was that her face softened; her perpetual scowl and glare disappeared. Over time, I periodically spoke with her in private for a few minutes after class. I used these opportunities to tell her I believed she had a lot of potential, and I really wanted to see her earn a passing grade in the class. Otherwise, she would have to make up the lost course credits by repeating the class.

One day her counselor, an African American woman, telephoned me and asked, "How did you do it? She used to hate your guts. She used to come in my office complaining about you all the time and begged me to transfer her to another class. Now, she loves you. How did you do it?"

At the end of the year, the student earned a passing grade in my class. Her writing skills had improved and she was writing poems about her life. We developed a strong bond, but I was surprised to hear that I had become her favorite teacher. Consequently, she asked if she could continue to work with me. During her junior and senior years she served as one of my student aides, and she shared more details about her life. She admitted that before moving from Los Angeles, she was involved in carjackings and other criminal activities. She told me never to leave my keys in the car at a gas station, because young gang members find this the easiest way to steal cars. She also gave me many other important safety tips. Before she graduated, we discussed our first meeting—that day, two years earlier, when my initial and instinctive assumption caused her to hate me. To my dismay, she admitted that my gut instinct had been correct. "I'm not going to say what it was," she admitted, "but I did have a weapon that day." Although she had no plans to use it, she felt she needed it because of her experiences in Los Angeles and because she still had gang ties.

Last year, I was driving to the beauty shop when I saw this former student of mine crossing a busy street. I made a U turn and went back to talk to her. We hugged each other, and she updated me on her life. She had married another of my former students, and they were the parents of a son. She proudly showed me a family photo and told me that her goal was to teach her son to read before he entered kindergarten.

More recently, on two occasions the topic of African American parents having a bad attitude came up. The first came from one of my graduate students, a Latina elementary school teacher. One night, she told the class she was disturbed by comments that her coworkers routinely made about African American parents. According to the student, her colleagues made it clear they did not want to be bothered with African American parents. They believed that African American parents were aggressive, boisterous, and problematic. Moreover, they bragged openly about preferring to deal with Latino parents, because they perceived them to be docile, nonassertive, and nonthreatening.

The second example took place at the end of March 2003. During a long-distance telephone conversation with Deborah, a friend whom I have known since third grade, the topic of bad attitudes came up. Of all of my friends, Deborah (a housewife and mother of three children, including twins) is among the most mild-mannered and jovial. However, the story that she shared with me during our conversation is indicative of why some African Americans are perceived to have a bad attitude.

Deborah has always been an advocate for her children, particularly her twins, a boy and a girl. They were born prematurely and experienced numerous setbacks during the first months of life. The most difficult challenges occurred during the days and hours immediately after their births. On several occasions, doctors told Deborah that her daughter would not live for more than two days. Each time the baby girl stopped breathing, doctors said it would be futile to attempt to resuscitate her. Deborah insisted they do so anyway. "I told them to do their jobs and God will do the rest," she stated.

After one resuscitation, an exasperated doctor told her it was the last time she would do so. That last time made the ultimate difference. In spite of the fact that she has mild cerebral palsy, today the little girl is a third grader who was identified as gifted by a psychologist at age three. Even with this label of giftedness, her parents have had to fight to ensure that she receives a quality education and is treated fairly by educators.

Although Deborah has shared many upsetting stories with me about her struggle as a parent advocate for her children in the predominantly white district in which they attend school, her daughter's experiences during third grade appeared to have resulted in the greatest transformation of Deborah's personality and how she interacted with educators. "I think the problem was that I was trying to be liked," she said. "Now, I don't care if they label me as a troublemaker."

Although they were the only African American third graders in the entire school and were placed in separate classes, Deborah's twins had an auspicious beginning during the 2002–03 school year. Deborah had "clothes to fold and a sink full of dirty dishes," but she continued to be active in her children's schooling and visible at the elementary school. In addition to serving as the room mother for her daughter's class, she served as a library volunteer twice a week, sent flowers and gifts to her children's teachers, and gave parties for the children. "I wanted to show the teachers that I appreciate what they do," she explained. "I know they work hard."

Things changed in November, when Deborah received a progress report. Her daughter had earned all E's (for excellence) in citizenship, an A in social studies, an A in reading, a B in writing, a C in cursive (as a result of fine-motor skill weakness related to her cerebral palsy), and a C in math. The progress report said her daughter had a problem with "processing abstract math concepts." Deborah became proactive. She began to work with her daughter specifically on the abstract concepts that the teacher said the child was struggling with. "When it's broken down into baby steps, my daughter gets it," Deborah said. "But when the teacher gives her a number line that includes 10, 20, 30, etc., and says 'Round it to the nearest ten,' then my daughter will say 18." In addition to hiring a tutor to work with her child, Deborah asked the teacher if the classroom aide assigned to work with her daughter (because she is a special needs child) could spend fifteen minutes three days each week working with her daughter on the problem areas. The teacher agreed.

Therefore, in February Deborah was surprised to receive a progress report indicating that her daughter was still struggling with abstract math concepts. Her surprise turned to dismay, and then anger, after she learned from the teacher that the aide was too busy filing papers and planning a whale-watching field trip to work with her daughter. Deborah told me:

> I went in and talked to the teacher. I asked her how things were going with the aide and told her that we were working with my daughter at home. The teacher told me that she had decided that it was not feasible for the aide to work with my child. I'm like "What? So, you're telling me that no one's been working with her?" The teacher said, "Surely, you don't expect me to be her personal tutor." I told her, "I'm not asking you to be her tutor; I'm just asking you to use the resources that are available to you." I told her, "I spent twenty minutes pouring my heart out to you about my kid way back in November, and if it was not working out, you should have told me."

Then Deborah suggested that the teacher permit the aide to work with her daughter during recess. After much resistance, the teacher relented. "She was not mad, but you could tell that she didn't want to do it, but she saw that I was not going to back down," Deborah stated. The last straw occurred a month later, when Deborah learned from the aide that the teacher, whom the aide labeled as "a control freak who is stubborn about her time and who doesn't want anyone else working with her class," had not kept her word. According to Deborah:

I asked the aide how things were going. She said, "To be honest with you, I haven't had any time to work with your daughter." You know I went off! I'm like, "What do you mean?" I turned to the teacher and she started this little nervous laugh of hers while she tried to think of what to say. She said, "Yes, we've been busy, preparing for the whale-watching trip." I said, "Wait a minute. I'm going to be raw. I'm pissed off. You're telling me that you don't care about my child getting extra help." She said, "Frankly, I'm overwhelmed by all of this." I said, "Why are you so overwhelmed? You have aides here to help you. No other third grade teacher has an aide." But she could not answer me.

After this meeting with the teacher, Deborah shared her frustration with the resource specialist and the school principal. Both made excuses for the teacher. The resource specialist even told her that her daughter needed to make more of an effort. "Her report card says she earned A's and B's in effort," Deborah replied, "but now, you're going to blame it on my child." Out of frustration, Deborah planned to transfer her children to another school. She kept her daughter out of school for several days. "I worked with her and we got so much done on those days," she said proudly. "I did not feel comfortable having my child in that woman's class." However, her husband, mother, and siblings dissuaded her from transferring the twins to another school, saying that it would be too difficult for the twins to adjust to a new school, new teacher, and new routines, and to find new friends midyear.

When it was time for her daughter to return to school, Deborah was too upset to drive her or walk her to class, as was her daily habit. "I had to cool off," she explained. "I had a major headache. It was draining and so consuming. I think it goes back to when the doctors told me that she was not going to live. If I had given up, then they would not have resuscitated her." At the end of the school day, when Deborah went to pick her children up from school, the teacher asked her if they could talk.

The teacher said, "Hopefully, we can talk and figure this out. I think that we can work together on what's best for your daughter." I looked at her and said to myself *You heifer!* because that's what I'd been asking for all along. I'm not asking for miracles. If they work with my child and she doesn't meet their goals, then that's fine. Now, I go up to the school and I have to walk through there like those people are invisible. I'm still angry and I have to pray about it. Girl, I tell you, those people are crazy! I feel really sorry for the kids who are severely handicapped and don't have anyone to fight for them. I know that there are some excellent teachers out there. My daughter's teacher isn't bad; she's just overwhelmed, but she's been teaching for more than five years. It hurts because I do so much for that school. I try to be involved but it doesn't make any difference. They don't care. That's why I'm so pissed. I know I have good kids who work hard, but the teachers don't want you to ask questions. It's been two weeks since my daughter returned to school, but there's still tension.

These stories contain some important messages to teachers about why some African Americans appear to have a bad attitude. The media, peer pressure, adoption of the cool pose as a self-protective measure, hormonal changes in adolescents, personal problems, and school factors are some of the possibilities. It is clear that teachers must not tolerate rudeness, defiance, or disrespect from any student or parent, but the stories indicate that when a bad attitude surfaces, teachers can become more effective with African American students and relate better to their parents if they take time to identify the possible causes of a bad attitude and examine how their own classroom policies and practices, and their own attitude and behavior, toward students and parents might create or exacerbate a problem. In Deborah's case, it was clear that she was extremely involved in her children's education. When she requested the assistance to which she was entitled, the teacher's lack of concern pushed Deborah to a point of frustration. As noted previously in this chapter, some African Americans become more forceful in their speech when they believe they are not being taken seriously. Deborah's story also illustrates how teachers can send mixed messages about parent involvement, and then appear to be totally oblivious to how their own behavior can create a hostile situation.

Are African American Teachers More Effective with African American Students Than Nonblack Teachers?

Throughout this book, I have shared numerous stories from my own teaching experience (and I have omitted many that are too embarrassing to tell). Some of the stories describe problems I had with African American and other students, and mistakes I made out of ignorance, stupidity, and insensitivity. Although I won an award for outstanding teaching and several awards from student groups, I was never a perfect teacher; today, as a university professor, my quest to improve my teaching skills continues. I am candid in sharing many of my failures and mistakes during the teacher trainings that I conduct, but the question inevitably arises, "Are African American teachers more effective with African American students than nonblack teachers?" In my opinion, the answer is simple: some African American teachers are more effective with African American students than some nonblack teachers. However, the converse is also true: some nonblack teachers are more effective than some African American teachers. It all depends on the teacher.

In *African American Teens Discuss Their Schooling Experiences* high school seniors described their best and worst teachers and the characteristics they associated with outstanding teachers. Some of the students also said that more African American teachers should be hired. Others said their best teachers happened to be African American. For example, a student who attended ninth and tenth grade in a school at which most of her teachers were African American spoke about the value of having teachers who cared about her personal and academic welfare, and who discussed culturally relevant issues with students. "They used to teach us stuff that was interesting," she said.[9] One of my conclusions in that book is that teacher education programs must actively seek to recruit African American prospective teachers, particularly at the middle school level, where a critical mass of African American teachers is needed.

In *What African American Parents Want Educators to Know*, the parents and guardians who participated in that study also spoke about African American teachers. A recurring theme was that most of the African American parents and guardians who attended racially segregated schools in the South believed they had better teachers than their children do. They considered having caring African American teachers who lived in their community an invaluable experience. For example, an African American who was a retired pediatric nurse attended segregated Texas schools; she credited her African American teachers with the accomplishments of her classmates and herself. "I praise God for those Black teachers," she said, "because those kids made it! They became teachers, counselors, everything that you can imagine. . . . Those Black teachers cared. They would discipline you. They would really teach you. . . . Those teachers were interested in the children. . . ."[10]

A mother of four who participated in the study also spoke highly of the African American teachers she had while attending segregated Oklahoma schools. After being bused to an integrated school, she decided to transfer to the predominantly black high school in her community: "I wanted to graduate from an all-black school. . . . [At the integrated school] we did not really have that much interaction with the white teachers other than during class. . . . But with the black teachers, it was different," she explained.[11] Years later, as the parent of four school-age children, she bemoaned the fact that her children's schools employed few African American teachers. "I think that if you want to give a child the best education and have the child become well-rounded," she said, "you should have a staff that reflects that. This district is not reflective [in the same way]. . . . I think my children need to see role models at all levels."[12]

In the same study, however, one parent complained about African American teachers. She felt both African American and nonblack teachers were unwilling to give struggling students the extra help they needed and complained that her children had been shortchanged academically, as she herself was during her K–12 schooling in California public schools. "Most of the parents, like me, when we went to high school, if we raised our hands and asked for extra help in math, we did not get that extra help, because we were black kids . . ." she said. "It was not only the white teachers; it was the black teachers too." Hence, she concluded, "If black teachers would stop acting like Uncle Toms, it would help. . . . Black teachers could step in and say . . . 'We have got to help our kids. . . .'"[13]

These conflicting messages about African American teachers also surfaced during a conversation I had with an African American mother, Mrs. Umrani, when I went to Chicago in 2003 to attend an educational conference. The mother of three adult children, she was the director of a university outreach program for high school students. Most of what she shared with me pertained to her youngest daughter's schooling experiences. This daughter, Annisah, had been identified as gifted at an early age, and Mrs. Umrani felt that her experiences illustrated that both good and bad African American teachers exist. In fact, according to Mrs. Umrani, Annisah's two best elementary teachers were African Americans—as were her two worst.

One of Annisah's worst teachers taught fourth grade. Among the numerous incidents that upset Mrs. Umrani was a comment the teacher made to her. According to Mrs. Umrani, the teacher said, "I know that they say that it's a sign of intelligence for a child to ask questions, but your daughter asks too many questions." Mrs. Umrani eventually grew so fed up with this woman's poor teaching practices and negative attitude that she transferred her daughter to another Chicago school, where Annisah ended up with two exemplary African American teachers. "They were black men," Mrs. Umrani stated. "One taught math and the other taught social studies. Annisah had come from one of the worst schools in the city and then she had these two male teachers who celebrated her accomplishments. It was like a breath of fresh air."

The following year, however, Annisah ended up with the second of her worst teachers, an African American woman who taught fifth grade math. One of the problems Mrs. Umrani described was that the teacher deliberately chose not to address Annisah by her correct name. According to Mrs. Umrani, the teacher asked her daughter, "Is your name Annisah (pronounced "Uh nee suh"), or is it 'Annie saw'?" When Annisah told the teacher the correct way to pronounce her name, the teacher replied, "Well, I like Annie saw better. That's what I'm going to call you."

The second problem was that the math teacher practiced gender discrimination. She placed the girls in the class in the lowest math groups and assumed that the boys deserved to be in the higher groups. When Annisah told the teacher she could do the more challenging math work, the teacher refused to move her to a higher group.

The third problem was that the teacher engaged in unfair grading practices. According to Mrs. Umrani:

Annisah got the highest scores of all of the fifth graders in the entire school on the Iowa Test of Basic Skills. The other kids in the class came in bragging, "Annisah got the highest scores! Annisah got the highest scores in reading and math!" The teacher said, "That doesn't mean that I'm going to give her anything higher than a D in this class." These experiences made me come up with the slogan, "It's Black-on-Black crime." Instead of celebrating her intelligence and promoting academic excellence, they preferred to put their foot on her neck and try to squelch her confident sense of who she was. I really do have issues with people who don't give our children their best. We have to fight white folks because they come to the table with biases. When black teachers give our kids the shaft educationally, I really do have a problem with that, too, because our kids deserve the same opportunities that everyone else gets. If you don't give a thousand percent to our kids, then I don't want you teaching our children.

I'll never be able to pay you what you're worth, but you
shouldn't take the job if you're not going to give it a thousand
percent.

In *Rock My Soul: Black People and Self Esteem*, bell hooks also wrote
about African American teachers and painted a poignant contrast
of her experiences attending racially segregated and integrated
schools. In the all-black schools, she felt less stress because she did
not have to fear violence from whites or prove she was intelligent,
since her black teachers assumed she was. She also had African
American boys as classmates and caring teachers. But in the integrated, mostly white school, she noticed that the black boys who
had been viewed as gifted in the black school were missing from
her classes. This was a "political" act that was designed to protect
the white female students, according to hooks. In summarizing
the effect that attending an integrated school had on her, hooks
wrote: "Often I would lay my head on the desk in history class and
weep. I wept for the world that had been taken from us, schools
where teachers loved us, where we were together, where no one
doubted our capacity to learn or called into question our interest in
learning."[14]

These examples indicate that good African American teachers
are needed and are invaluable. They also underscore the point I
made at the beginning of this section: some African American
teachers are more effective with African American students and
some are not. It depends on the teacher. Bad African American,
white, Latino, or Asian American teachers do not belong in the
classroom. In "Preparing Teachers for Diversity: A Dilemma of
Quality and Quantity," Gandara and Maxwell-Jolley said, "While
there is no body of research that concludes that teachers of the
same ethnicity or social background necessarily produce superior
academic outcomes for ethnic minority students, a substantial literature indicates the positive influences of teachers on students
with whom they share a common background."[15]

Despite the fact that race and ethnicity do not necessarily ensure that African American teachers will be more successful with African American students than nonblack teachers, there is clearly a greater likelihood of African American teachers sharing cultural commonalities and insights with the students that nonblack teachers might not share. One of my African American doctoral students made this point recently. One afternoon, she came to class frustrated. When she told me why, I too became frustrated. She had been observing a kindergarten classroom for a study she was conducting. Her frustration came from the fact that she saw the teacher, a white woman, regularly singling out an African American boy for punishment. "He's so cute and so intelligent," the student told me, "but the teacher criticizes everything that he does. In her eyes, he can't do anything right. She's always sending him to the corner or she's always criticizing him." The fact that the African American graduate student perceived the child in a positive light and the teacher perceived him negatively illustrates one of the reasons why some people believe more African American teachers are needed to help African American students succeed in schools.

Because of the onslaught of negative information that most Americans internalize about African Americans, particularly about black males, too many educators look for deficits instead of strengths in African American students. They often get what they are looking for. As this example demonstrates, the "deficit-finding mission" can start as early as preschool or kindergarten, when children are most vulnerable to being damaged by negative labels—labels that will undoubtedly follow them for the duration of their schooling.

However, I stress that only well-qualified and caring African American teachers are needed. Nonblack teachers may benefit from discussing concerns they have with effective African American teachers. When culturally gray issues involving African American students arise in the classroom, nonblack teachers can consult African American teachers to get a different perspective and suggestions. In *Black Teachers on Teaching*, Michele Foster presented the results of interviews she conducted with exemplary African American teachers.[16] The book can be used as a resource for teachers who want to learn more about the experiences, attitudes, and pedagogies of effective black teachers.

Unfortunately, some researchers, such as Murrell[17] and Delpit,[18] have found that nonblack teachers may refuse to hear the voices of their African American colleagues because of racism and ethnocentrism. Often, the result is that these teachers fail dismally with African American students.

Conclusion

Can Beliefs Be Changed?

The formal training of teachers ostensibly begins in a teacher training program. In most cases, this training occurs at a university, but it usually does not end there. Of course, the real training occurs in the classroom. Teachers often find they have learned numerous theories about teaching, but putting those theories into practice in the classroom is another matter. For this reason, many teachers find their first years of teaching are extremely stressful. Classroom management (which was discussed at length in Chapter Three), planning effective lessons (discussed in Chapter Two), effective time management, dealing with students from diverse backgrounds, and other professional as well as personal obligations contribute to this stress. In *Crossing over to Canaan: The Journey of New Teachers in Diverse Classrooms*, Ladson-Billings stated that "few teacher education programs prepare teachers to be effective in urban classrooms serving diverse groups of students."[1] Furthermore, she asserted, although "the K-12 student population is becoming increasingly diverse, the prospective teaching population is becoming increasingly monocultural, that is white, middle class, and monolingual English."[2] In Cattani's *A Classroom of Her Own*,[3] Nieto's *Affirming Diversity: The Sociopolitical Context of Multicultural Education*,[4] and the U.S. Department of Education's "Eliminating Barriers to Improving Teaching,"[5] the authors all reached a similar conclusion about the large number of teachers who are ill-equipped to meet the needs of students from diverse backgrounds.

One way education officials have attempted to reduce some of the stressors that teachers experience and at the same time ensure that formal teacher training does not begin and end at the university is to require teachers to complete a certain number of professional development hours each year. This can occur at school sites, at education conferences, or through additional university course work. Moreover, to prevent some of the problems already mentioned in this book, teacher training programs tend to require courses that focus on issues pertaining to cultural awareness, diversity, and multiculturalism. The problem, as Fullan stated, is "you can't mandate what matters."[6] New teachers, prospective teachers, and veteran teachers are often resistant to courses and professional development workshops that address these issues. Consequently, they leave these courses[7] and workshops with the same attitudes and beliefs with which they arrived. Since teacher training institutions and professional development workshops are failing to change attitudes and beliefs, and since no legislation can change them, it becomes the responsibility of teachers to do this work for themselves.

As noted in the Introduction, many school administrators and teachers throughout the nation are searching for ways to increase their efficacy with African American students; the No Child Left Behind Act[8] has sparked a sense of urgency in this regard. During the last five years, I have been invited to conduct numerous inservices and workshops at schools to provide educators with professional development in various areas, but recently the number of invitations to do workshops that focus specifically on how teachers can increase their efficacy with African American students has increased tremendously.

The school administrators (a middle school principal and three high school principals) who invited me to conduct professional development inservices at their schools during summer 2002 were in this group (see Appendix I). Although they realized that inviting an African American researcher to conduct an inservice at schools in which the majority of teachers were white could be problematic, they believed that the problems many of their teachers were experiencing with African American students made the inservices imperative.

Although the four school principals were eager to find ways to improve the academic achievement of African American students, the question that remained was, "How would the 175 middle school and high school teachers react to their principals' efforts to address issues pertaining to African American students by inviting an African American scholar to share related research and strategies?"

Like readers of this book, during each inservice participants had the opportunity to hear theories, research, and personal stories. They heard numerous theories posited to explain why many African American students are underachievers, and they were given specific instructional strategies. They also heard some of the reasons African Americans are disproportionately represented among the students who are perceived to be discipline problems, and they were presented with classroom management strategies.

The inservice also addressed the culturally sensitive issues that are presented in this book. The participants heard details about differences between Ebonics and slang, and reasons why many African Americans continue to speak Ebonics. As I have done throughout this book, I underscored the need for teachers to use an additive approach that rests on a foundation of respect for the students' home language and culture. I also shared information and recommendations concerning the use of the N word in class, why students need a culturally relevant curriculum, and how a teacher might handle being accused of being racist by his or her African American students. Moreover, I presented the information in Chapter Four about how teachers can reach students from challenging backgrounds. In addition to hearing most of the information discussed in this book throughout the inservice day, the teachers from the four schools had a chance to offer feedback, through their questions and comments as well as on the questionnaire I distributed at the end of the inservice. The results yielded data about their pre-inservice and post-inservice attitudes and beliefs on several topics, and they contain important information about professional development practices. A summary of the teachers' pre- and post-inservice attitudes and beliefs follows.

Participants' Pre-Inservice Attitudes

The questionnaire results revealed that the 175 participants could be divided into three groups (resentful, open-minded but not enthusiastic, and eager to learn) according to their pre-inservice attitudes about having to attend an inservice that focused exclusively on African American students. This information came from three questionnaire statements, which required the use of a four-point Likert scale (strongly agree, agree, disagree, or strongly disagree). The first statement said, "Prior to attending the inservice, I was eager to learn as much as I could about improving my efficacy with African American students." The second statement said, "Prior to attending this inservice, I was open-minded, but not enthusiastic about the inservice topic." The third statement said, "Prior to attending this inservice, I was resentful about having to attend a workshop that only focused on African American students." My goal was to find out how teachers really felt. Realizing that some teachers might attend the inservice for more than one reason, I sought to present different dimensions of their attitudes. Therefore the three statements could result in teachers fitting into two groups, instead of being forced into only one group. Because the groups were not mutually exclusive, the percentages in the three groups add up to more than one hundred.

Although slightly more than three quarters of the participants said that prior to attending the inservice they were eager to learn as much as they could about African American students, 15 percent admitted that they were actually resentful about having to attend the inservice. Moreover, because nearly half of the participants said that they had been open-minded but not enthusiastic about the inservice topic, there was clearly some overlap among the three groups. However, stepwise multiple regression analysis indicated the resentful group and the open-minded-but-not-enthusiastic group tended to be characterized by negative factors. For example, both groups were more likely than the eager-to-learn group to blame parents and guardians for African American student underachievement, and both were more likely to believe that African American students do not want to succeed academically. Consequently, the data suggest that participants in these two groups may have consciously or unconsciously relinquished their professional responsibilities by blaming the "victims" (parents and students). Furthermore, the fact that they were resentful about attending an inservice that focused on research and strategies pertaining to African American students, or unenthusiastic about the topic, also suggests that they not only held negative beliefs about African American parents and students but may have actually felt hopeless about the possibility of increasing their efficacy with African American students. Of course, other explanations are possible.

Two other interesting findings were that individuals in the resentful group were more likely to have a full credential and to perceive themselves to be colorblind to racial, ethnic, and cultural differences. (In fact, 29 percent of the participants considered themselves to be colorblind.) One plausible explanation is that participants who had a full credential may have believed that they already knew enough information about how to teach African American students effectively. Another possibility is that these teachers— like many teachers—believed that most professional development inservices are a waste of time. A third possibility is that these teachers were resentful by nature or as a result of negative experiences. In this case, it is probable that they would have been resentful about attending any inservice about any topic, even one that did not pertain to racial issues.

The link between perceived colorblindness and feeling resentful about having to attend the inservice is more difficult to explain.

One possibility is that these teachers were racist. In American society, when it comes to African Americans no one is colorblind. Often, individuals who are quick to proclaim "I do not see race; I only see people" are merely in denial. When an African American male walks into a classroom, a teacher who claims that she sees no difference between that student and a blond, blue-eyed white male student is not only in denial but is being dishonest as well. Moreover, the moment that I walked into each of the two inservice sites (the middle school and the one high school where the inservice for the three high schools was conducted), the participants did not merely see an American or a female; they saw an African American. The fact that one of the high school teachers uttered a racial slur that was directed at me indicates that even before I entered the auditorium this teacher saw an African American, instead of a raceless or colorless being. Cattani, who wrote A Classroom of Her Own, an ethnographic study about the professional lives of six young white teachers, said: "Race is an inescapable part of classroom interaction and teachers ignore it at their own—and their students' peril. . . . White teachers may be particularly uncomfortable acknowledging differences in race and may prefer to adopt a color-blind stance."[9] Recently, a white elementary school principal mentioned to me that the most difficult teachers to work with at her predominantly Latino school are the ones who consider themselves to be colorblind. However, another possibility is that the "colorblind" inservice participants could have truly believed that they were oblivious to racial and ethnic differences.

Another finding from the questionnaire data was that although the overwhelming majority of participants stated that they had positive relationships with most of their African American students, only 55 percent said they considered themselves to be outstanding teachers of African American students. Therefore the responses of nearly half of the participants indicated that they realized they were in need of improvement when it came to educating African American students. Tables A.1, A.2, and A.3 in Appendix I contain related information about these findings.

Who Was Affected and Who Was Not? The Teachers' Post-Inservice Attitudes, Beliefs, and Plans

The questionnaire results illustrate two very important points about the teachers who were affected and those who were not affected by the inservice. The first point is that the inservice appeared to have made a positive short-term impact on most of the participants, particularly in examining their beliefs about African Americans in general. However, the results also indicate that changing educators' negative perceptions of African American parents and students may be a lot more difficult. The results also indicated that at the end of the inservice most participants appeared to believe that the inservice would improve their teaching methods; an even higher percentage of participants said that they planned to use some of the instructional strategies that were presented. This suggests that some of the participants who may have been doubtful, skeptical, or disbelieving that the strategies could improve their instructional practices were willing to try them nonetheless. A similar message surfaced about classroom management. There was a discrepancy between the percentage of participants who said they planned to use some of the classroom management strategies that were presented (92 percent) and those who said they did not believe that the strategies would result in a reduction in discipline problems among African American students (11 percent). This suggests that some of the participants who were doubtful or who did not believe that the strategies would yield positive results might have still been willing to try them.

Whereas 10 percent of the participants agreed that "Teachers should not be required to attend inservices that focus on only one racial/ethnic group," only 5 percent said that it is wrong to acknowledge racial, ethnic, and cultural differences among students. This is an interesting finding because nearly 30 percent of the participants said that prior to attending the inservice they considered themselves to be colorblind to racial, ethnic, and cultural differences. One of the most positive results to emerge from the data was that the majority of participants said they planned to continue their professional growth pertaining to African American students, and nearly two-thirds planned to use the long-term professional growth model that was included in the inservice handbook. (The model is presented at the end of this chapter.)

The second main theme that emerged from the data was that whereas the inservice model appeared to produce many positive results, the participants' prior attitudes and beliefs were the best predictor of the short-term impact of the inservice on them. There were two recurring related findings. First, participants who said that prior to attending the inservice they were eager to learn all they could about increasing their efficacy with African American students, and those who said that prior to attending the inservice they were unaware of how their attitudes and beliefs affected the quality of instruction that African American students received, were more likely than others to indicate that various aspects of the inservice had resulted in a positive effect on them. The second related finding was that participants who said that prior to attending the inservice they were resentful about attending were more likely than others to indicate that the inservice had failed to have a positive effect on their beliefs about African Americans, on their desire to use the strategies that were presented, and on their desire to continue their professional growth pertaining to African American students. Table A.4 in Appendix I contains more information about these findings.

The results imply that short-term professional development training seeking to address issues that teachers constantly wrestle with is a good start. However, logic suggests it can never suffice for the much-needed, ongoing, long-term professional development that is crucial to helping teachers examine the deeply entrenched attitudes and beliefs that are so damaging to African Americans and other students. Moreover, since the questionnaires were collected before the teachers returned to their classrooms and actually had a chance to try the strategies and apply the presented information to their pedagogy and African American students, it is possible that participants who gave favorable responses failed to actually use the information and the strategies. An obvious limitation of this study, therefore, is that it did not include longitudinal data.

Closing Thoughts

On a personal level, my experiences when I arrived at each inservice site and while conducting each inservice, plus the questionnaire results, have caused me to draw some conclusions that might be beneficial to other researchers who are planning to conduct similar work in schools. The good news, in my opinion, is that many educators appear to sincerely want to do a better job of instructing and relating to African American students. I inferred this from many favorable responses to positive statements on the inservice questionnaire and from the comments and questions from numerous participants during the inservices, during the short breaks, and at the end of the inservices. But the fact that you can lead a horse to water but you cannot force it to drink was also obvious from the body language of some participants, and from negative responses to some questionnaire statements.

Another message that became clear is that just as some educators naïvely assume that they are colorblind to racial, ethnic, and cultural differences, some educators—no matter how they try to hide it—are racist. This point was underscored in at least two ways. The first was that a white vice principal told me that, when I arrived at the site where the inservice for the three high schools would be conducted, unbeknownst to me a teacher had directed a racial slur at me. A second indicator is that three of the high school teachers who sat together were so rude and disruptive throughout the inservice that I actually had to ask them to refrain from their distracting behavior. Although their behavior did not change, their rudeness, in my opinion, spoke volumes. Their behavior "shouted" that they did not want to hear anything that I had to say, and they were resentful about having to listen to me. Undoubtedly, an overly optimistic individual or a person who deludes himself or herself into believing that he or she is colorblind would justify such behavior by saying that racism had nothing to do with it. Of course, it is possible that these teachers might have been just as rude to a white, Latina, or Asian American scholar as well. In other words, they might have been rude by nature, or they could have been frustrated by previous professional development inservices.

However, my own perspective is that this example might be related to a third conclusion, which pertains to some of my past teaching experiences as a university professor. As I mentioned previously, in some of my classes I have encountered K–12 teachers (graduate students) who resented having an African American professor as an instructor. Like the three teachers at the high school inservice, one student, a white male, was so resentful that he became disruptive on the first night of class and continued to behave badly throughout the quarter. When I asked him to refrain from talking to his neighbors and from passing notes during my lectures, he retaliated by trying to coerce students into signing a petition, stating that I had discriminated against him for being a "conservative white male." In another case, out of anger at having to refer to me as "Dr. Thompson," one white student, a veteran teacher who challenged nearly everything that I tried to teach, refused to permit me to call her by her first name.

These examples, in my opinion, confirm bell hooks's statements about some whites being resentful of having to listen to an African American woman speak directly and honestly, particularly about culturally sensitive issues.[11] As in the case when half of my white students became upset about being required to read Delpit's *Other People's Children*,[12] and in the case where a young white teacher insisted that I stop discussing racial issues in a multicultural literature class, I have learned that some white teachers would much rather silence the messenger by any means necessary than to face their own issues about African Americans. Instead of being receptive to information that might increase their efficacy with African American students, they attempt to project their hidden or overt racism and their fear of what self-examination may uncover onto the messenger, or onto African American parents and African American students.

In February 2003, during a presentation for educators about recurring themes in *African American Teens Discuss Their Schooling Experiences*[13] and *What African American Parents Want Educators to Know*,[14] I described some of the aforementioned examples of resistance and racism that I have encountered from teachers. One of my former doctoral students, a white man who does diversity training and who seeks to bring about racial reconciliation in churches, attended the presentation. After I mentioned his work to the audience, a retired African American professor suggested that the student and I consider doing presentations together in schools. She said that she suggested this because she believed that teachers who are racist and those who are resentful about having to listen to an African American woman speak would probably be willing to listen to the same information if it came from a white man.

Although I do not know for certain, I suspect that the retired professor might be right. There is a great probability that teachers who are resentful about having to listen to an African American woman might indeed receive the same information from someone who has more in common with them. In fact, I have heard three white males who do diversity training in schools say that they can get away with making certain statements to predominantly white audiences that a person of color could never make. However, during the inservice for the high schools several white teachers told me that during my presentation I had made statements that they could never make. As an African American, they believed that I could make comments about African American culture that would have been misunderstood if a white person had made them.

In short, my experiences and the questionnaire results suggest that much work remains to be done. More studies need to be conducted. More inservices, particularly for much longer duration, need to take place to give teachers information and strategies that will result in better schooling outcomes for African Americans and other students of color. However, in addition to long-term professional development, teachers need ongoing support as they attempt to incorporate new strategies into their curricula, and as they undergo the process of examining the effects of their beliefs, attitudes, and behaviors on the schooling experiences of African American students. Moreover, teachers need to be able to engage in this personal and professional growth process in a nonthreatening manner. Another important point is that educators who truly want to increase their efficacy with African American students must develop an intrinsic motivation to seek the information that they need, and continue to work on their personal and professional growth. The three-part long-term professional growth plan at the end of this chapter is designed to help educators begin this process.

Finally, in spite of the racism and resentment that they will undoubtedly encounter, researchers must continue to share what they know about African American students and other students of color with teachers and school administrators. They must become more proactive about getting their work into the hands of teacher trainers, prospective teachers, and veteran teachers. This can be done through professional development inservices and workshops.

I designed the three-part long-term professional development plan that follows specifically for educators who are courageous enough to go beyond the reading of this book in order to improve their efficacy with African American students—teachers who want to become powerful and influential, like Mrs. Tessem in Chapter Four. The plan will permit these individuals to continue to examine their attitudes, beliefs, and practices by looking through the "ebony eyes" of myself and other researchers who have attempted to explain what teachers need to know about African American students.

Where Do We Go from Here? A Three-Part, Long-Term Professional Development Plan for Educators

Teachers who want to increase their efficacy with African American students must examine their own beliefs and attitudes toward African American students. Gandara and Maxwell-Jolly refer to this, in *Preparing Teachers for Diversity* (2000), as a "self-knowledge strategy." The goal should be to identify beliefs that influence the curriculum and quality of instruction students receive. The process I recommend requires a long-term commitment and a journal that is used exclusively for this program. These exercises can also be used for professional development workshops at school sites. The program entails these three components:

1. A self-assessment that begins with a writing assignment and analysis

2. Writing and analyzing responses to recommended readings

3. Creating an action plan that is based on analyses of responses to the first two exercises

Self-Analysis, Part One: Examining My Core Beliefs About African American Students

Directions: Read each question, and in your journal write a response as quickly as you can. Do not merely write the politically correct answer; write what you really believe in the deepest recesses of your mind. Continue to write until you run out of ideas.

1. Do I truly believe that all students can learn?

2. What are the main reasons many African American students do not succeed academically in school?

3. What are my core beliefs about African American females?

4. What are my core beliefs about African American males?

5. What are my core beliefs about my former and current African American students?

6. During my upbringing, what did I learn about African American culture?

7. When an African American student speaks Ebonics in my class, how do I feel and react?

8. What are the recurring themes in my conversations with my colleagues about African American students?

9. What are my beliefs about African American parents?

10. What are the stereotypes and negative messages about African Americans that I have internalized from the media and my upbringing?

After you have completed the writing assignment, analyze your answers by writing a summary paragraph for each question. The summary should describe what your answers reveal regarding your core beliefs about African American students, parents, and African American culture. One of the most important sections to focus on is "What are the main reasons many African American students do not succeed academically in school?" If your answers mainly blame the students for innate deficiencies, their culture, their styles of discourse, and their parents, then it is important to note that these beliefs will probably prevent you from working effectively with African American students. If you internalized negative messages that African Americans are dangerous, lazy, or inferior, these messages will be detected by your students. These beliefs may become self-fulfilling prophecies in your classroom.

Self-Analysis, Part Two: Reading Research About African Americans

Read each of the books listed here. As you read, record your thoughts, emotions, and specific teaching strategies in your journal.

Other People's Children, by Lisa Delpit

Bad Boys: Public Schools in the Making of Black Masculinity, by Ann Arnett Ferguson

African American Teens Discuss Their Schooling Experiences, by Gail Thompson

Two Nations: Black and White, Separate, Hostile, Unequal, by Andrew Hacker

The Dreamkeepers: Successful Teachers of African American Children, by Gloria Ladson-Billings

The Miseducation of the Negro, by Carter G. Woodson

Countering the Conspiracy to Destroy Black Boys (volumes one, two, and three), by Jawanza Kunjufu

What African American Parents Want Educators to Know, by Gail Thompson

Learning While Black, by Janice E. Hale

The Skin That We Speak, by Lisa Delpit and Joanne Kilgour Dowdy

Aptitude Revisited, by David E. Drew

Black Teachers on Teaching, by Michele Foster

Young, Gifted, and Black: Promoting High Achievement Among African American Students, by Theresa Perry, Claude Steele, and Asa Hilliard III

Improving Schools for African American Students, edited by Sheryl Denbo and Lynson Moore Beaulieu

Culturally Responsive Teaching: Theory, Research and Practice, by Geneva Gay

Afterwards, analyze your responses to each book and record them in your journal. Determine:

- Which book made you angriest, and why?
- Which was easiest to read, and why?
- With which points did you most agree or disagree, and why?
- What did you learn from each book that can improve how you view and instruct African American students?

- Which of the references in those books should you add to your own list of future reading?

Self-Analysis, Part Three: Creating an Action Plan

1. Examine your responses to Parts One and Two.

2. Identify the recurring beliefs and themes that surfaced.

3. Create an action plan that includes specific steps that you can take to improve your beliefs about African Americans, as well as your instructional practices and classroom management strategies. This might include additional reading; attending workshops and conferences; dialoguing with African American educators, parents, students, and community leaders; and enrolling in classes pertaining to African American history and culture.

4. Implement your action plan.

5. In your journal, describe how your action plan has affected your relationships with African American students and its impact on your instructional practices and classroom management practices. How has your action plan affected African American student achievement?

6. Determine the aspects of your action plan that need to be revised.

7. Determine what steps you need to take to continue increasing your efficacy with African American students.

8. Determine how the plan can be modified to increase your efficacy with other students of color.

Notes

Introduction

1. Walker, E. W. "Conflict in the House: Interethnic Conflict as Change Agent: Change as Conflict Instigator." *Journal of Negro Education*, 1999, 68(4), 486–495.

2. U.S. Department of Education. *Tools for Schools: School Reform Models Supported by the National Institute on the Education of At-Risk Students*. Washington, D.C.: Office of Educational Research and Improvement, 1998.

3. Goertz, M. E., Floden, R. E., and O'Day, J. *Systemic Reform*. Washington, D.C.: U.S. Department of Education Office of Educational Research and Improvement, 1996.

4. Shipler, D. K. *A Country of Strangers: Blacks and Whites in America*. New York: Knopf, 1997.

5. Hacker, A. *Two Nations: Black and White, Separate, Hostile, Unequal*. New York: Ballantine, 1992.

6. Dupuis, J. "California Lawsuit Notes Unequal Access to AP Courses." *Rethinking Schools Online*, 1999, 14(1).

7. Welner, K. G. "They Retard What They Cannot Repel: Examining the Role Teachers Sometimes Play in Subverting Equity-Minded Reforms." *Journal of Negro Education*, 1999, 68(2), 200–212.

8. Walker, E. W. "Conflict in the House: Interethnic Conflict as Change Agent—Change as Conflict Instigator." *Journal of Negro Education*, 1999, 68(4), 486–495.

9. Glasser, W. *Every Student Can Succeed*. Chatsworth, Calif.: William Glasser, 2000.

10. Orange, C., and Horowitz, R. "An Academic Standoff: Literacy Task Preferences of African and Mexican American Male Adolescents Versus Teacher-Expected Preferences." *Journal of Adolescent and Adult Literacy*, 1999, 43(1), 28–39.

11. U.S. Department of Education. *No Child Left Behind*. Washington, D.C.: Office of the Secretary, 2001.

Chapter One

1. Gould, S. J. *The Mismeasure of Man*. New York: Norton, 1981.

2. Comer, J. P. "My View." In S. Denbo and L. Beaulieu (eds.), *Improving Schools for African American Students*. Springfield, Ill.: Charles C. Thomas, 2002, p. 6.

3. Loewen, J. W. *Lies My Teacher Told Me: Everything Your American History Textbook Got Wrong*. New York: New Press, 1995, p. 137.

4. Au, K. *Literacy Instruction in Multicultural Settings*. Orlando: Harcourt Brace, 1993.

5. Ibid.

6. Ibid.

7. Oakes, J. "Limiting Students' School Success and Life Chances: The Impact of Tracking." In A. C. Ornstein and L. S. Behar-Horenstein (eds.), *Contemporary Issues in Curriculum* (2nd ed.). Needham Heights, Mass.: Allyn & Bacon, 1999.

8. Ibid.

9. Hacker (1992).

10. Au (1993).

11. Ladson-Billings, G. *Crossing over to Canaan: The Journey of New Teachers in Diverse Classrooms*. San Francisco: Jossey-Bass, 2001, p. 167.

12. Cattani, D. H. *A Classroom of Her Own*. Thousand Oaks, Calif.: Corwin Press, 2002, p. 123.

13. Gay, G. *Culturally Responsive Teaching: Theory, Research, and Practice*. New York: Teachers College Press, 2000, p. 20.

14. Ibid., p. 29.

15. Kunjufu, J. *Countering the Conspiracy to Destroy Black Boys* (Vol. 1). Chicago: African American Images, 1985.

16. Ferguson, A. A. *Bad Boys: Public Schools in the Making of Black Masculinity*. Ann Arbor: University of Michigan Press, 2001, p. 204.

17. Fordham, S. "Racelessness as a Factor in Black Students' School Success: Pragmatic Strategy or Pyrrhic Victory?" *Harvard Educational Review*, 1988, 58(1), 54–84.

18. Ferguson (2001), p. 203.

19. Majors, R., and Mancini-Billson, J. *Cool Pose: The Dilemmas of Black Manhood in America*. New York: Touchstone, 1992, p. 9.

20. Ibid.

21. Thompson, G. *What African American Parents Want Educators to Know*. Westport, Conn.: Praeger, Greenwood Press, 2003.

22. Ibid., p. 175.

23. Ibid., p. 175.

24. Ibid., p. 173.

25. Ibid., p. 173.

26. Kitwana, B. *The Hip-Hop Generation: Young Blacks and the Crisis in African American Culture*. New York: Basic Books, 2002, p. 7.

27. Ibid., p. 6.

28. Ibid., p. 48.

29. Ibid., p. 46.

30. Ibid., p. 179.

31. Ibid.

32. U.S. Department of Education. *Family Involvement in Children's Education: An Idea Book* (abridged version). Jessup, Md.: Office of Educational Research and Improvement, 2001.

33. Thompson (2003).

34. Thompson, G. *African American Teens Discuss Their Schooling Experiences.* Westport, Conn.: Greenwood Press, 2002.

35. Thompson (2003).

36. Thompson (2002).

37. Thompson (2003).

38. Ibid., pp. 58–59.

39. Ibid., p. 59.

40. Ibid., p. 59.

41. Ibid.

42. Hale, J. E. *Learning While Black: Creating Educational Excellence for African American Children.* Baltimore, Md.: Johns Hopkins University Press, 2001, p. xv.

43. Ibid., p. 7.

44. Ibid., p. 7.

45. *No Child Left Behind* (U.S. Department of Education, 2001).

46. Paige, R. "Meeting the Highly Qualified Teacher Challenge: The Secretary's Annual Report on Teacher Quality." Jessup, Md.: U.S. Department of Education, Office of Postsecondary Education, 2002.

47. Ingersoll, R. M. "The Problem of Underqualified Teachers in American Secondary Schools." *Educational Researcher*, 1999, *28*(2), p. 27.

48. Ibid.

49. U.S. Department of Education. *Eliminating Barriers to Improving Teaching*. Washington, D.C.: U.S. Department of Education, 2000, p. iii.

50. Ibid., p. iii.

51. Hale (2001), p. xx.

52. Gay (2000).

53. Collins, M. *Ordinary Children, Extraordinary Teachers*. Charlottesville, Va.: Hampton Roads, 1992.

54. Oakes, J., and Rogers, J. "Diploma Penalty Misplaces Blame." *Los Angeles Times*, Oct. 8, 2002, p. M2.

55. Delpit, L. *Other People's Children: Cultural Conflict in the Classroom*. New York: New Press, 1995, p. 172.

56. Nieto, S. *Affirming Diversity: The Sociopolitical Context of Multicultural Education* (3rd ed.). White Plains, N.Y.: Longman, 2000, p. 2.

57. Thompson (2002).

58. Gay (2000), p. 56.

59. Comer (2000), p. 9.

60. Hale (2001).

61. Cattani (2002).

62. Collins (1992).

63. Boykin, A. W. "Talent Development, Cultural Deep Structure, and School Reform: Implications for African Immersion Initiatives." In S. J. Denbo and L. Moore Beaulieu (eds.), *Improving Schools for African American Students: A Reader for Educational Leaders*. Springfield, Ill.: Charles C. Thomas, 2002.

64. Ibid., p. 87.

Chapter Two

1. Ladson-Billings (2001), p. 8.

2. Hale (2001) p. xvi.

3. Ibid.

4. Ibid., p. 114.

5. Ibid., p. 122.

6. Thompson (2003).

7. Thompson (2002).

8. Manzo, K. K. "Phonics Is Back: California Ditches Whole Language Texts and Returns to the Basics." *Teacher*, Feb. 1997, pp. 10–11.

9. U.S. Department of Education. *National Assessment of Educational Progress: NAEP Trends in Academic Progress*. Washington, D.C.: National Center for Education Statistics, 2000.

10. Thompson, G. "California Educators Discuss the Reading Crisis." *Educational Forum*, Spring 2000, 64, pp. 229–234.

11. Kozol, J. *Illiterate America*. New York: Penguin Books, 1986.

12. Queen, J. A. *Curriculum Practice in the Elementary and Middle School*. Upper Saddle River, N.J.: Prentice Hall, 1999.

13. Thompson, G. "Stories from the Field: What Prospective and Beginning Secondary Teachers Learned from Working with Struggling Third and Fourth Grade Readers." *Educational Horizons*, Fall 2000, pp. 19–25.

14. Roe, B. D., Stoodt, B. D., and Burns, P. C. *Secondary School Literacy Instruction: The Content Areas* (6th ed.). Boston: Houghton Mifflin, 1998.

15. Thompson (2003).

16. Thompson (2002).

17. Ibid.

18. Drew, D. E. *Aptitude Revisited: Rethinking Math and Science Education for America's Next Century.* Baltimore: Johns Hopkins University Press, 1996.

19. Drew, D. E. "Tell Students: Yes, You Can." *USA Today,* Feb. 7, 2001.

20. Drew (1996), p. 2.

21. Ibid., p. 15.

22. Ibid., p. 15.

23. Thompson (2002)..

24. Hale (2001).

25. U.S. Department of Education. *The Nation's Report Card Mathematics 2000.* Washington, D.C.: National Center for Education Statistics, 2001.

26. Ibid.

27. Ibid.

28. Ibid.

29. Ibid.

30. Drew (1996).

31. American Association of University Women. *Shortchanging Girls, Shortchanging America: Executive Summary.* Washington, D.C.: American Association of University Women, 1991.

32. *No Child Left Behind* (U.S. Department of Education, 2001).

Chapter Three

1. Thompson (2003).

2. Ibid., p. 76.

3. Gordon, D. T. "Turning Frustration to Fulfillment: New Teachers Need More Help with Discipline." *Harvard Education Letter*, 1999, *15*(5), 2–3.

4. *Eliminating Barriers to Improving Teaching* (U.S. Department of Education, 2000).

5. Murrell, P., Jr. "Responsive Teaching for African American Male Adolescents." In V. C. Polite and J. E. Davis (eds.) *African American Males in School and Society: Practices and Policies for Effective Education*. New York: Teachers College Press, 1999.

6. "White Teachers Fleeing Black Schools." Jan. 13, 2003. (www.CNN.com/EducationMonday)

7. "Teacher Suspended for Controversial Letter." Oct. 22, 2002. (www.kca19.com)

8. Thompson, G (2002). "African American Students in Schools: Research and Effective Instruction." (Introduction to themed issue.) *Educational Horizons*, Spring 2002, 105–108.

9. *Eliminating Barriers to Improving Teaching* (U.S. Department of Education, 2000).

10. Cattani (2002).

11. Ibid., p. 6.

12. hooks, b. *Rock My Soul: Black People and Self-Esteem*. New York: Atria Books, Simon & Schuster, 2003.

13. Ibid., p. 21.

14. Canada, G. *Fist Stick Knife Gun: A Personal History of Violence in America*. Boston: Beacon Press, 1995.

15. Ibid.

16. Skiba, R., and Peterson, R. "The Dark Side of Zero Tolerance: Can Punishment Lead to Safe Schools?" *Phi Delta Kappan* online, 1999. (www.pdkintl.org/kappan/kski9901.htm).

17. Thompson (2003).

18. Majors and Mancini-Billson (1992), p. 34.

19. Ibid., p.33.

20. Centers for Disease Control. *National Center for Chronic Disease Prevention and Health Promotion Adolescent and School Health Youth Risk Behavior Surveillance System*. 2001. (www.cdc.gov/nccdphp/dash/yrbs/index.htm)

21. Simmons, R. *Odd Girl out: The Hidden Culture of Aggression in Girls*. Orlando: Harcourt Brace, 2002, p. 8.

22. Ibid., p. 3.

23. Ibid.

24. Ibid., p. 3.

25. Ibid., p. 3.

26. Ibid., p. 177.

27. Ibid., p. 178.

28. Canada (1995).

29. Simmons (2002), p. 194.

30. Ibid., pp. 178–179.

31. Hale (2001).

32. Comer (2002), pp. 5–11.

33. Thompson (2003).

34. Ibid., p. 64.

35. Thompson (2002).

36. Kunjufu, J. *Countering the Conspiracy to Destroy Black Boys* (Vol. 3). Chicago: African American Images, 1990, p. 23.

37. Ibid., p. 41.

38. American Association of University Women (1991), p. 8.

39. Ibid., p. 8.

40. Ibid., p. 10.

41. Ibid., p. 10.

42. Ibid.

43. hooks, b. *Rock My Soul: Black People and Self-Esteem*. New York: Atria Books, Simon & Schuster, p. 12.

44. Ibid., p. 13.

45. Ibid., p. 16.

46. Thompson (2002).

47. Ibid., p. 23.

48. Ladson-Billings, G. "I Ain't Writin' Nuttin': Permissions to Fail and Demands to Succeed in Urban Classrooms." In L. Delpit and J. Kilgour Dowdy (eds.), *The Skin That We Speak: Thoughts on Language and Culture in the Classroom*. New York: New Press, 2002.

49. Ibid., p. 110.

50. Ibid., p. 110.

51. Jones, L., Newman, L., and Isay, D. *Our America: Life and Death on the South Side of Chicago*. New York: Scribner, 1997.

52. Ibid., p. 123.

53. Thompson (2003).

54. Thompson (2002).

55. Thompson (2003).

56. Ibid., pp. 9–10.

57. Ibid., p. 78.

58. Hale (2001).

59. Ibid., p. 51.

60. Ibid., p. 60.

61. Ibid., p. 62.

62. Ibid.

63. Gay (2000), p. 54.

64. Thompson (2002).

65. Thompson (2003).

66. Ibid., p. 7.

67. Delpit (1995).

68. Thompson (2003).

69. Ibid., p. 10.

70. Ibid., p. 7.

71. Ibid., p. 64.

72. Payne, R. K. *A Framework for Understanding Poverty*. Highlands, Tex.: RFT, 1998.

73. Hale (2001).

74. Delpit (1995).

75. *No Child Left Behind* (U.S. Department of Education, 2001).

Chapter Four

1. Thompson, G. *Predictors of Resilience Among African American Adults*. Unpublished doctoral dissertation, Claremont Graduate University, 1998.

2. U.S. Census Bureau. *Statistical Abstract of the United States: 2000* (120th ed.). Washington, D.C.: U.S. Census Bureau, 2000.

3. Thompson (2002).

Chapter Five

1. Johnson, K. R. "The Language of Black Children: Instructional Implications." In R. L. Green (ed.), *Racial Crisis in American Education*. River Grove, Ill.: Follett, 1969.

2. Traugott, E. "Pidgins, Creoles, and the Origins of Vernacular Black English." In T. Trabasso and D. Sears-Harrison (eds.), *Black English: A Seminar*. New York: Wiley, 1976.

3. Haskins, J., and Butts, H. F. *Psychology of Black Language*. New York: Hippocrene Books, 1973, p. 40.

4. Gilman, C. "Black Identity, Homeostasis, and Survival: African and Metropolitan Speech Varieties in the New World." In S. S. Mufwene (ed.), *Africanisms in Afro-American Language Varieties*. Athens: University of Georgia Press, 1993.

5. Sprauve, G. A. "Toward the Parameters of Black English." In T. Trabasso and D. Sears-Harrison (eds.), *Black English: A Seminar*. New York: Wiley, 1976.

6. Haskins, J., and Butts, H. F. *Psychology of Black Language*. New York: Hippocrene Books, 1973.

7. "Most Popular Words of the New Generation." *Ebony*, Aug. 2000, p. 158.

8. Dillard, J. *Black English: Its History and Usage in the United States*. New York: Random House, 1972.

9. Smith, E. A. "Bilingualism and the African-American Child." In M. A. Ice and M. A. Saunders-Lucas (eds.), *Reading: The Blending of Theory and Practice*. Bakersfield: California State University, 1995.

10. Dillard (1972).

11. Carroll, J. B. "Linguistic Relativity: Any Relevance to Black English?" In T. Trabasso and D. Sears-Harrison (eds.), *Black English: A Seminar*. New York: Wiley, 1976.

12. Smitherman, G. *Talkin' and Testifyin': The Language of Black America*. Detroit: Wayne State University Press, 1977.

13. Traugott, E. "Pidgins, Creoles, and the Origins of Vernacular Black English." In T. Trabasso and D. Sears-Harrison (eds.), *Black English: A Seminar*. New York: Wiley, 1976.

14. Ibid.

15. Smitherman (1977).

16. Thompson (2003).

17. Smitherman (1977).

18. Dillard (1972).

19. Traugott (1976).

20. Johnson (1969).

21. Smitherman (1977).

22. Ibid.

23. Johnson (1969).

24. Smitherman (1977).

25. Ibid., p. 18.

26. Fasold, R. W., and Wolfram, W. "Some Linguistic Features of Negro Dialect." In P. Stoller (ed.), *Black American English: Its Background and Its Usage in the Schools and in Literature*. New York: Dell, 1975.

27. Ibid., p. 69.

28. Ibid., p. 69.

29. Smitherman (1977).

30. Labov, W. *Language in the Inner City: Studies in the Black English Vernacular*. Philadelphia: University of Pennsylvania Press, 1972, p. 73.

31. Haskins and Butts (1973), p. 41.

32. Ibid., p. 41.

33. Thompson (2000).

34. Delpit, L. "No Kinda Sense." In L. Delpit and J. Kilgour Dowdy (eds.), *The Skin That We Speak: Thoughts on Language and Culture in the Classroom*. New York: New Press, 2002, p. 47.

35. Delpit (1995).

36. Delpit, L., and Kilgour Dowdy, J. *The Skin That We Speak: Thoughts on Language and Culture in the Classroom*. New York: New Press, 2002.

37. Wynne, J. "We Do Not Talk Right. You Ask Him." In L. Delpit and J. Kilgour Dowdy (eds.), *The Skin That We Speak: Thoughts on Language and Culture in the Classroom*. New York: New Press, 2002, p. 208.

38. Ibid., p. 208.

39. Purcell-Gates, V. "As Soon as She Opened Her Mouth! Issues of Language, Literacy, and Power." In L. Delpit and J. Kilgour Dowdy (eds.), *The Skin That We Speak: Thoughts on Language and Culture in the Classroom*. New York: New Press, 2002, p. 134.

40. Kohl, H. "Topsy-Turvies: Teacher Talk and Student Talk." In L. Delpit and J. Kilgour Dowdy (Eds.), *The Skin That We Speak: Thoughts on Language and Culture in the Classroom*. New York: New Press, 2002, p. 147.

41. Hilliard, A. "Language, Culture, and the Assessment of African American Children." In L. Delpit and J. Kilgour Dowdy (eds.), *The Skin That We Speak: Thoughts on Language and Culture in the Classroom*. New York: New Press, 2002, p. 101.

42. Delpit (1995).

43. Smith, E. "Ebonics: A Case History." In L. Delpit and J. Kilgour Dowdy (eds.), *The Skin That We Speak: Thoughts on Language and Culture in the Classroom*. New York: New Press, 2002.

44. Delpit (2002), p. 47.

45. Delpit (1995).

46. Baker, J. "Trilingualism." In L. Delpit and J. Kilgour Dowdy (eds.), *The Skin That We Speak: Thoughts on Language and Culture in the Classroom*. New York: New Press, 2002.

47. Purcell-Gates (2002).

48. Delpit (2002).

49. Baker (2002).

50. Ibid., p. 53.

51. Ibid., p. 56.

52. Nieto (2000), p. 4.

Chapter Six

1. Fineman, H. "Ghosts of the Past." *Newsweek*, Dec. 23, 2002, pp. 22–25.

2. Kennedy, R. *Nigger: The Strange Career of a Troublesome Word*. New York: Pantheon, 2002.

3. Ibid.

4. Isaac, M. *Mommie, What Is a Nigger? The Case of the Centuries*. Columbia, S.C.: IGIA, 1996.

5. Kennedy (2002), p. 4.

6. Ibid., p. 5.

7. Ibid., p. 33.

8. Ibid., p. 9.

9. Ibid., pp. 9–12.

10. Ibid., p. 12.

11. Ibid., p. 38.

12. Ibid., p. 41.

13. Ibid.

14. Ibid., p. 32.

15. Ibid., pp. 48–49.

16. Ibid., p. 37.

17. Ibid., p. 45.

18. Ibid., p. 50.

19. Wright, R. *Black Boy* (reissued). Upper Saddle River, N.J.: Prentice Hall, 1986.

20. Twain, M. *The Adventures of Huckleberry Finn*. New York: Penguin, 1986.

21. Lawton, W. Y. "Multicultural Lessons and Respect." *Oregonian*, Nov. 13, 2002. (www.oregonlive.com/morenews/oregonia/index.ssf)

22. Ibid.

Chapter Seven

1. Giovanni, N. *Racism 101*. New York: William Morrow, 1994, p. 143.

2. Fredrickson, G. M. *Racism: A Short History*. Princeton, N.J.: Princeton University Press, 2002, p. 5.

3. Ibid., p. 5.

4. Murrell, P. C. *African-Centered Pedagogy: Developing Schools of Achievement for African American Children*. Albany: State University of New York Press, 2002, p. 34.

5. Nieto (2000).

6. Loewen (1995), p. 136.

7. Ibid., p. 137.

8. Ibid., p. 137.

9. Thompson (2002).

10. Ibid.

11. Ibid.

12. Thompson (2003).

13. Thompson (2002).

14. Oakes and Rogers (2002).

15. Thompson (2002).

16. Murrell (2002).

17. Hale (2001), p. 52.

18. Drew (1996).

19. Comer, J. P., and Poussaint, A. F. *Raising Black Children: Two Leading Psychiatrists Confront the Educational, Social, and Emotional Problems Facing Black Children*. New York: Penguin Books, 1992.

20. Hale (2001), p. xx.

21. Ibid., p. 2.

22. Nieto (2000), p. 5.

23. Wright (1986).

24. Guy, R. *The Friends*. New York: Dell, 1973.

Chapter Eight

1. Hacker (1992).

2. Kozol, J. *Savage Inequalities*. New York: Harper Perennial, 1991.

3. Chideya, F. *Don't Believe the Hype*. New York: Penguin Books, 1995.

4. Moore, M. *Stupid White Men: And Other Sorry Excuses for the State of the Nation!* New York: HarperCollins, 2001.

5. Chideya (1995).

6. Bond, H. M. *Black American Scholars*. Detroit, Mich.: Balamp, 1972.

7. Woodson, C. G. *The Miseducation of the Negro*. Washington, D.C.: Associated Publishers, 1933.

8. Loewen (1995).

9. Nieto (2000), p. 5.

10. Bennett, C. I. *Comprehensive Multicultural Education: Theory and Practice* (4th ed.). Needham Heights, Mass.: Allyn and Bacon, 1999.

11. Diamond, B. J., and Moore, M. A. *Multicultural Literacy: Mirroring the Reality of the Classroom*. White Plains, N.Y.: Longman, 1995.

12. Manning, M. L., and Baruth, L. G. *Multicultural Education of Children and Adolescents* (3rd ed.). Boston: Allyn and Bacon, 2000.

13. Nieto (2000).

14. Au (1993).

15. Delpit (1995).

16. Au (1993).

17. Delpit (1995).

18. Wright (1986).

19. Jimenez, F. *The Circuit: Stories from the Life of a Migrant Child.* Albuquerque: University of New Mexico Press, 1997.

20. Herron, C. *Nappy Hair.* New York: Knopf, 1997.

21. "Nappy Hair! Oh, My! Almost as Silly as 'Niggardly.'" Dec. 5, 2002. (www. adversity.net/special/nappy_hair.htm)

22. Ibid.

23. Thompson (2003), p. 190.

24. Murrell (2002).

25. Gay (2000), p. 14.

26. Ladson-Billings (2002), p. 111.

27. Ibid., p. 111.

28. Ibid.

29. Ibid., p. 111.

30. Ibid., p. 111.

31. Gay (2000).

32. Boykin (2002), p. 91.

Chapter Nine

1. Gould (1981).

2. Isaac (1996), p. 235.

3. Cattani (2002).

4. Ibid.

5. Delpit (1995).

6. Wiley, R. *Why Black People Tend to Shout: Cold Facts and Wry Views from a Black Man's World.* New York: Penguin Books, 1991, p. 2.

7. Moore (2001).

8. Hale (2001).

9. Thompson (2002), p. 52.

10. Thompson (2003), p. 62.

11. Ibid., p. 155.

12. Ibid., p. 155.

13. Ibid., p. 6.

14. hooks (2003), p. 15.

15. Gandara, P., and Maxwell-Jolly, J. *Preparing Teachers for Diversity: A Dilemma of Quality and Quantity.* Davis: Linguistic Minority Research Institute Education Policy Center, University of California, 2000, p. 7.

16. Foster, M. *Black Teachers on Teaching.* New York: New Press, 1998.

17. Murrell (2002).

18. Delpit (1995).

Conclusion

1. Ladson-Billings (2001), p. 3.

2. Ibid., p. 4.

3. Cattani (2002).

4. Nieto (2000).

5. *Eliminating Barriers to Improving Teaching* (U.S. Department of Education, 2000).

6. Fullan, M. *Change Forces*. London: Falmer Press, 1993, p. 21.

7. Gandara and Maxwell-Jolly (2000).

8. *No Child Left Behind* (U.S. Department of Education, 2001).

9. Cattani (2002), p. 122.

10. Gandara and Maxwell-Jolly (2000).

11. hooks (2003).

12. Delpit (1995).

13. Thompson (2002).

14. Thompson (2003).

Appendix A

The Time Line Project

(adapted from Professor Diane Schuster)

Introduce this assignment to your students by following these steps and presenting your own time line to the class on the first day of school. Then ask the students to follow these guidelines.

1. Make a list of the ten most important events that have occurred in your life. This list can consist of good and bad experiences.

2. Design a colorful and creative time line of these events. The time line should include:

   A brief description of each event

   The year when the event occurred

   Your age at the time the event occurred

   A pictograph or symbol that describes the event

3. Plan to share your time line with the entire class during a short oral presentation.

4. All time lines should be displayed in class after the presentations.

Appendix B

The All About Me Project

Find a creative way to share this information with the class:

1. Describe what you like most about yourself.
2. Describe the music, way of dressing, hobbies, way of talking, and foods that you enjoy.
3. Describe your role models and the people you admire and respect most. Explain why you admire them.
4. What are your future plans and goals? How do you plan to accomplish them?
5. What do you do for fun?
6. Describe your best friends.
7. Describe your favorite places.
8. Add any additional information you would like to share about yourself.

Appendix C

The Cultural Awareness Project

The purpose of this assignment is for you to share information about your culture in an interesting and creative manner. Your presentation should include details about

1. The history and origins of your culture
2. Unique customs that pertain to your culture
3. Titles of books about your culture
4. Contributions that your culture has made to American society
5. Foods that are popular in your culture
6. Music that relates to or originated from your culture
7. Artwork that depicts your culture
8. Any additional information you would like to share about your culture

Appendix D

The Community Problem-Solving Project

The purpose of this project is for you to identify a problem in your community and develop an action plan for solving it.

Complete each step. Be prepared to share your project with the entire class.

1. Make a list of what are, in your opinion, the five biggest problems in your community.

2. Select the problem that is most important to you. This problem will be the focal point of your project.

3. Write ten to fifteen questions about this problem (regarding the causes, consequences, and solutions) that you would like to ask members of your community.

4. Revise and finalize your questions.

5. Interview ten to fifteen members of your community (schoolmates, parents, neighbors, church officials, politicians, and so on) using the questions as your guide.

6. Look for similarities among the responses to your questions.

7. Write a seven-paragraph essay that includes these sections:

A description of the problem

An explanation of the causes of the problem

Examples of some consequences of the problem

Some solutions to the problem

8. Produce a chart, poster, or video (or some other creative outlet) to display this information during an oral presentation to the class.

Appendix E

Writing About Music

Here are some suggested writing assignments for your students concerning music.

1. Ask your students to make a list of their favorite songs.
2. Ask them to select one of the songs from the list.
3. Ask them to write a paragraph about why they like this song.
4. Ask them to revise, rewrite, and proofread their paragraph.
5. Ask them to share their paragraph with a classmate, a small group of classmates, or the entire class.

Writing to Music

1. Tell your students that they will listen to a song.
2. Afterward, ask them to write a paragraph about the song (why they liked or disliked it, what it reminded them of, or what the main message is).
3. Ask them to revise and proofread their paragraph.
4. Ask them to share their paragraph with a classmate.

Appendix F

Using Writing Assignments and Student Artwork to Create a Class Anthology

Here are some steps you might take to compile a class anthology of student work.

1. Give students an opportunity to use the writing process (prewriting, drafting, sharing, revising, rewriting, and proofreading) to create an original story, research paper, or essay.

2. Ask them to draw a related illustration for each story.

3. Compile the stories into a class anthology.

4. Submit the class anthology to writing contests.

5. If you are unable to give each student a copy of the anthology, allow students to borrow it from the class library for a short period of time to share with their family members.

Appendix G

Using "Quotes of the Week" for Writing Assignments and to Improve Critical Thinking Skills

(adapted from Susan Tessem)

"Quotes of the Week" are a great resource for writing assignments and discussion topics. Here are some suggested ways you might use them in the classroom.

1. Each Monday, write a famous quote on the board, such as:

   Every shut eye ain't sleep; every goodbye ain't gone. (African American proverb)

   It takes a village to raise a child. (African proverb)

   Never judge a man until you have walked a mile in his moccasins. (Native American proverb)

   Power concedes nothing without a fight. (Frederick Douglass, paraphrased)

   Fool me once, shame on you; fool me twice, shame on me. (Chinese proverb)

   To err is human, to forgive divine. (Alexander Pope)

   Ah, but a man's reach should exceed his grasp or what's a heaven for. (Robert Browning)

   To avoid criticism, say nothing, do nothing, be nothing. (unknown)

It's not the falling down that means failure but the staying down. (unknown)

Fall seven times; stand up eight. (unknown)

The thief doth fear each bush an officer. (Shakespeare)

No one can make you feel inferior without your consent. (Eleanor Roosevelt)

The mind is its own place and in itself can make a hell of heaven or a heaven of hell. (John Milton)

2. Tell your students to study the quote each day during the week, and to try to interpret its meaning.

3. Encourage students to discuss the quote with classmates, friends, and family members.

4. On Friday, have students write a paragraph in which they explain the meaning of the quote. (This can be used as a warmup activity.)

5. Have them revise, rewrite, and proofread the paragraph.

6. Ask volunteers to share their work with the entire class.

Appendix H

Vocabulary Building Strategies

Here are some suggested practices to build your students' vocabulary skills.

1. Use key words and concepts from textbooks and required readings for vocabulary lists.

2. Give students multiple opportunities to be exposed to each list of vocabulary words before formally assessing their knowledge of these words.

3. Use affixes (prefixes and suffixes) to expand the students' vocabulary.

4. Empower students by having them use the vocabulary words in multiple ways, including asking them to develop their own:

   Crossword puzzles and answer keys

   Multiple-choice tests and answer keys

   Vocabulary clusters

   Fill-in-the-blank tests and answer keys

   Pictographs (defining the words through symbols and drawings)

   Word searches

5. Have students play vocabulary games ("Jeopardy," "Upwords," "Scrabble").

6. Have students develop individual or group projects, such as their own original games, that are based on vocabulary lists.

7. Require students to use key vocabulary words in their writing assignments.

8. Give students class time to use the dictionary regularly. (Some students do not have access to a dictionary or computer at home.)

9. Tell students why they need to know the selected words and how this knowledge will benefit them.

10. Have students make flashcards of the vocabulary words, and encourage them to review the flashcards regularly.

11. Award extra credit to students who use the vocabulary words during class discussions.

Appendix I

The Six-Hour Inservice and the Four Schools

In the summer of 2002, I conducted inservice trainings for teachers at a middle school and three high schools. This Appendix describes the schools, the training participants, and the inservice trainings in some detail. Four tables at the end of the Appendix present data about factors predicting or correlating to the participants' pre-inservice and post-inservice attitudes and beliefs, about their having to attend the inservice, and about their attitudes and beliefs regarding African American students (Tables A.1 through A.3), as well as the short-term impact of various aspects of the inservice (Table A.4) on the participants.

The Four Schools

In this Appendix, the schools are referred to as "the Middle School," "High School A," "High School B," and "High School C."

The Middle School

The middle school, which the California Department of Education described as a "large city school," is located in a central California city. The school, which includes grades six through eight, is part of a unified school district composed of ninety-nine schools, including fifteen middle schools. There were a total of 295 schools in the county.

During the preceding year (the most recent year for which data were reported), the district had a 6 percent high school dropout rate, which exceeded both the county rate and the state dropout rate. The average class size was higher than that of the district, the county, and the state.[1]

Shortly before I arrived to conduct the inservice, the school underwent several major changes. The school principal, who was Latino, described himself as an advocate for children. After realizing that many parents of color were uncomfortable about coming to the school, the principal decided to go to the parents. As a result, periodically he held heavily attended parent meetings in local apartment complexes in which many of the middle school students lived. He also regularly visited students' homes to discuss both positive and negative student behaviors with their parents. However, his candor and style of leadership prompted several teachers to criticize him and to complain about him to the Teachers' Union. In most cases, according to the principal, these teachers were angry at his insistence that children of color be treated respectfully and humanely. During faculty meetings, some teachers "wrote down every word" he said and were constantly looking for excuses to report him to the Teachers' Union. From the principal's perspective, most of the disgruntled teachers represented the city's "old guard." The real issue, according to the principal, was that they did not want to teach children of color. Moreover, he stated that whereas some of the disgruntled teachers were cautious about making derogatory remarks about Latino students in his presence, they were openly critical of African American students, a growing population at the school.

By the time of my arrival to conduct the inservice, the principal had lost all of his assistant principals (for reasons that were not divulged to me), and he had just gotten a new administrative team. Among them was the school's sole African American certificated employee, one of the new assistant principals. Furthermore, many of the disgruntled teachers had left. Therefore, the principal had hired several new teachers. As one Latina teacher who had worked at the school for many years told me, "This is a good thing, because we want our school to be a positive place for all students."

The Middle School Inservice Participants. During the 2000–01 school year, there were twenty-two teachers at the school. Thirty teachers, counselors, and administrators attended the inservice that I conducted. Females made up sixty-seven percent of the individuals in attendance. Sixty-seven percent of the participants had a full credential, which was far less than the district percentage (94), the county percentage (91), and the state percentage (86). However, 7 percent of the inservice participants did not respond to this questionnaire item. The average teacher had taught for seven to nine years; 40 percent had taught for ten or more years, but 13 percent had taught for less than four years. Fifty percent of the participants had only a bachelor's degree, 43 percent had a master's degree, and 7 percent did not respond to this question.

White teachers accounted for 73 percent of the participants, which was equal to the district percentage. Latino teachers totaled 17 percent of the inservice participants, which was slightly higher than their rate districtwide. Although nearly 6 percent of the teachers employed by the district were Asian American; there were no Asian American teachers at this school. Although African Americans constituted 4 percent of the teachers districtwide, at this particular middle school there were no African American teachers. The new African American assistant principal did attend the inservice.

The Middle School Students. During the 2001–02 school year, more than eighty-one thousand students were enrolled in the school district. At the middle school, the total enrollment was approximately nine hundred students, who were primarily students of color. Thirty-four percent of the students were designated as "English learners." Whites were only 7 percent of the student population, which was much lower than their district, county, and state totals.

Latinos were the largest group of students (61 percent). African Americans made up the second largest group (18 percent), and Asian Americans were the third largest group of students (13 percent).

The percentage of students who were eligible for free or reduced-price meals (88 percent) exceeded the district total (74 percent), the county total (63 percent), and the state total (47 percent). However, the proportion of students whose families received public assistance (27 percent) was lower than the district total (32 percent), but higher than the county total (20 percent) and the state total (11 percent). Only four of the fifteen middle schools in the district had standardized test scores that exceeded the base score of the middle school that participated in the inservice. Moreover, during the previous year the participating middle school had shown school-wide improvement in its standardized test scores.

The High Schools

The three high schools that participated in the inservices are located in a high desert region of southern California. The city had been home to a military base that closed in 1992. The school district consists of three junior high and middle schools, three high schools (including one continuation school), and two charter schools for students in grades seven through twelve. During the 2001–02 academic year, more than nine thousand students were enrolled in the district, but nearly four hundred thousand were enrolled in schools throughout the county. Forty-four percent of the students in the district qualified for reduced-price or free meals, and 12 percent came from families that received public assistance. The two regular high schools and the continuation school participated in the inservice that I conducted.

High School A. During the telephone conversation in which she invited me to come to her school, the principal of High School A, a woman who had been on the job for only a few months, shared numerous examples of challenges pertaining to African American students at her school. They included low standardized test scores and discipline problems. As she spoke, I grew increasingly amazed at her candor and insight, especially when she spoke about the impact of teachers' cultural ignorance on African American students. However, at the moment she was extremely concerned about how teachers reacted to African American students who "talk loud" (a topic discussed in Chapters Three and Nine) and the number of teachers who referred African American students to the office for "minor" offenses. "When black parents come to this school," she stated, "I get embarrassed, because I know they wonder why the office is always full of black kids."

The California Department of Education described High School A as a "rural area metropolitan" school that consisted of nearly four hundred classes. During the 2001–02 school year, the average class size (thirty-four) was slightly higher than the district average, the county average, and the state average. The school's four-year dropout rate (26 percent) was much higher than the district rate (18 percent) and more than twice as high as the county and state rates. During the previous year alone, 7 percent of the students had dropped out.

High School A Inservice Participants. During the 2001–02 school year, 109 teachers were employed at High School A. Seventy-four teachers from this school handed in an inservice evaluation questionnaire. Females were 51 percent of the participants. Sixty-one percent of the participants had a full teaching credential, which was lower than the district, county, and state totals. The average participant had taught for at least ten years. Fifty-five percent had taught for ten or more years, and only 8 percent had taught for less than four years. Forty-three percent of the participants reported that a master's degree was their highest degree; 5 percent had earned a doctorate.

Sixty-four percent of the participants were white, which was less than the district, county, and state totals. The percentage of Latino participants (15 percent), the second largest group of inservice participants from High School A, exceeded the district total (9 percent). The percentage of African Americans (5 percent), the third largest group of participants, was higher than the district total (4 percent) but equal to the county and state totals.

High School A Students. During the 2001–02 school year, twenty-seven hundred students were enrolled at High School A. Students of color accounted for 63 percent of the students, and 5 percent of the students were English language learners. The three largest racial or ethnic groups were Latinos (39 percent), whites (37 percent), and African Americans (17 percent). Although they constituted less than 1 percent of the student population, Pacific Islanders and American Indians and Alaska Natives were overrepresented among the dropouts at High School A. African Americans made up the third largest group of dropouts. Forty-three percent of the students at High School A were eligible for free or reduced-price meals, and 13 percent were from families that received public assistance.

Students at High School A took numerous standardized tests during the 2000–01 school year. These tests included the Stanford Achievement Test, the California High School Exit Exam, and the Scholastic Aptitude Test (SAT). The Stanford Achievement Test results indicated that the entire school district did poorly, with only 37 percent of the students scoring at or above the 50th national percentile ranking (NPR) in math and only 33 percent scoring at or above the 50th NPR in reading. However, at High School A, 42 percent of the students scored at or above the 50th NPR in math, but only 29 percent scored at or above the 50th NPR in reading. These scores were lower than the statewide total of 53 percent and 44 percent, respectively. At High School A, when the scores were disaggregated by race or ethnicity, African American students were disproportionately represented among the students who scored below the 50th NPR. Only 30 percent of the African American students scored at or above the 50th NPR in math, and only 17 percent scored at or above the 50th NPR in reading. The high school seniors' SAT scores showed a similar pattern in that African American students had lower average math and reading scores than all of the other racial or ethnic groups for whom results were reported. Conversely, on the California High School Exit Exam, among the racial and ethnic groups for whom scores were reported, a higher percentage of African American students passed the math exam (39 percent) and English language arts exam (54 percent) than Latinos.

High School B.   High School B was the only participating school that had an African American principal. The California Department of Education described High School B as being on the "urban fringe of a large city"; it consisted of nearly 269 classes. During the 2001–02 school year, the average class size (thirty-two) was higher than the district average, the county average, and the state average. The school's four-year dropout rate (10 percent) was lower than the district, county, and state totals. During the previous year, 3 percent of the students had dropped out.

High School B Inservice Participants.   During the 2001–02 school year, eighty-eight teachers were employed at High School B. Fifty-two teachers from this school handed in an inservice evaluation questionnaire. Males were 52 percent of the participants. Fifty-eight percent of the participants had a full teaching credential, which was much lower than the district, county, and state totals (though nearly one-fourth of the participants failed to respond to this question). The average participant had taught for at least ten years. Sixty-four percent had taught for ten or more years, and only 8 percent had taught for less than four years. Forty-four percent of the participants reported that a master's degree was their highest degree, and 4 percent had earned a doctorate. However, 13 percent of the participants did not respond to this questionnaire item.

Sixty percent of the participants were white, which was less than the district, county, and state totals. The percentage of Latino participants (23 percent), the second largest group of inservice participants from High School B, was more than twice the district total. There were more American Indian participants from High

School B than from any other participating school; they constituted 6 percent of the High School B participants. Districtwide, American Indian and Alaska Natives made up less than 2 percent of the teachers; countywide and statewide, they totaled less than 1 percent. The percentage of African Americans (4 percent), the fourth largest group of participants, was comparable to the district total, slightly less than the county total, and less than the state total (5 percent).

High School B Students. During the 2001–02 school year, more than twenty-two hundred students were enrolled at High School B. Students of color accounted for 63 percent of the students, and 8 percent of the students were English language learners. The three largest racial and ethnic groups were Latinos (40 percent), whites (37 percent), and African Americans (18 percent). American Indians, Alaska Natives, and Filipinos were overrepresented among the dropouts at High School B. Latinos were the third largest group of dropouts. Forty-five percent of the students at High School B were eligible for free or reduced-price meals, and 18 percent were from families that received public assistance.

Thirty-five percent of the students at High School B had Stanford Achievement Test scores that were at or above the 50th NPR in math, and 29 percent had scores that were at or above the 50th NPR in reading. Again, when scores were disaggregated by race or ethnicity, a lower percentage of African Americans scored at or above the 50th NPR in math (19 percent) and in reading (17 percent). During the 2000–01 school year, only eight African American students at High School B took the SAT college entrance exam. Therefore, because of this small number, their scores were not published. However, the 2002 California High School Exit Exam results indicated that whereas 29 percent of the African American students passed the English language arts exam, only 15 percent passed the math exam. For both exams, a lower percentage of African Americans passed than the percentages of whites and Latinos.

High School C. High School C was the only continuation school
that participated in the inservices, and it was the smallest school in
terms of the number of participating educators as well as student enrollment. The California Department of Education described High
School C as being on the "urban fringe of a large city"; it consisted
of eight classes. During the 2001–02 school year, the average class
size (thirty) was lower than the district average, but higher than the
county and state averages. The school's four-year dropout rate (33
percent) far exceeded the district, county, and state rates. During
the previous year, 8 percent of the students had dropped out.

High School C Inservice Participants. During the 2001–02 school
year, fourteen teachers were employed at High School C. Seven
teachers from this school handed in an inservice evaluation questionnaire. Three males and three females from High School C participated; one participant did not specify his or her gender. Five of
the participants had a full teaching credential, and two had a Professional Growth Credential. All of the participants had taught for
at least seven years; two had taught for more than fifteen years. Five
of the participants had earned a master's degree. Five of the seven
participants were white. There was one African American, and one participant did not specify his or her race or ethnicity.

High School C Students. During the 2001–02 school year, 258 students were enrolled at High School C. Students of color accounted
for 73 percent of the students, and 8 percent were English language
learners. The three largest racial or ethnic groups were Latinos (49
percent), whites (27 percent), and African Americans (21 percent).
American Indians, Alaska Natives, and African Americans made up
the largest groups of dropouts at High School C. Sixty-one percent
of the students at High School C were eligible for free or reduced-
price meals, and 12 percent were from families that received public
assistance.

Seven percent of the students at High School C had Stanford
Achievement Test scores that were at or above the 50th NPR in

math, and 11 percent had scores that were at or above the 50th NPR in reading. Again, when scores were disaggregated by race and ethnicity, a lower percentage of African Americans scored at or above the 50th NPR in math (6 percent) and in reading (6 percent). During the 2000–01 school year, SAT scores were not reported for High School C, a standard procedure for schools at which fewer than ten students are tested. The 2002 California High School Exit Exam results indicated that among the African American students who took the math exam, only one student passed. However, among the African American students who took the English language arts exam, 67 percent passed. Whereas the African American student pass rate for math was lower than for other groups, their English language arts exam pass rate was higher.

Summary of the Schools

The background information about the schools and the participants reveal several interesting details. All of the schools were "servicing" a high percentage of students from lower socioeconomic backgrounds, but at the middle school nearly 90 percent of the students were in this category. There was an obvious racial and ethnic mismatch between the teachers and the students at all three schools, in that—as is the case nationwide—white teachers were the largest group even though students of color formed the bulk of the student body. Moreover, at two of the three high schools, there were only a few African American teachers, and at the continuation school there was just one. At the middle school, despite the fact that African American students amounted to nearly one-fifth of the student population, there were no African American teachers.

The students' test scores shed some light on one of the primary reasons why the school principals were interested in having their teachers participate in an inservice that focused exclusively on African American students. Although several groups did poorly on standardized tests, in most cases a lower percentage of African American students had passing scores. Another factor was that two of the high schools had extremely high dropout rates.

TABLE A.1. Factors That Predicted or Were Correlated to the Participants' Pre-Inservice Attitudes About Having to Attend the Inservice.

Attitude (Percentage)	Factors
Resentful (15)	Having a full teaching credential Perceiving oneself to be colorblind Being unaware of the link between teachers' attitudes and expectations and the quality of instruction that African American students receive Believing that African American students do not want to succeed academically Blaming parents and guardians for African American students' underachievement
Neutral; open-minded but not enthusiastic (48)	Believing that African American students do not want to succeed academically Blaming parents and guardians for African American student underachievement
Eager to learn (76)	Teaching higher academic tracks

Note: n = 175

TABLE A.2. Inservice Participants'
Pre-Inservice Beliefs and Attitudes.

Attitude or Belief	Percentage
Having positive relationships with most African American students	93
Considering oneself to be an outstanding teacher of African American students	55
Blaming parents and guardians for African American students' underachievement	34
Perceived colorblindness	29
Being unaware of the impact of teachers' attitudes and expectations on instruction	14
Believing that African American students do not want to succeed academically	10
Having low expectations for African American students	9

Note: n = 175

TABLE A.3. Factors That Predicted or Were Correlated
to the Participants' Pre-Inservice Attitudes and Beliefs
About African American Students.

Attitude or Belief	Factor
Perceived colorblindness	Blaming parents and guardians Not having low expectations Feeling resentful about having to attend the inservice Having taught for more years than other participants Teaching higher academic tracks
Having a positive relationship with most African American students	Believing oneself to be an outstanding teacher of African American students Being aware of the link between teachers' attitudes and expectations and the quality of instruction students receive Believing that most African American students do want to succeed academically Teaching higher academic tracks Not having low expectations for African American students Not blaming parents and guardians for African American students' under-achievement Not feeling resentful about having to attend the inservice Teaching a higher academic track
Considering oneself to be an outstanding teacher of African American students	Having positive relationships with most African American students Believing that most African American students do want to succeed academically
Having low expectations	Blaming parents and guardians Being unaware of the link between teachers' attitudes and expectations and the quality of instruction students receive

TABLE A.3. Factors That Predicted or Were Correlated to the Participants' Pre-Inservice Attitudes and Beliefs About African American Students, Cont'd.

Attitude or Belief	Factor
	Not having positive relationships with most African American students Believing that most African American students do not want to succeed academically Not considering oneself to be an outstanding teacher of African American students
Being unaware of the link between teachers' attitudes and expectations and the quality of instruction that African American students receive	Not having positive relationships with most African American students Feeling resentful about having to attend the inservice Having low expectations for African American students Blaming parents and guardians Not considering oneself to be an outstanding teacher of African American students
Believing that African American students do not want to succeed academically	Blaming parents and guardians Not having positive relationships with most African American students Feeling resentful about having to attend the inservice Being open-minded but not enthusiastic about the inservice Having low expectations for African American students Being unaware of the impact of teachers' attitudes and expectations on instruction

TABLE A.3. Factors That Predicted or Were Correlated to the Participants' Pre-Inservice Attitudes and Beliefs About African American Students, Cont'd.

Attitude or Belief	Factor
Blaming parents and guardians for African American students' underachievement	Believing that most African American students do not want to succeed academically
	Having low expectations for African American students
	Believing oneself to be colorblind
	Being open-minded but not enthusiastic about the inservice topic
	Having the least years of teaching experience
	Feeling resentful about having to attend the inservice
	Not having positive relationships with most African American students
	Being unaware of the impact of teachers' attitudes and expectations on instruction

Note: $n = 175$

TABLE A.4. The Short-Term Impact of Various Aspects of the Inservice.

Attitude or Belief	Participants' Responses (by Percentage)				
	Strongly Disagree	Disagree	Agree	Strongly Agree	No Answer
This inservice has helped me to examine some of my attitudes and beliefs about African Americans.	1	8	57	30	4
This inservice will not make a significant impact on the way in which I view African American students.	27	49	11	5	8
This inservice will not make a significant impact on my views about African American parents.	23	47	18	3	9
Instructional Practices					
This inservice will improve the way in which I instruct my African American students.	1	7	57	30	5
I plan to incorporate some of the instructional strategies that I learned from this inservice into my curriculum.	1	1	53	39	6
This inservice will not make a significant impact on the way in which I instruct African American students.	27	48	14	4	7

Classroom Management

I plan to use some of the classroom management strategies that were presented during this inservice.	1	1	57	35	6
I do not believe that the classroom management strategies that were presented will reduce the number of discipline problems among my African American students.	29	51	9	2	9

Professional Growth

As a result of this inservice, I will continue my professional growth in order to increase my efficacy with African American students.	1	9	52	26	12
I plan to follow the professional growth plan that is outlined at the end of the inservice handbook.	2	18	55	8	17

Other Topics

Teachers should not be required to attend inservices that focus on one racial or ethnic group.	47	36	7	3	7
I believe that it is wrong to acknowledge that racial, ethnic, and cultural differences exist among students.	57	31	3	2	7

Note: n = 175

Note

1. Source for all background information on schools, school districts, average class size, dropout rates, information on race and ethnicity of teachers in school districts, and the like (at district, county, and state levels) other than data clearly derived from the inservice trainings that are the subject of this Appendix is California Department of Education (2002).

Index

A

Ability grouping, 15

Academic problems, misbehavior as cover-up for, 91–93

Academic standoff, 3

Achievement gap, black-white: "acting white" theory of, 17–18; classroom management and, 104–105; communication and language problems and, 145–146; cultural discontinuity theory of, 15–16; deficit-deprivation theory of, 14, 34–35; "fourth grade failure syndrome" theory of, 16–17; low teacher expectations and, 27–29, 35; lure-of-street-life theory of, 19–22; parents-are-at-fault theory of, 22–26; peer pressure theory of, 19–22; persistence of, 3–4, 6, 63–64; research categories on, 33–34; structural inequality theory of, 14–15; teacher underpreparation factor in, 26–27; teachers' negative beliefs about African American students and, 29–33, 34–35; theories of, 6, 13–37; tracking and, 15

Achievement test scores, of inservice participant schools, 300–301, 303–304

ACT scores, 225

Acting black, 141–142

Acting white: fears of being seen as, 18; speech and, 141–142; theory of achievement gap, 13, 17–18

Action plan, for teacher self-improvement 252–253, 256

Active approach to learning, 37

Active sentences, 137

Additive pedagogy, 36–37, 147, 148

Administrators: influence of, on teacher expectations, 28–29; inservice training and, 242–243; support of, for classroom discipline, 69, 85

Adventures of Huckleberry Finn, The (Twain), 157–158

Adversity, childhood. See Childhood adversity

Advocacy, parent, 229–234

Affective filter blocking, 143

Affirming Diversity (Nieto), 241–242

Africa and Africans: Ebonics and languages of, 135–136; loudness in, 216; negative messages about, 81–82; terms for African Americans and, 210–211

African American female students: aggression styles of, 78–79; jealousy among, 82; low self-esteem in, 82

African American male students: "acting white" theory and, 17–18; aggression and violence of, 74–77; classroom discomfort of, 94–96; "cool pose" coping mechanism of, 17–18, 76; "fourth grade failure syndrome" in, 16–17; low self-esteem in, 79, 82–83; misunderstandings between teachers and, 3; negative beliefs about, 33, 74–75, 239; socialization of, 75–76

Discussion Questions for *Through Ebony Eyes*

1. Which theory of African American underachievement resonated with you the most and why?

2. What are Gail Thompson's main messages on effective instructional practices for African American students? Which (if any) of these practices have you used in the classroom? Describe your experience.

3. Discuss the author's key points on effective classroom management. In your own experience, which of these methods have you found to be most effective?

4. How does Mrs. Tessem differ from the other elementary school teachers?

5. Describe additional strategies teachers can use to reach students from challenging backgrounds.

6. How would you define *Ebonics*? What are some of the reasons so many African Americans continue to speak Ebonics?

7. How can teachers show respect for students' home language or dialect and still motivate them to learn the use of standard English?

8. What reasons does the author give on why teachers should not allow use of the N word in the classroom? Describe how you feel about this.

9. Describe strategies teachers can use to dissuade students from using the N word and other offensive language in school.

10. What evidence may an African American student cite in claims that a teacher exhibits racist behavior?

11. How should a teacher respond to a possibly unfair accusation of racism?

12. What is a *culturally relevant education*? How do African American students benefit from this kind of education?

Teaching with Fire
Poetry that Sustains
the Courage to Teach

SAM M. INTRATOR AND MEGAN SCRIBNER

Cloth / 256 pages / 2003
ISBN: 0-7879-6970-2

"Teaching with Fire is a glorious collection of the poetry that has restored the faith of teachers in the highest, most transcendent values of their work with children . . . . Those who want us to believe that teaching is a technocratic and robotic skill devoid of art or joy or beauty need to read this powerful collection. So, for that matter, do we all."

—Jonathan Kozol, author of *Amazing Grace* and *Savage Inequalities*

Those of us who care about the young and their education must find ways to remember what teaching and learning are really about. We must find ways to keep our hearts alive as we serve our students. Poetry has the power to keep us vital and focused on what really matters in life and in schooling.

Teaching with Fire is a wonderful collection of eighty-eight poems from well-loved poets such as Walt Whitman, Langston Hughes, Billy Collins, Emily Dickinson, and Pablo Neruda. Each of these evocative poems is accompanied by a brief story from a teacher explaining the significance of the poem in his or her life's work. This beautiful book also includes an essay that describes how poetry can be used to grow both personally and professionally.

Teaching with Fire was written in partnership with the Center for Teacher Formation and the Bill & Melinda Gates Foundation. Royalties will be used to fund scholarship opportunities for teachers to grow and learn.

Sam M. Intrator is assistant professor of education and child study at Smith College. He is a former high school teacher and administrator and the son of two public school teachers. He is the editor of *Stories of the Courage to Teach* and author of *Tuned In and Fired Up: How Teaching Can Inspire Real Learning in the Classroom*.

Megan Scribner is a freelance writer, editor, and program evaluator who has conducted research on what sustains and empowers the lives of teachers. She is the mother of two children and PTA president of their elementary school in Takoma Park, Maryland.

The Dreamkeepers

Successful Teachers of African American Children

GLORIA LADSON-BILLINGS

Paperback / 208 Pages /
ISBN: 0-7879-0338-8

"Education, like electricity, needs a conduit, a teacher, through which to transmit its power, i.e., the discovery and continuity of information, knowledge, wisdom, experience, and culture. Through the stories and experiences of eight successful teacher-transmitters, The Dreamkeepers keeps hope alive for educating young African Americans."

—Reverend Jesse L. Jackson, president and founder,

National Rainbow Coalition

Ladson-Billings's portraits, interwoven with personal reflections, challenge readers to envision intellectually rigorous and culturally relevant classrooms that have the power to improve the lives of not just African American students but all children. Quality education remains an elusive dream for most African American children. Historically, they have been denied schooling, subject to separate and unequal education, and forced into unsafe, unhealthy, substandard schools.

In *The Dreamkeepers*, Gloria Ladson-Billings explores the positive signs for the future. Who are the successful teachers of African American students? What do they do? And how can we learn from them? Her portraits of eight exemplary teachers who differ in personal style and methods but share an approach to teaching that affirms and strengthens cultural identity are inspiring and full of hope. Written in three voices, that of an African American scholar and researcher, an African American teacher, and an African American parent and active community member, this book is a mixture of scholarship and storytelling. Ladson-Billings's portraits, interwoven with personal reflections, challenge readers to envision intellectually rigorous and culturally relevant classrooms that have the power to improve the lives of not just African American students, but all children.

Gloria Ladson-Billings is a professor of education at the University of Wisconsin, Madison. She has served on the faculties of Santa Clara University and Stanford University, and has spent over ten years working as a teacher and consultant in the Philadelphia public school system.

The Exceptional Teacher

Transforming Traditional Teaching Through Thoughtful Practice

Elizabeth Aaronsohn

Paperback / 304 pages / 2003
ISBN: 0-7879-6576-6

"Using inspiring stories from her own classroom, heart-felt student responses, and current educational research, Liz Aaronsohn challenges readers to prepare a new generation of teachers who dare to know themselves, love their students, question the system, and rock the boat. If we heed her advice, we will all— teachers, students, and teacher educators—be better as a result."

—Sonia Nieto, University of Massachusetts, Amherst

In *The Exceptional Teacher*, veteran K-12 teacher Elizabeth Aaronsohn examines three important questions: What do our teachers really want our children to get out of school? How do their own schooling experiences inhibit them from achieving these goals? How can a teacher education program give beginning teachers a framework for thinking differently about the whole process of teaching?

The Exceptional Teacher offers the guidance that teacher educators need to help their students become teachers who are knowledgeable and skillful practitioners, while also developing the ability to be reflective, imaginative, courageous, and flexible in the classroom— a model for the students they are instructing. In this inspiring book, Aaronsohn shows that becoming an exceptional teacher can be a difficult but rewarding journey. She explains that success begins in understanding one's self and societal and cultural experiences. Based on qualitative research from student writings and workshops, the author offers practical advice to help beginning teachers move beyond their own internalized assumptions, and become educators who will transform their classrooms.

Aaronsohn encourages teachers to develop the practice of honest reflection on their attitudes, thinking, and practices, and especially to develop the capacity to assume the perspective of another person. These practices can be nurtured through the process of in-depth writing, which helps to make meaning of experiences and brings teachers to a new level of consciousness about themselves, the world, and the mission of teaching.

Elizabeth Aaronsohn is an associate professor of teacher education at Central Connecticut State University in New Britain, Connecticut. She has taught eight years each at three levels: high school English; college English, speech, and women's studies; and early elementary school. She is the author of *Going Against the Grain: Supporting the Student-Centered Teacher*.

Becoming Multicultural Educators

Personal Journey Toward Professional Agency

GENEVA GAY

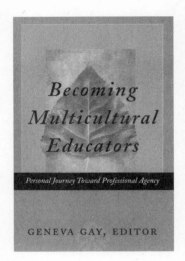

Paperback / 368 pages / 2003
ISBN: 0-7879-6514-6

"Exceptional and insightful book for teachers, counselors, and administrators about the personal and professional transformations that we all must go through in order to become caring, multicultural educators for all students. A must read."

—Valerie Ooka Pang, professor of education, San Diego State University

One of the most daunting tasks facing teachers today is learning how to work with students from a wide range of ethnic, cultural, and social backgrounds. Teachers are eager to improve their skills, but good multicultural teaching cannot be learned in a single education course or in-service workshop. It is something that evolves over time as a teacher accumulates critical self-awareness, cultural knowledge, and teaching skills.

To help both new and seasoned teachers become more effective with their students from diverse backgrounds, *Becoming Multicultural Educators* edited by Geneva Gay offers fourteen compelling stories from different regions, cultures, ethnic groups, and stages of professional and personal growth in developing multicultural awareness, knowledge, and skills. One contributing author declares community participation and social activism are the keys to his professional growth. For another, multicultural understanding comes when she learns to unveil the masks of insidious negative stereotypes. Through these stories, we share their struggles as these educators come to understand diversity among ethnic groups and cultures, resolve conflicts between curricular and multicultural goals, and find authentic models and mentors for their students. But most important, we learn how this laudatory group of educators has come to realize that they need to know themselves if they are to truly know their students.

Well-grounded in education theory, *Becoming Multicultural Educators* is both personal and inspiring. This is the book that will help teachers, and those who prepare them, blossom as educators and human beings.

Geneva Gay is professor of education at the University of Washington, Seattle. She is nationally and internationally known for her scholarship in multicultural education. She is the author of numerous articles and books, including *Culturally Responsive Teaching*, which received the 2001 Outstanding Writing Award from the American Association of Colleges for Teacher Education (AACTE).